Firebrand Waves of Digital Activism 1994–2014

Firebrand Waves of Digital Activism 1994–2014

The Rise and Spread of Hacktivism and Cyberconflict

Athina Karatzogianni
University of Leicester, UK

First published 2015 by
PALGRAVE MACMILLAN

Palgrave Macmillan in the UK is an imprint of Macmillan Publishers Limited, registered in England, company number 785998, of Houndmills, Basingstoke, Hampshire RG21 6XS.

Palgrave Macmillan in the US is a division of St Martin's Press LLC, 175 Fifth Avenue, New York, NY 10010.

Palgrave Macmillan is the global academic imprint of the above companies and has companies and representatives throughout the world.

Palgrave® and Macmillan® are registered trademarks in the United States, the United Kingdom, Europe and other countries.

ISBN: 978–0–230–24246–3

This book is printed on paper suitable for recycling and made from fully managed and sustained forest sources. Logging, pulping and manufacturing processes are expected to conform to the environmental regulations of the country of origin.

A catalogue record for this book is available from the British Library.

Library of Congress Cataloging-in-Publication Data
Karatzogianni, Athina.
    Firebrand waves of digital activism 1994–2014: the rise and spread of hacktivism and cyberconflict / Athina Karatzogianni.
        pages cm
    Includes bibliographical references.
    ISBN 978–0–230–24246–3 (hardback)
    1. Internet – Political aspects. 2. Cyberspace – Political aspects.
    3. Hackers. 4. Political activists. 5. Political participation – Technological innovations. I. Title.
HM851.K367 2015
303.48'34—dc23   2015015586

Contents

Preface and Acknowledgements

The research for this book was conducted between 2007 and 2014, in what was a period of intense cyberactivism in the global political arena: proliferation of socio-political activist networks; social-media-enabled political protests and mobilizations leading to social or political change; and increased resistance to surveillance and censorship of global communications, including leaks from government employees uncovering significant problems in the use of ICT by both states and corporations. This book brings together work specifically relevant to media movements and radical politics and the interaction between states and corporations with these movements.

In engaging with this work, I have incurred many intellectual debts. I extend my lasting thanks to all my colleagues at Hull and Leicester, who I often stopped in corridors to talk to between writing sessions. My list of gratitude for stimulating intellectual exchanges over the years includes Noel O'Sullivan, Andrew Robinson, Michael Schandorf, Christiana Gregoriou, Gillian Youngs, Cony Beyer, Phoebe Moore, Bev Orton, Mike Brayshaw, Adi Kuntsman, Korina Patelis, Petros Ioannidis, Popi Aggeli, Ming-Yeh, Gary Rawnsley, George Michaelides, Christos Sideras, Eugenia Siapera, Anthimos Tsirigotis, Artur Alves, Michel Bauwens, Zizi Papacharissi, Geert Lovink, Gabriella Coleman, Martin Gak, Patricia Clough, Rafael-Cohen Almagor, Richard Aldrich, James Zborowski, Maria Karanika, Marie-Hélène Bourcier, Mayra Rodrigues Gomes, Simon Willmetts, Peter Wilkin, James Connelly, David Lonsdale, Peter Young, Luke O'Sullivan and Panagiota Tsatsou. In addition, I extend my gratitude to my students for many inspiring conversations.

I have benefited from material support from the EU FP 7 MIG@NET project (http://www.mignetproject.eu/). I am grateful to this body for enabling me to travel widely for research; as well as to the University of Illinois in Chicago and the University of São Paulo for inviting me to visit and engage with staff and students. I am also grateful to the University of Hull for allowing me research leave, and to the University of Leicester for continuous support. I am thankful for the ESRC grant The Common Good: Ethics and Rights in Cyber Security (ERCS), which supported my research into the Snowden affair. I must also thank all the publishers and editors who have supported my work over the years and the editorial team for this book. And no book on digital activism should omit thanks to online friends, who are too numerous to mention!

I have published parts of the case studies included in this book over the past seven years (Karatzogianni, 2010; 2012a; 2012b; 2012c; 2013; Karatzogianni and Michaelides, 2009; Karatzogianni and Robinson, 2014; 2016), and I am grateful to colleagues, editors and publishers for permission to use the material again. I have indicated in the text when this is the case and where the relevant study originally appeared. In doing so, I am opening my modest and often inadequate research vault in the hope that scholars of digital activism and cyberconflict might discover continuities, patterns and discontinuities, as well as paradoxes to aid the analysis of future cases, for they are virtually certain to emerge.

This book is dedicated to my family in Greece, my son Sebastian and his dad, Tim Hawkins, who is still tolerant of my frequent absent-mindedness, travelling and smashing of kitchenware.

Introduction: Four Phases of Digital Activism and Cyberconflict

This book introduces four waves of digital activism and cyberconflict. Digital activism began in 1994, was transformed by the events of 9/11, peaked in 2011 with the Arab Spring uprisings and then entered a transformative phase of control, mainstreaming and co-optation, accentuated by the Snowden revelations in 2013. Digital activism is defined here as political participation, activities and protests organized in digital networks beyond representational politics. It refers to political conduct aiming for reform or revolution by non-state actors and new socio-political formations such as social movements, protest organizations and individuals and groups from the civil society, that is by social actors outside government and corporate influence. Cyberconflict is defined as conflict in computer-mediated environments and it includes interactions between actors engaged in digital activism to raise awareness for a specific cause and struggles against government and corporate actors, as well as conflicts between governments, states and corporations. The rationale for distinguishing these phases is based solely on political effects, rather than technological developments.

The first phase, covering the years 1994–2001, encompasses the origins of two phenomena. With the invention of the World Wide Web in 1991 by Tim Berners Lee, the digitization of production in the 1980s could finally be networked, and many-to-many broadcasting was no longer a far-fetched reality. The optimism of the early 1990s that digitality would bring an economic, socio-political and cultural revolution ended in the last years of that decade with the bursting of the dot.com bubble, which caused a rethink.

Nevertheless, consumers were able and eager to interact and participate in the creative process and this was changing the relationship between

1

existing industries, technologies, audiences and markets. The communication landscape of the 1990s was effectively described by McLuhan's 'global village' (1989); De Sola Pool's (1983) argument about the artificiality of a media separation based on political economy rather than technological characteristics; Rheingold's (1994) first take on the power of virtual communities; Jenkins' (2006) convergence theory explaining the shifting of balance with the intertwining of grassroots and corporate media; and Castells' (2000) 'network society'. Activism during that period included the alternative peer-produced Linux operating system started by Linus Torvalds in 1991 (the road had been opened by Richard Stallman's free software in the 1980s); the online transfer of ethnoreligious conflicts (the Falun Gong in China, the Tamil in Sri Lanka, the Kosovo war, the Israel-Palestine conflict); the use of ICTs by social movements and protests, such as the Zapatista movement in Mexico, which dropped guerrilla war in favour of digital engagement in 1994; the birth of IndyMedia during the anti-globalization protests in Seattle in 1999; and the overthrow of Estrada through the use of mobile phones in 2001. By the first year of the new Millennium, digital activism was a global force to be reckoned with.

The second phase is from 9/11 to 2007. It starts with 9/11, because the Al Qaeda network's attack on the Twin Towers in the US not only had a profound impact on news coverage (the internet's audience skyrocketed and the media industry was transformed) but also prompted political transformations both in the US and at the global level that led to the War on Terror, a crackdown on civil liberties, securitization and militainment, among other phenomena. The subsequent Afghanistan and Iraq wars heightened the impact of internet politics on the global public sphere and increased digital activism in the form of anti-war protest, in which ICT was used to accelerate its mobilization. The Iraq war (2003–2011) came to be known as the first internet war, because the digital revolution ensured that independent voices and new media actors were able to challenge the official narrative of the War on Terror and offer an alternative. The Afghanistan and Iraq wars were the dominant spheres of digital activism and cyberconflict in that period, but there were other notable examples: the socio-political mobilization in Ukraine's Orange Revolutions (2004–2005); hacktivism during the Republican Convention in the US 2004; the Madrid and London Al Qaeda bombings; continuing resistance in China; the ICT impact on the Lebanon war in 2006; and the Estonian cyberattacks of 2007.

The third phase, from 2007 to 2010, started with the South Ossetia conflict. In 2008, Senator Barack Obama exploited the power of social media activism to win the US presidential election, becoming the first black president of the United States. It was also one of the first instances of the blending between political participation and digital activism, in which ICT had a decisive impact on representative politics. This period includes the formation of the Green Movement after the 2009 elections in Iran in an attempt to overthrow Mahmoud Ahmadinejad, and the bloody crackdown on organized protests and in embassies around the world, which were deemed the biggest since the 1979 revolution. This was followed by the Google-China incident in 2010 and the birth of the anti-austerity protest movement in Syntagma Square in Athens in May of the same year. I focus in this book primarily on case studies relating to Russia and China (see also Karatzogianni and Robinson, 2014).

The fourth phase (2010–2014) of digital activism starts with the WikiLeaks video release in the summer of 2010, the 'Arab Spring' revolutions in the MENA region, the Occupy Wall Street movement in 2011 and the spread of Occupy across the globe, with Occupy Central leading protests in Hong Kong in September 2014. The years 2011–2014 witness protests in countries as diverse as Portugal, Spain, Brazil, Turkey, Nigeria and India, to name but a few, as well as digital activism relating to feminist, LGBT, environmental and politics of food issues. This period is also crucially marked by the Snowden revelations in the summer of 2013, which provide significant evidence for the crackdown on digital activism by the United States and the United Kingdom and the allegedly forced cooperation of tech corporations. The Sony hack at the end of 2014 seems to have pushed digital activism and cyberconflict into a new phase. In this fourth phase the book focuses on WikiLeaks, the Arab Spring and the Snowden affair.

The book's thesis is that there is a constant transformation of digital activism beyond its symbolic and mobilizational qualities, as we have experienced it since 1994. Digital activism is likely to enter a phase of mainstreaming, becoming part of 'politics as usual': an established element in the fabric of political life with no exceptional qualities, normalized and mainstreamed by governments through collaboration with corporations, the co-optation of NGOs and the resistance of new socio-political formations. Cyberconflict will revolve more around high-level information warfare, attacking infrastructure, rather than just being used as a weapon in largely symbolic low-level societal attacks. The higher-level character of conflict in digital networks will intensify to the extent that the digital activism and cyberconflict of the last two decades will pale into insignificance.

To support this thesis, the book follows a simple logic. In the first chapter, I provide a brief overview of the first (1994–2001) and second (2001–2007) phases of digital activism and cyberconflict. I provide a more detailed account of specific cases of digital activism in two further phases: 2007–2010 in the second chapter and 2010–2014 in the third chapter. In the fourth and concluding chapter, I argue that the mainstreaming of digital activism will render it ineffective and inconsequential in the long term. Finally, I offer my thoughts on how high-level information warfare will impact on network power in the future targeting infrastructure and grids rather than information content and network connections.

1
Origins and Rise of Digital Activism (1994–2007)

1.1 First phase (1994–2001): the origins of digital activism

Knowledge communities and the FLOSS movement

I place the birth of digital activism in virtual knowledge communities, particularly those used to create alternative software products engaging in peer production, as starting with the free/libre/open software movement. They descended from the first hackers of the 1960s: the first dreamers of the power to divert technology from its original purpose to extend it and make it do the impossible.

And yet there is a very long line of lineage in the human condition tracking back in time to knowledge networks at the forefront of human innovation. Ancient Athens was an innovative democracy before the hegemonic decline brought about by the domination of the polis by warfare (Karatzogianni, 2012a). In the cited work, I offer Ober's analysis from *Democracy and Knowledge: Innovation and Learning in Classical Athens* (2010), and it is worth reusing that material here. Ober puts forward the hypothesis that democratic Athens competed successfully over time against hierarchical rivals:

> because the costs of participatory political practices were overbalanced by superior returns to social cooperation, resulting from useful knowledge, as it was organized and deployed in the simultaneously innovation-promoting and learning-based context of democratic institutions and culture. (37)

Various intriguing arguments stemming from social network and organizational theory are utilized by Ober to understand the superiority of the Athenian system. For instance, process innovation, highly valued by knowledge-based organizations, is thought to be impeded by hierarchies, as they favour learning as routinization at the expense of learning as innovation, which is paramount in highly competitive environments (ibid., 106). The Athenian system was operating in flexible small teams in horizontal governmental structures, where the mentality of peer production prevailed over rigid hierarchy. Moreover, in the participatory Athenian context, social knowledge served as a sorting device: 'Experienced citizens learned habits of discrimination, of recognizing whom to attend to and whose opinion to trust in what context' (ibid., 120). Ober identifies two features of Athenian decision-making institutions, which conjoin the innovation-promoting and routinizing aspects of organizational learning: social/knowledge networks and task-specific work teams (ibid., 123). By serving in rotation and being educated in the democratic machine, the Athenian system made experts out of lifelong learning amateurs: 'Through its day-to-day operations, the Athenian system sought to identify and make effective use of experts in many different knowledge domains' (ibid., 31). As he puts it,

> By participating in 'working the machine' of democracy, the individual Athenian was both encouraged to share his own useful knowledge, and given the chance to develop and deepen various shorts of politically relevant expertise ... learning as socialization helped to sustain democracy by granting it ideological legitimacy in the eyes of the citizenry. Predictability, standardization, and legitimacy all lowered transaction costs and thereby reduced the friction inherent within every complex system. (ibid., 273)

Cleisthenes is credited with making the most important of the democratic reforms in Athens, significantly enabling the golden era of participatory democracy by creating institutions built for knowledge sharing, lowering communication costs, and context-sensitive information sorting. He did this first of all by creating the weak ties that were crucial to uniting local strong ties across Attica, bridges that were essential to knowledge aggregation. The blatantly artificial tribes in his system drew from three areas, communities located in coastal, inland, and urbanized regions of Athenian territory, whereby a stable local identity was linked to a desired national identity, the participatory citizen of Athens (ibid., 138). According to Ober, the Athenian system intermixed Athenians from different geographic/economic zones in a variety of psychologically powerful activities, such as fighting, sacrificing, eating, and dancing, which led to a strengthened collective identity at the level of the polis (ibid., 142). Athenian citizens acted as individuals bridging holes in the network, linking subnetworks and gaining social capital in the process, similar to the process described in Ron Burt's (1992) theory on structural holes (ibid., 146). The ability of the Athenian citizen to learn and be part of a knowledge network runs contrary to the ignorant-mob assumption often put forward by historians (Ober, 2010, 162).

In terms of leadership, the Athenian polis did not depend on authoritarian leaders or hierarchy and rejected Spartan-style hypersocialization. Athens relied instead on choices freely made by free citizens to gain its public ends: 'intermixing the four mechanisms...for facilitating complex coordination: first choice, informed leader, procedural rules, and credible commitments' (ibid., 179). For example leadership would shift readily depending on which individuals or groups happened to know something useful, with consensus following from plurality and alignment (ibid., 174). Balancing elite and non-elite preferences meant, for example, that someone like Themistocles in the debates leading to the Athenian decision to fight the Persians at Salamis in 480 BC were able to assume leadership roles by advocating and carrying through innovative policies (ibid., 182). It was indeed his genius in Salamis of using the change of wing direction at a specific time of the day that enabled the small, agile Greek ships to devastate the larger and more inflexible Persian fleet. Lastly, Athenians valued innovation as a good in itself, because it was a manifestation of their communal identity, of what they supposed was special and excellent about themselves as a people – as well as valuing innovation as an instrument (ibid., 275).

A giant leap forward to the 1960s and the birth of the hacker movement, whereby radical geeks argued for free information and open collaborative knowledge networks. The enthusiastic computer virtuosos dreaming of a world where information and knowledge could be produced and accessed by anyone at any time openly and freely, such as Ted Nelson and his Xanadu project of hyperlinked text, and with greater and greater speeds within flows of time and space compression in Gibson's cyberspace, were no longer dreaming.

The digital revolution saw the term 'hackers' used as an umbrella term for any computer intrusion or illegal activity relating to digital networks, from cybercrime (e.g., identity theft, online fraud, ATM attacks) to cyberprotest, (e.g., electronic civil disobedience, symbolic defacements, network disruption) to cyberterrorism (e.g., cyber activities relating to individuals and groups who commit violence against civilians). All these terms and examples are continuously debated, of course, and by no means am I offering here a definitive solution to ideological and ontological preferences. The point is that 'in the popular press, however, the connotations of "hacker" are most often negative, or at minimum refer to illegal intrusion of computer systems' (Coleman, 2014).

Broadly speaking, a hacker is involved in an act that is against the rules and involves sophisticated technical knowledge. The literature on hackers has looked at reasons for hacking, such as feelings of addiction, the urge of curiosity, boredom with the educational system, enjoyment of a feeling of power, peer recognition, and political motivations. The more political hackers believe that electronic communications are unsafe, with governments legally tapping data lines, copying electronic mail, and suspecting hacking often enough to get search warrants or confiscate equipment. Taylor and Jordan (2004) argue that overidentification with technical means over political ends and their parasitic relationship to various technological systems means that although they are at the heart of the exercise of power, they remain in an ultimately powerless dependent relationship. This point is reserved for a later discussion about the third phase of digital activism because it relates to WikiLeaks, Anonymous, and other examples.

I am following a long line of scholars who think that the first successful example of digital activism originated from the free/libre open-source software movement (FLOSS) (Wark, 2004; Weber, 2004; Blenkler, 2006). In collaboration with George Michaelides who works in organizational behaviour at Birbeck, we theoretically explored conflict and governance in this movement (Karatzogianni and Michaelides, 2009). In communities that exist at the interface between order and randomness (at the edge of chaos), conflict and crisis can act as a catalyst or a defence mechanism toward establishing governance structures or, failing that, disintegration. Conflict is a catalyst, in the sense of enabling the morphosis of cryptohierarchies, and a defence mechanism, in the sense of forcing communities to separate. Through negotiation and soft control, the community can develop new structures in order to cope with conflict, creating core and periphery groups and cryptohierarchies. In another scenario, due to extreme group polarization, the community is unable to create new structures but branches out and uses conflict as a defence mechanism to avoid centralization. Or, in the worst case scenario, the community separates into two (forking the code), and there is no collaboration between original and fork, in which case the conflict can be constructive or destructive depending on the evolution of the communities and groups involved.

In these communities, conflict and self-organization play a critical role in the emergence of structures: leadership emergence, the bifurcation into core and peripheral groups, and soft control by cryptohierarchies (intracommunal cyberconflict); different levels of group polarization and conflict between communities negotiating their identity, strategy, coordination, and complexity (intercommunal cyberconflict); and lastly, the dynamic relationships between hierarchies and networks. These dynamics are forcing open-source communities and, more often than not, networked communities to exist at the edge of chaos and to constantly engage in lines of flight and resistance from the system of global control while ignoring current capitalist practices and 'growing their own' models of self-organizing knowledge creation and exchange (e.g., peer production in open software or hardware communities).

Michel Bauwens (20 October 2007) of the P2P foundation talked of peer-to-peer processes as bottom-up processes whereby agents in a distributed network can freely and voluntarily engage in common pursuits without external coercion, where anyone can access, anyone can use, and any change to the commons belongs to the commons. Peer governance-based leadership on reputational capital is the order of the day: 'Within the teams, decision making is participative and consensual, and the global coordination is voluntarily accepted and today technically feasible. Small tribes, the victims of civilizational hierarchies, are re-enabled in the new format of affinity-based cyber-collectives' (ibid.). Postmonetary, postdemocratic, postcapitalist modes of value and exchange, embedded or not in the system, are the answer and solution to the structural crisis of contemporary capitalism (see also Bauwens, 2009).

And yet, very much like ancient Athens (with its exclusion of migrants, foreigners, and women), the open-source and/or free software movement is mistakenly romanticized as the ultimate democratic, egalitarian, and horizontal system of governance:

People often see in the open source software movement the politics that they would like to see – a libertarian reverie, a perfect meritocracy, a utopian gift culture that celebrates an economics of abundance instead of scarcity, a virtual or electronic existence proof of communitarian ideals, a political movement aimed at replacing obsolete nineteenth-century capitalist structures with 'new relations of production' more suited to the Information Age. ... It is almost too easy to criticize some of the more lavish claims. ... The hype should be partly forgiven. ... Unlike the shooting star that was Napster, the roots of open source go back to the beginning of modern computing; it is a productive movement ultimately linked to the mainstream economy;

and it is developing and growing an increasingly self-conscious identification as a community that specifies its own norms and values.
(Weber, 2004, 7)

On the down side, structurelessness is masking power in these communities. The equivalent in open source could be the distribution of knowledge sharing spectacularly skewed (huge gap between core and peripheral
developers' contributions). Is soft control by cryptohierarchies necessary
to provide the social glue and facilitate the creation of technical infrastructures and decision-making mechanisms?

Weber argues that open source poses three interesting questions for
political economy, which can be summarized as follows: *motivation* of
individuals (why do talented programmers chose to spend time on a
project for which they will not be compensated); *coordination* ('how does
the open source sustain coordinated cooperation among large numbers
of contributors, outside the bounds of hierarchical or market mechanisms'); and *complexity* ('what is the nature of governance within the
open source process that enables this community to manage the implications of Brooks's Law' – this is the observation that when manpower
is added to a software project, the project falls even further behind –
'and perform successfully with such complex systems?') (2004, 11–12).
Incorporating Weber's foci of analysis, the open-source community/
ies and the socioeconomic and politico-economic cyberconflicts
(Karatzogianni, 2006) that arise can be described firstly as ultracreative,
intracommunal conflicts between individuals in an open-source community. This can lead to much more diverse knowledge creation, or, in the
worst case scenario, code forking. Forking, were the code is replicated
and continued by another team of developers is different from code
branching. What is interesting in intracommunal conflicts are issues
of personal freedom, the right to fork, ownership, leadership direction,
competitive technical visions/ideologies, reputational risk of the original
project, and fork leader recruitment. For the purpose of this discussion,
it is also interesting for intracommunal conflicts to explore group polarization, cryptohierarchies, and what Weber terms the 'winner-takes-all
dynamic within certain kinds of open source projects' (2004, 160).

Secondly, *intercommunal* conflicts, between different open-source
communities, raise questions of coordination (too much and too little),
complexity (how much the community can handle), and ideology
(different political visions for the open source, expressing all inclina-
tions, from anarcho-syndicalism to libertarianism and even to right-wing
ideologies, with free software emphasizing the freedom aspect and the

Open Source Initiative establishing links with business). In the bigger picture, there is a general conflict between the open-source community and aligned proprietary software companies supporting open-source initiatives against the Microsoft monopoly and other proprietary players. Here macro-organizational structures and the dynamics of the IT industry are important, as well as questions of identity, strategy (framing), and structure (hierarchy vs network or hybrid, such as the Linux case, when Torvalds started rerouting submissions to lieutenants). Within this bigger picture, a metaconflict occurs synchronously, bringing all these different levels together and posing them in direct and intense contact and contrast to the current global system of capitalist accumulation.

The edge of chaos is defined as a state of a system where the system undergoes a phase transition; that is, its behaviour shifts from one state to another. In social systems, the edge of chaos refers to the conceptual region between order and chaos. It refers to a system being at a 'self-organized' state. In open-source communities, and possibly other network structures, the edge of chaos is captured in two ways in which the system can self-organize. First, open-source communities exhibit a power law distribution (e.g., Healy and Schussman, 29 January 2003; Madey, Freeh, and Tyran, 2005). The power law distribution in the Internet literature comes up in the study of links on the Internet, and as Benkler points out, 'if a tiny minority of sites gets a large number of links, then the vast majority gets few or no links, it will be very difficult to be seen unless you are on the highly visible site'. Not only that, but the emergent new hierarchy is becoming 'a more intractable challenge to the claim that the networked information economy will democratize the public sphere' (Benkler, 2006, 241–242). Every successful community tends to be organized into a two-tier structure with a core and a periphery group (Michaelides, 2006). The significance of these two forms of self-organization in this discussion is that this is not only unavoidable, but also a necessary component to the success of the community. First, networks that follow power law distributions tend to be more robust and are more adaptable to environmental disturbances (e.g., Barabási, 2002). Second, the fact that communities tend to separate into core and periphery enables them to effectively exploit and integrate knowledge from diverse sources (Michaelides, 2006). Issues of leadership and soft control are equally relevant to the different types of conflict occurring on the intracommunal, intercommunal, and metaconflict levels, when conflict becomes a catalyst for self-organization, or a defence mechanism against the emergence of cryptohierarchies or explicit hierarchies in the form of core and periphery.

Group polarization occurs when 'members of a deliberating group move toward a more extreme point in whatever direction is indicated by the members' predeliberation tendency' (Sunstein, 1999). Online communities tend to be more polarized, while the bazaar empowers louder and more aggressive individuals (Raymond, 1998), often exacerbating online conflicts, leaving out people who disagree, while empowering people with a common cause, and the opinion of the mediocrity gets adopted, having reached a critical mass. This is directly linked to social cascades and cryptohierarchies both informational and reputational. Familiar and long-debated issues do not depolarize easily (so in Open Source Software (OSS) political/ideological issues do not depolarize easily, but technical issues do). Polarization increases when the group defines itself by contrast to another group; when there is some sense of identity (reinforcing group consensus, rather than complicating things, e.g., XFree86 fork X.org). On the other hand, depolarization can occur if there is external shock (new members, new arguments, new information).

The lesson from group polarization is that social homogeneity can be damaging to good deliberation, something proven by better knowledge exchange in communities where conflict actually occurs. Intercommunal conflicts occur, for instance the free software versus open source, simply because not all peer communities are the same, and they do not have the same collective identity or strategy. More importantly, they certainly do not understand their ideological position (if they have one) in relation to other communities – the FLOSS movement as a whole, the latter's role in the IT industry, or in the global justice movement discourse – in the same way. This is also true because the FLOSS movement, or the peer revolution, if you will, is a hybrid, a mosaic. It is a bit of a social movement, a bit formal organization, a bit volunteer and virtual organization, and a bit virtual community of practice (Healy and Schussman, 2003; Michaelides, 2006). The stylized image of this movement is of an egalitarian network of developers free of hierarchical organization and centralized control. However, adhering to power law distributions, participation is spectacularly stratified. Soft control, flaming, and file killing, in the guise of quality control, is observed, for example, 'We won't wait for your code'. Meanwhile, the distribution of projects can be skewed, and huge diversity exists even among successful projects.

Another parameter in relation to conflict in these communities and the constant threat of the fundamental right of forking is leadership. In fact all three kinds of issues identified by Weber – who makes the final decision, who gets credit, and who can legitimately fork (2004, 89) – are ultimately connected to leadership (visible structure) and the core developers/cryptohierarchies (invisible decision making) issue. In 1998, due to an excessive workload, Linus Torvalds could not cope and incorporate patches to the code in time. Programmers at Linux became frustrated and even started to doubt the capacity of their leader, Linus Torvalds, to respond to them, which almost resulted in a major fork of the Linux code. A particular mirror site set up by Dave Miller called VGER at Rutgers University was incorporating patches that Torvalds was not, and from then on an argument erupted between the two, which was described by Raymond (the unofficial anthropologist of open source) as a test of open source under stress, not a personal battle between Torvalds, Miller, or anyone else (Weber, 2004, 118). Bitkeeper, a commercial source management software, kick-started the discussion of resolving the workflow and organizational problems and taking some pressure off Torvalds. When the main protagonists met in Silicon Valley in 1998, they agreed on what Weber calls a somewhat more formal pyramidal structure for the flow of patches and software submissions:

> The key players had in effect, looked straight into the eye of a major fork and turned back from it. The heated conflict took place out in the open, on emailing lists accessible to the entire community. The resulting bargains and most of the negotiations were public. The vehemence of the conflict was de-escalated by a common language around technology. And the fight did not drag on forever; in fact the acute phase lasted less than a week. The conflict management system of then open source process was becoming more defined. (Weber, 2004, 119)

To put it in different words, the number of patches submitted to Linus Torvalds reached the critical level in the self-organizing criticality sense. As a consequence, the community had to restructure itself in order for Linus to be able to cope with the increasing number of submitted patches. The result of this is a real hierarchy of decision making, where Torvalds relies on 'lieutenants' who rely on maintainers. It is not clear at any given time who is in which group. In the Berkeley Software Distribution (BSD), they organize governance around concentric circles, while 'a small core group controls final access to the code base. This group grants (or revokes) the rights to the concentric circle, who can modify code or commit new mode to the core base. These are the committers for evaluation. The boundaries of the circles are generally more definite: FreeBSD, for example, has a core of 16 and about 180 committers in the second circle' (Weber, 2004, 92).

What is really inspiring inside the political romanticism of cybercommunism, anarchism, libertarianism, and ethical capitalism is that these ideas are playing on the interface between hierarchies and networks, and the increasingly dense relationships between the two. States are becoming more networked to deal with the current networked resistances, be they sociopolitical or ethnoreligious, or with open source, politico-economic. These networked resistances are now more conscious of their hosting environment, reversing from networks toward cryptohierarchies to establish a common interface with hierarchies.

The potential contained in network forms of social organization, first found in open source, for constructing resistances to repressive apparatuses and to the world system as a system of global control is no longer just a potential but has become a reality, especially with social media enabling uprisings and protests around the world.

Both hierarchies and networks coexist, and the interface between them is a fascinating study. Open source, among other network(ed) communities, has provided an empirical window to how the global system and its subsystems resolve problems of structural complexity, how networks evolve, connect, and create complex dynamics within diverse nodes and rhizomes. The self-organization dynamic, sustaining this movement, creating order out of chaos, can help and is helping us to analyse network(ed) movements, communities, and resistances around the world and the dialogue between diverse systems of knowledge management, organization, mobilization, and leadership/decision-making structures. More importantly, despite governance immaturity, the influence of the stubborn FLOSS example on the global justice movement proved immense. This is where we now turn in the history of digital activism.

Hacktivism (hackers + activism) was coined as a term for when hackers attack virtually chosen political targets: a kind of electronic disobedience in which activists break into governmental, corporate, or organizational computer systems. Another definition includes when individuals organize through the Internet to protest, or when they use networking technologies to convey a political message. The very first hacktivists were the Zapatistas, who gave up guerrilla warfare in favour of online activism. Jordan (2001) explains that hacktivists have found two uses of the Internet: mass virtual direct action (MVDA) – simultaneous use by many people, such as the virtual sit-in for the Zapatista cause, where 10,000 people delivered 600,000 hits to the site of the then Mexican president Zedillo, the Pentagon, and the Frankfurt stock exchange – and individual virtual direct action (IVDA), which can take the form of defacements, denial of service, or network penetrations. During the anti-WTO demonstrations in Seattle in 1999, protestors used cell phones, direct transmissions from independent media feeding to the Internet, and wireless computers broadcasting live video. Hacktivists acquired the URL of the WTO and turned it into a parody WTO site, criticizing its policies. A virtual sit-in by the Electrohippies slowed down and halted the original WTO site.

However, there is an ethical debate in hacktivism. There are hacktivists who claim that defacements and similar hacktions are against other people's freedom of speech. There are others who view these actions as the only way to get the public's attention. For example, hackers around the world (The Cult of the Dead Cow, !Hispahack, Phrack, etc.) argued that this has nothing to do with hacktivism or hacker ethics and is nothing a hacker should be proud of. These hacktivists see the development and use of technology as opportunities to foster human rights and the open exchange of information. Hacktivists brought together by antiglobalization protests and the indymedia network have developed their own network of skills sharing, free software, and solidarity (see 'Sociopolitical Cyberconflict' in Karatzogianni, 2006, 121–153).

1.2   Second phase (2001–2007): the rise of digital activism

Ethnoreligious and sociopolitical cyberconflicts

The catastrophic terrorist attacks on the Twin Towers in New York in September 2001 (9/11) initiated a devastating polarization in global politics and a crackdown on activism in cyberspace. The network resistances based on reactive affect and desire for destruction in the form of the Al-Qaeda network saw the rise of closed fixed identities based on hierarchical notions of race, religion, nationality, and patriarchy. The U.S. and Western reaction to the attacks followed a similar social hierarchical logic of network closure, with the crackdown on civil liberties at home and conduct that violated human rights abroad. The reverberation of the fear and uncertainty that American and Western hegemony faced because of 9/11 fuelled nationalistic and ethnic politics sustained by patriarchal discourses and had a devastating effect on democratic politics. As we will see in the following phase (2007–2014), the WikiLeaks and Snowden revelations, among others, point to the killing of journalists by the multinational force in Iraq, the Guantanamo files point to torture, while pervasive surveillance of a matrix of foreign populations by the National Security Agency (NSA) in the United States and the Global Communication Head Quarters (GCHQ) in the United Kingdom was organized during this period.

When I started my doctoral research on the politics of cyberconflict in September 2000, which empirically covered the rise of digital activism, the two main groups I identified were those fighting for ethnoreligious causes such as the Israeli-Palestinian and Indian-Pakistani cyberconflicts of 2001–2002 and those fighting for sociopolitical causes, such as the antiglobalization movement in Seattle in 1999. I used a theoretical framework which I called 'cyberconflict theory', synthesized from a combination of social movement, conflict, and media theoretical elements, to help in the analysis of these conflicts. Still, I argued that these movements had modernist aims such as power, participation, and democracy in a medium that was postmodern, in that it was not just a medium in the classical mass communication sense but another place altogether: a network of networks, in which only postmodern theory could help us theorize. Predictably, I turned to network theory first and subsequently to the philosophy of Gilles Deleuze and Felix Guattari (1987). The result of this theoretical synthesis was the following frame:

1. Environment of cyberconflict (CC): the reversal argument
   (a) Ethnoreligious CCs represent loyalties of hierarchical apparatuses while.
   (b) Sociopolitical CCs are empowering network forms of organization.
   (c) Actors in ethnoreligious CCs need to operate in a more *network* fashion if they are fighting network forms of terrorism or resistance.
   (d) Actors in sociopolitical CCs need to operate in a more *organized* fashion and be more conscious of the rest of their hosting network if they are to engage with the present global political system.
2. Sociopolitical cyberconflicts: impact of information communication technologies (ICTs) on
   (a) mobilizing structures (network style of movements using the Internet, participation, recruitment, tactics, goals);
   (b) framing processes (issues, strategy, identity, the effect of the Internet on these processes);
   (c) political opportunity structure (the Internet as a component of this structure); and
   (d) hacktivism.
3. Ethnoreligious cyberconflicts: elements of analysis
   (a) ethnic/religious affiliation, chauvinism, national identity;
   (b) discourses of inclusion and exclusion;

(c) information warfare, the use of the Internet as a weapon (hacking), propaganda, and mobilizational resource; and

(d) conflict resolution, which depends on the legal and organizational framework, the number of parties and issues, the distribution of power, and the content of values and beliefs.

4. Media components:
   (a) analysing discourses (representations of the world, constructions of social identities and social relations);
   (b) control of information, level of censorship, alternative sources;
   (c) Wolfsfeld (1997): political contest model among antagonists: the ability to initiate and control events, dominate political discourse, mobilize supporters; and
   (d) media effects on policy (strategic, tactical, representational).

Cyberconflict theory was devised between 2001 and 2005 to help me as a scholar to situate conflict in digital networks in a historical, geosociopolitical, and communications context (for the three theories and their integration, see Karatzogianni, 2006, 53–93). It was initially developed to explain pre-Web 2.0 and pre-social media uses of the Internet as a resource or weapon of propaganda wars. Cyberconflicts of that period acted as a 'barometer' of real-life conflicts of the participating groups. The protagonists in sociopolitical cyberconflicts fought for participation, power, and democracy, while the groups in enthoreligious cyberconflicts used the Internet as a propaganda tool and to coordinate and fund attacks on the enemy.

Evident in the antiglobalization and anticapitalist movement was an alternative programme for the reform of society, asking for democracy and more participation from the 'underdogs', be they in the West or in the developing world. In the antiwar movement of 2003, which was a single-issue movement, the demand was for a change in power relations in favour of those that believed the war to be unjustified. In new social movements, the Internet linked diverse communities such as labour, feminist, ecological, peace, and anticapitalist groups with the aim of challenging public opinion and battling for media access and coverage. Groups were brought together like a parallelogram of forces, following a swarm logic, indicating a web of horizontal solidarities to which power might be devolved or even dissolved. The Internet began to encourage a version of the commons that was ungoverned and ungovernable, either by corporate interests or by leaders and parties.

Ethnoreligious cyberconflicts primarily included hacking enemy sites and creating sites for propaganda and mobilizational purposes.

In ethnoreligious cyberconflicts, despite the fact that patriotic hackers can network, there is a greater reliance on traditional ideas, such as protecting the nation or fatherland and attacking for nationalist reasons. The 'Other' is portrayed as the enemy, through closed, fixed, and primordialist ideas of belonging to an imagined community, such as the fatherland.

During 2001–2002, the Israeli-Palestinian cyberconflict saw the use of national symbols (like the Israeli flag, Hebrew text, and even a recording of the Israeli national anthem) when hacking the Hezbollah home page. This explicitly draws attention to issues of national identity, nationalism, and ethnicity. Also, the language used by these nationalist hackers relied on an 'us' and 'them' mentality, where Israelis and their American supporters, or else Palestinians and Muslims, are portrayed as barbaric, reflecting classic discourses of inclusion and exclusion. The Internet in this cyberconflict became a battleground and was used as a weapon by both sides, and full-scale action by thousands of Israeli and Palestinian youngsters involved both racist e-mails and the circulation of instructions on how to crush the enemy's websites. Similarly, in the Indian-Pakistani cyberconflict of the same period, the Indian army's website was set up as a propaganda tool, and hacked pictures of alleged torture of Kashmiris by Indians were placed on the site in a similar propaganda tactic. Also, the Internet was used as a weapon when the worm Yaha was released by Indian hackers. In particular discourses, religion is mentioned (religious affiliation), as well as the word 'brothers' (collective identity and solidarity), 'our country', and a promised land (for a detailed analysis of ethnoreligious cyberconflicts of this period, see Karatzogianni, 2006, 154–173).

A central part of the cyberconflict environment of this period was cyberterrorism: computer-based attacks intended to intimidate or coerce governments or societies in pursuit of goals that are political, religious, or ideological. Arquilla and Ronfeldt (2001) argued that conflicts increasingly revolved around knowledge and the use of soft power. This would come about with the help of information age ideologies in which identities and loyalties shift from the nation-state to the transnational level of global civil society. Additionally, they used the term 'netwar' to refer to low, societal struggles, and 'cyberwar' to refer to high-information warfare, that is, attacks on grids and infrastructure.

Besides the ad hoc ethnoreligious/nationalist assemblages and ultra right-wing groups using ICTs, there was 'terrorist media' used to create fear in the populace, mobilize support, increase recruitments and funds, and disrupt governments' efforts at 'counterterrorism' during what was ludicrously termed 'The war on Terror'. Terrorist stories tend to raise audience rates, and the media often provide data on terrorist targets and organizations to intelligence services. The Internet became a new media battleground in itself, which could potentially give away battlefield positions of the warring parties and could pressure governments to react prematurely. Between 2001 and 2007, terrorism coverage created a self-help ethics, especially in the environment of cyberspace and fast live 24/7 ICTs; policies of censorship and statutory regulation were unsuccessful, with the ethics training of journalists remaining low in the priority of the media industry if the News of the World phone hacking scandal is anything to go by.

During this period, militant groups such as Al-Qaeda relied on the web to recruit new adherents. The web's growing centrality in Al-Qaeda-related operations led analysts such as former CIA director John E. McLaughlin to describe the movement as primarily driven today by 'ideology and the Internet' (Coll and Glasser, 7 August 2005). The web's shapeless disregard for national boundaries and ethnic markers fits exactly with bin Laden's original vision for Al-Qaeda, which he founded to stimulate revolt among the worldwide Muslim *ummah*, or community of believers. In November 2001, as the Taliban collapsed and Al-Qaeda lost its Afghan sanctuary, Osama bin Laden biographer Hamid Mir watched 'every second Al-Qaeda member carrying a laptop computer along with Kalashnikov' (ibid.) as they prepared to scatter into hiding and exile. Al-Qaeda's innovation on the web 'erodes the ability of our security services to hit them when they are most vulnerable, when they are moving', as Michael Sheuer, former CIA chief of the unit that tracked bin Laden, explained. 'It used to be they had to go to Sudan, they had to go to Yemen, they had to go to Afghanistan to train. An Al-Qaeda operative no longer has to carry anything that is incriminating. He doesn't need his schematics, he doesn't need his blueprints, he doesn't need anything that is incriminating'. Everything is posted on the web or 'can be sent ahead by encrypted Internet, and it gets lost in the billions of messages that are out there' (ibid.). Al-Qaeda militants defied a crackdown and the loss of senior leaders in Saudi Arabia by using the Internet to win over new recruits in Osama bin Laden's birthplace.

Al-Qaeda was quite a unique case in point, because it used the Internet in all sorts of resourceful ways, to fund and coordinate attacks, to replace leaders, and so on. A possible explanation for this is that their ideology does not rest on national identity, so it is open to international networking. The Al-Qaeda network and its ideology relies more on common religious affiliation and kinship networks than strict national identity, which fits well with the borderless and network character of the Internet. The Internet was used as a primary mobilizational tool before 9/11, especially after the breakdown of cells in Afghanistan, Saudi Arabia, and Pakistan. On the Internet, Al-Qaeda was replicating recruitment and training techniques and evading security services because they cannot be physically intercepted due to the virtuality of their networks. The Internet was used as a propaganda tool via electronic magazines, training manuals, and general recruitment sites, and as a weapon for financial disruptions aimed at financing operations or stealing data and blueprints.

Post 9/11, the U.S. military was consistently advised by think tanks to exploit new information technologies and create and sustain a more network-based approach to warfare, utilizing psychological and information warfare and 'winning the hearts and minds of the population'. Especially with the wars in Afghanistan and Iraq, the United States was forced to recognize the need to utilize new media and social networking technologies to tap into a younger American audience and to recruit and mobilize global public opinion under a more favourable light of how the Iraq war was fought and why.

The second most significant event of the 2001–2007 phase of digital activism and cyberconflict was the 'first Internet war': the Iraq War in 2003. When we look at the March 2003 Iraq conflict, the Internet's role in the conflict is studied in terms of its effect on the organization and spread of the movement and its impact on war coverage and war-related cyberconflicts. These last involved hacking between antiwar and prowar hacktivists (sociopolitical cyberconflict), but also between pro-Islamic and anti-Islamic hackers (ethnoreligious cyberconflict) (see Karatzogianni, 2006, 174–191).

On the sociopolitical cyberconflict field, the Internet played a distinctive role in the spread of the peace movement, in war coverage, and in war-related cyberconflicts, rendering the full potential of the new medium in politics and information undisputable. In the months preceding the actual war in Iraq, a plenitude of phenomena on and off the Internet emerged, which in previous international conflicts were only embryonic. Peace groups organized demonstrations and events through the Internet, to the effect that ten million people protested against the war globally, with the net speeding up mobilization remarkably. It helped mobilization in loose coalitions of small groups that organized very quickly, at the same time preserving the particularity of distinct groups in network forms of organization. Antiwar groups used e-mail lists and websites, group text messages, and chat rooms to organize protests, and in some cases to engage in symbolic hacking against the opposite viewpoint. Accordingly, the antiwar movement succeeded in this respect at gradually building their own image of the Americans and their allies and framing their message (no WMD, dodgy dossiers, humanitarian concerns, etc.). The integration of the Internet into mainstream media, the effect of online material challenging official government sources and the mainstream media, and blogging challenged the primacy of American hegemony, their allies, and their representations in the global public sphere.

Mobilization structures, for instance, were affected by the Internet, since the peace groups used the Internet to organize demonstrations and events, to mobilize in loose coalitions of small groups that organize very quickly, and to preserve the particularity of distinct groups in network forms of organization. Moreover, the framing process was also affected, since e-mail lists and websites are used to mobilize, changing the framing of the message to suit the new medium. Antiwar groups used e-mail lists and websites, group text messages, and chat-rooms to organize protests, making politics more accessible to an unprecedented number of people from all backgrounds who normally would not or could not get involved to such a degree. In only one weekend of 15 and 16 February 2003 (or F-15, in activist parlance), about ten million people protested globally against the war, rendering them the biggest peace protests since the anti-Vietnam War protests of the 1960s/1970s. Ruth Rosen wrote in the *San Francisco Chronicle*, 'Never before in human history has an anti-war movement grown so fast and spread so quickly' (Kahney, 21 January 2003); Sarah Sloan, an organizer with International ANSWER argued that the Internet played a very significant role because 'it made a major difference in getting our message out there especially because the mainstream media is not covering the anti-war movement' (ibid.). Rayman Elamine, organizer with Direct Action to Stop the War, said, 'Groups wouldn't have been able to do some of the logistical and other planning without the aid of the Internet for getting the message out' (Glasner, 19 March 2003). Howard Rheingold argued at the time, 'Instead of having some hierarchical top-down coalition, it's possible to have loose coalitions of small groups that organize very quickly' (ibid.).

What became possible was a mass mobilization without leaders – a digital swarm – by allowing mobilization to emerge from free-wheeling amorphous groups, rather than top-down hierarchies, the net changed protests in a more fundamental way. As Todd Gitlin explained at the time, 'It took four and a half years to multiply the size of the Vietnam protests twenty fold. This time the same thing has happened in six months'. Besides the use of websites in countries such as Germany (www.resistthewar.de), Britain (www.reclaimthebases.org.uk, www.peaceuk.net), France (www.mvtpaix.org), and Spain (www.pazahora.org), and the global Independent Media Center (legacy from Seattle) (www.indymedia.org), there was a 'Virtual March' on Washington when tens of thousands of people bombarded the switchboard of the White House and other U.S. government offices with protest calls and e-mails, halting much business in the capital. The coalition of 32 organizations that organized the action claimed that more than 400,000 people registered to participate in the campaign.

In that early period of Internet use for mobilization, concerns were already expressed. For instance, Stewart Nusbaumer, coordinator of Veterans Against the War, said at the time, 'On the one hand, [the Internet] gives you larger numbers of people. But I've also noticed it's not great for a specific demonstration somewhere. I get emails from people who say: I live 2,000 miles away' (Glasner, 19 March 2003). Because of the much lower digital development of that era, it seemed that the leaderless and dispersed nature of online activism could render it ineffective in that it ultimately would fail to reach the vast majority of the world, where many activists in developing countries had little or no access to the Internet or ICTs in general. The other issue with digital activism was that the epic qualities of major demonstrations both in size and drama could be lost when in cyberspace.

During the Iraq War, the Internet was used not only to mobilize international civil society, but also to offer alternative coverage of the conflict. Various developments included the integration of the Internet into mainstream media, the effect of online material challenging official government sources and mainstream media, and the 'blogging' phenomenon, which gave birth to citizen journalism. As Mitch Gelman, executive producer of CNN, put it, 'You are combining the speed of television with the depth of print. This could define how future wars are covered' (Swartz, 18 March 2003).

Because U.S. media mostly followed the government line with patriotic fervour, Americans turned to non-U.S. sources by using the Internet. The war coverage setup used journalists embedded with troops, so it was difficult for war correspondents not embedded with troops to get nonofficial stories out. Their reporting was based in large part on handouts from U.S. occupation officials, or material gained while 'embedded' with U.S. military units supplemented by on-the-spot accounts and interviews obtained by Iraqi 'stringers', who risked their lives for a fraction of the salary paid to their Western counterparts. Iraq was notoriously dangerous for war correspondents; '[t]he figures in Iraq tell a terrible story. Fifteen media people dead, with two missing, presumed dead. If you consider how short the campaign was, Iraq will be notorious as the most dangerous war for journalists ever' (Knightley, 14 June 2003). There were significant concerns raised on the targeting of journalists by the U.S. Army: 'We can only conclude that the U.S. Army deliberately and without warning targeted journalists' (Reporters without Borders); 'We believe these attacks violate the Geneva conventions' (Committee to Protect Journalists in a letter to Defense Secretary Donald Rumsfeld, 8 April 2003); the attacks on journalists 'look very much like murder' (Robert Fisk of the London *Independent*, 3 March 2003). Eason Jordan, CNN's chief news executive, suggested at the World Economic Forum in Switzerland that some of the 63 journalists killed in Iraq had been specifically targeted by U.S. troops. The president of the 35,000-member Newspaper Guild asserted that U.S. troops were deliberately killing journalists in Iraq. Meanwhile, several national and local media figures in the United States found their jobs jeopardized, either explicitly or implicitly, because of the critical views they expressed on the war.

Despite the official U.S. government warning against patriotic hacking, the most notorious incident occurred when the Al-Jazeera website was knocked offline by an American web designer. Al-Jazeera became the Internet's number one search query for 48 hours, according to web portal Lycos. People were hunting for video footage that Al-Jazeera had aired of dead American soldiers and U.S. prisoners being interrogated by their Iraqi captors – including gruesome images that American TV networks mostly declined to show. Cyberattacks were occurring as early as October 2002, debating virtually the situation in Iraq. London-based computer security firm mi2g said October 2002 was the worst month for digital attacks since its records began in 1995. It estimated that 16,559 attacks were carried out on computer systems and websites during that month (BBC News, 29 October 2003). When the war actually started, Zone-H, a firm that records and monitors hackings, reported 20,000 defacements in the first week of the war. Hundreds of U.S. and British business, government, and municipal websites were defaced with antiwar messages. Roberto Preatoni: '[t]his is the future of protest. If you take down Al-Jazeera, everybody around the world knows it. And you never have to leave your house' (Reuters, 28 March 2003). As a result of the escalating conflict, thousands of websites were the target of denial-of-service attacks, defacement, worms, and viruses. Jason Halloway of F-Secure put it this way: 'I have never seen that level of political hacktivism before, nor so many defacements in such a short time'. (For an extensive discussion see 'The Effects of the Internet on the Iraq War' in Karatzogianni, 2006, 176–191).

In the same period, dissidents against governments were able to use a variety of Internet-based techniques (e-mail lists, e-mail spamming, bulletin boards, peer-to-peer networks, and e-magazines) to spread alternative frames for events and a possible alternative online democratic public sphere. An example of dissidents' use of the Internet is spamming e-magazines to an unprecedented number of people in China, a method that provides recipients with 'plausible deniability'. Also, proxy servers and file-trading networks like Kazaa and Gnutella helped dissidents communicate. Those using the Internet against their governments seek power, participation, and democracy, prompting counterstrategies to crack down on cyberdissidents. In countries such as Iran, China, and Vietnam, dissidents were bypassing censorship and transmitting banned themes: ideologies, revolution, reform, massacres, and historical events of repression and conflict.

Despite the unsuccessful Orange Revolution in 2005 (Morozov, 2011), people around the world started to believe in the power of the medium to organize to promote a single use, to fight for global justice and against authoritarian regimes. Significantly, the Internet was also used to coordinate and organize violent insurgent networks as witnessed by the Madrid (2004) and London (2005) bombings (on global justice and violent insurgencies and ICTs, see various studies, such as De Armond, 2001; Papacharissi, 2002; 2004; Chase and Mulvenon, 2002; Jenkins and Thorburn, 2003; McCaughey and Ayers, 2003; Vegh, 2003; Diani and McAdam, 2003; Le Grignou and Patou, 2004; Van Aelst and Walgrave, 2004; Van De Donk et al., 2004; Calabrese and Sparks, 2004; Berry and Moss, 2005; Longman, 2005; Shane, 2005; Denning, 2006; Pickard, 2006; Chadwick, 2006).

In new social movements, networking through the Internet links diverse communities such as labour, feminist, ecological, peace, and anticapitalist groups, with the aim of challenging public opinion and battling for media access and coverage. This is enabling civil society actors to the extent that a reformatting of politics is taking place (Dean, Anderson, and Lovink, 2006). It is at the interface, the spectrum and the clash between hierarchies and networks, that revolutionary change occurs. In complexity theory terms, this happens when a system is at the edge of chaos. It is herein that networks/rhizomes fight against hierarchies/arborescent systems to disrupt the closure of space in the global system in the fields of governance, knowledge production, convergence culture, and digital citizenship in a new public sphere (Karatzogianni and Robinson, 2010).

2
The Third Phase (2007–2010): Spread of Digital Activism

2.1 Russia-related ethnonational digital activism and cyberconflicts

I place the start of the third phase in 2007 with the Estonian cyberconflict because it pointed to the deficiency of the international community to regulate cyberconflict and to create mechanisms for defining and reacting to cyberattacks conducted against a state, especially one linked to NATO and the EU, and in a sensitive geopolitical area. Keeping the socioeconomic implications in mind, the real impact of the Estonian cyberconflict operates on multiple political levels. It was initially speculated whether the attacks were by the Russian government, Russian diasporic communities, or more likely ethnic Russians in Estonia. It is also a problem, even when the guilty party is confirmed, to decide whether to treat cyberattacks as 'real' military attacks. The other problem it pointed to is how to understand the differences between cyberprotest, cyberterrorism, and cybercrime.

Information communication technologies (ICTs) are a very convenient and cost-effective tool for protest, but the real spark is the uncertainty about the enemy within and the anxiety about the always incomplete project of national purity so that 'these geographies are the spatial outcome of complex interactions between faraway events and proximate fears, between old histories and new provocations, between rewritten borders and unwritten orders', as Appadurai (2006) puts it. This cultural struggle, which integrates war and politics at the borders with vigilance and purification at the centres, is exacerbated by the media in general and by new communication technologies in particular. The fight to win the global war of messages, propaganda, and ideas has often produced unpredictable results, especially in cyberspace. In essence, patriots are defending the purity of their national space, and they do so by skilfully using online media technologies. To put it simply, globalization and its technologies can expose pathologies in the sacred ideologies of nationhood.

As today's ethnic groups number in the hundreds and thousands, their mixtures, cultural style, and media representations 'create profound doubts about who exactly are among the "we" and who are among the "they" in the context of rapid migration or refugee movements, how many of "them are now among us"' (Appadurai, 2006). The statue and its removal in Estonia, and the cyberconflict that ensued, is a reflection of the instability of the EU enlargement project, especially in relation to Russia's hegemonic aspirations, energy disputes, and legacy in the region, pointing to an emerging second cold asymmetric war by Russia, such as disputes with the United States and Russia's relentless involvement in the region as a whole (e.g., supporting secessionist states in South Ossetia and the recent Ukraine conflict in 2013).

Appadurai's notion that a geography of anger is fuelled by the media, but its spark is the uncertainty about the enemy within and the anxiety about the always incomplete project of national purity, is the frame that could be used successfully to explain cyberattacks by ethnic and nationalist hackers: 'These geographies are the spatial outcome of complex interactions between faraway events and proximate fears, between old histories and new provocations, between rewritten borders and unwritten orders' (Appadurai, 2006, 100). Appadurai, although he recognizes that we still live in a vertebrate world, albeit one in which the state is not the only game in town, argues that 'alongside this exists the cellular world, whose parts multiply by association and opportunity rather than by legislation or by design. It is also a product of globalization – of the new information technologies, of the speed of finance and the velocity of the news, of the movement of capital and the circulation of refugees' (Appadurai, 2006, 129). And, more importantly, 'We need to watch them, for the coming crisis of the nation-state may lie not in the dark cellularities of terror but in the utopian cellularities of these new transnational organizational forms' (ibid., 137).

In 'How Small Are Small Numbers in Cyberspace?' (2009) I argued that established mainstream media and their online equivalents usually support what different theorists call state-like, hierarchical, or vertebrate political forms of organization crucial to state/status quo survival. Second, independent, alternative, or peer-to-peer networked media usually support transnational, rhizomatic, cellular networks, such as ethnoreligious and sociopolitical movements or diasporic minorities and dissident networks within. Third, small states and minorities are especially vulnerable to both of these modalities, as they are frequently too small, too new, or too insignificant to have been adequately mass-mediated in the past, so any representations by the mass media are registered automatically as negotiated in the global public sphere.

It is likely that minorities and small numbers benefit from ICTs far more than their powerful enemies. In all these places, the mainstream media tended either to represent them as 'trouble in paradise', sided with the status quo state in cases of secession, or failed to engage seriously with the deeper roots of the conflict. In the advocacy or action websites, what is called currently by the popular press in France 'the 5th power of the Internet' enabled players to punch above their weight and at least enter the competition for the battle for the ears of global public opinion.

For instance, there are the continuities in the coverage of Russian hackers and links made in the global media between intelligence, cyberespionage, cybercrime, and patriotic hacking, which implicated Russian hackers and Russia in the Climategate hack. The Climategate hack revealed tensions and pressures in understanding the transfer of physical conflict to cyberspace, essentially lurking in the following plateaus: cultural perceptions of electronic crime, hackers and hacktivism, and un-nuanced media representations of such perceptions; difficulties in defining the often subtle or otherwise ideological distinctions behind ad hoc assemblages engaging in cyberconflict, hacktivism, cybercrime and the media portrayal of such events; the overall presence in culture and the media of a residual, politicized, and ideological discourse, indiscriminately portraying individuals, which nevertheless engage in fundamentally diverse ways, in order to effect change, to protest electronically, to support ethno-national causes or to engage in criminal activities in cyberspace; and the effect of such discourses on diplomacy, global politics, and the question of defining and regulating cyberconflict, cyberprotest, and cybercrime at a global level.

Although Russians *are* involved in cybercrime and cyberconflict incidents – as are other nationals by participating in cybercrime gangs, ad hoc patriotic assemblages, or even hacking dissident media organizations to reinforce the government line – they are also portrayed by the majority of the global media as *the* perpetrators of everything under the sun (unless the crimes are attributed to China or Chinese hackers). Russians were accused relentlessly of the Climategate hack under a new Cold War rhetoric spurred on by Russia's energy interests and motivations. In contrast to the overwhelming blame that Russian hackers are made to bear, there are other possible competing explanations: involvement of oppositional bloggers and scientists invested in the Climategate debate, or a computer security failure at East Anglia University's network.

The Estonian and Georgian cyberconflicts were of the ethnonational type, revealing cultural struggles due to Russia's alleged continuing intervention in the political life of these countries. The hacker groups involved in these conflicts and their systems of belief and organization aspire to hierarchical apparatuses (nation, ethnicity, identification with parties and leaders). The Climategate hack case, on the other hand, had sociopolitical and economic aspects, as it is an issue that is global in nature in terms of content. However, the Climategate case also pointed to ethnic and national issues in the coverage, as geopolitical narratives involved the main protagonists in the Climategate debate and the actual groups blamed for the hack. In mapping the environment of cyberconflict, the relationships between military and security, politicians and media, and geopolitical dimensions need to be addressed.

For the article 'Blame It on the Russians: Tracking the Portrayal of Hackers in Cyberconflict Incidents', which was published in *Digital Icons* (2010) and subsequently in *Violence and War in Culture and the Media* (2012), I surveyed approximately 130 news articles and blogs collected between 2007 and 2010. The articles were sampled manually by using the keyword 'Russian hackers' on two different web search engines, Google and Yahoo, while also snowballing to include other items that followed the initial searches. The study includes sources from mainstream media (online versions of newspapers, magazines, and TV outlets, such as *The Guardian, New York Times, Wall Street Journal, The New Scientist, The Independent, Le Monde, BBC,* AFP, and Reuters); country- and incident-specific media and blogs (such as the *Georgian Times, Russia Today,* and climate sceptic blogs); and IT business, security, and military sites and blogs commenting on cybersecurity and on technical aspects of the cyberconflicts under discussion (such as *National Defence Magazine, Wired Magazine, Asian Computers, PC World,* and Villeneuve's blog).

The Estonia cyberattacks lasted roughly a month (beginning on 27 April 2007) and handicapped Estonian government, media, and bank sites. The attacks served as a protest platform for ethnic Russians objecting to the relocation of the Bronze Soldier of Tallinn and included defacement of websites, denial-of-service attacks and the use of botnets previously used for spam. The real-life event that sparked the cyberconflict in Estonia was the removal of a Soviet war hero statue from Tallinn's square and the subsequent riots that took place in Estonia for several days around 26 April 2007, leading to several casualties.

By 20 April 2007, although the real-world riots had calmed down, the country's digital infrastructure was crumbling from cyberattacks. The statue incident reflected deeper tensions and the cultural conflict between the Estonian state and ethnic Russians in Estonia, who made up around one-quarter of the Baltic republic's population of 1.34 million (1 January 2015 figure at 1.31).

Estonia is considered to be an Internet success story due to its e-commerce, and it also has a strong e-government presence. The Estonian cyberconflict included denial-of-service attacks, clogging the country's servers and routers, infiltrating the world with botnets, and banding computers together and transforming them into 'zombies' hijacked by viruses to take part in such raids without their owners' knowledge. Multiple sources flowed into the system, and the attackers even rented time in botnets. The attacks lasted three weeks. The plans of the attackers were posted in Russian-language chat rooms with instructions on how to send disruptive messages and which websites to target. The attacks targeted all levels of the social, political, and economic infrastructure: the Estonian presidency and its Parliament, almost all of the country's government ministries and political parties, three of the country's six big news organizations, two of the biggest banks, and other firms specializing in communications.

Blaming the Russian state for the attacks, the Estonian authorities rapidly mobilized to fight the war, utilizing contacts in several countries and requesting NATO and the EU for help. The Estonian government was also portrayed as going through a 'panic attack', exaggerating the situation when its networks were attacked in cyber space: 'Faced with DDoS and nationalistic, cross-border hacktivism – nuisances that have plagued the rest of the wired world for the better part of a decade – Estonia's leaders lost perspective' (Poulsen, 22 August 2007).

To use the lens of cyberconflict theory, the Estonian case points to ethnonational and cultural elements, with ethnic Russians utilizing ICTs to protest their anger at the treatment of Russians in Estonia. The use of patriotic hacking as a facet of hacktivism creates questions in terms of how the groups were organized, their mobilization, framing, and the organization of the attacks. Similar elements of organizing are found in sociopolitical cyberconflicts. At the same time, wider issues of cultural conflict and geopolitical tensions need to be explored. Article 5 in NATO's charter states that if a NATO ally is the victim of an armed attack, each and every other member of the alliance should consider this act of violence as an armed attack against all members and should take the actions it deems necessary to assist the ally attacked. As NATO did not define electronic attacks as military action, it could not intervene even when the origin of the attack could be proven. Also, the use of information communication technologies is a very convenient and cost-effective tool for protest, usually related to hacktivism and the ethical debates surrounding it. Linked to the real-life protests and their online incarnation is the uncertainty about the 'enemy within' and the anxiety about the always incomplete project of national purity, as manifested in the lives of the ethnic Russians in Estonia and elsewhere. These cultural struggles are exacerbated by the media and propaganda, with groups defending the purity of their national space using online technologies.

The South Ossetian-Georgian cyberconflict occurred right before and during the actual armed conflict in August 2008 between Georgia and Russia. On 7 August, Georgia launched a military attack in South Ossetia in an attempt to reestablish control of the area. Russia retaliated by bombing and occupying Georgian cities. The war ended after five days; in the aftermath, Russia supported the independence of South Ossetia and Abkhazia (another region seeking independence from Georgia), keeping troops in the areas. The cyberconflict began several days before the actual war, when the virtual infrastructures of various South Ossetian, Russian, and Georgian organizations were attacked, leading to defacement of websites, denial-of-service attacks, and botnets. According to Internet rumours, the Russian Business Network (RBN), a well-known cybercrime gang linked to malicious software and hacking, was involved in the attacks, together with the Russian security services. Several governments such as Estonia, Poland, and Ukraine offered assistance to Georgia.

In November 2009, the 'Climategate hack', as it was termed by the media, was discovered: thousands of e-mails, files, and other communications among scientists at the Climate Research Unit (CRU) at the University of East Anglia were hacked into, and the materials were posted on a Siberian server. The controversy, which portrayed climate change scientists as manipulating data and the peer-review process, coincided with the Copenhagen Summit, where world leaders were meeting to discuss climate change. Three independent inquiries in the United Kingdom rejected allegations of wrongdoing by the scientists involved, though it was found there was room for improvement in the CRU's working practices (Gillis, 7 July 2010).

Many of the online news articles addressed here consistently described Russian hackers as highly educated and talented people who, upon unemployment, are forced to turn to illegal activities. Examples of this type of explanation are plenty. For instance, a local media outlet in the

United States called *Elk Grove Citizen* presented a story in which special agent LuAnna Harmon of the FBI's Sacramento division visits a high school to talk about cybercrime and frequently mentions Russian cybercrimes as her examples. When asked by the students about the reasons cybercrimes happen in Russia, she blames the situation on highly educated people who turn to crime since there are few jobs for them (Macdonald, 13 April 2010). In another report by the *Register*, Dmitry Zakharov, director of communications at the Russian Association of Electronic Communications, is quoted saying, '[W]e are not able to offer talented technology people jobs. So they get involved in illegal activity' (Leyden, 12 April 2010).

Russia is consistently portrayed as a nation of superhackers, responsible for sophisticated attacks. Various media reports involve interviews with security professionals and Russian hackers about their background and motivations. For example, in the BBC interview with Evgeny Kaspersky, the 'computer security guru' and an owner of Internet security firm Kaspersky Labs, the reporter refers to the Russian city of Tomsk as a centre for producing hackers (Rainsford, 11 March 2010). Tomsk is mentioned because the files relating to the Climategate hack were leaked and posted on a server there. In fact, the files were originally uploaded to Turkish and Saudi Arabian servers before Tomsk. In the interview, Kaspersky describes Russia as a nation of 'superhackers' and attributes their abilities to good technical education. The graduates at Tomsk are described in the article as facing a choice of either creating sophisticated information protection systems or joining the ranks of Russia's hackers for hire. However, this description of unemployment as the main reason for hacking in Russia is not always consistent. For instance, *National Defence* magazine features a former U.S. intelligence officer's description of Vladimir, who comes from a well-educated Russian family and who could be anything he wanted to be, but chose instead to be a cyberthief (Magnuson, May 2010).

Another theme in describing Russia as a nation of hackers is the portrayal of Russia and its relationship to its homegrown hackers and cybercrime gangs. Russia is presented as one of the top five countries from where international hacking attacks originate, and as a growing centre of cybercrime. Russia is also portrayed as a top cybersecurity concern in a Cold War-style discourse, a topic to which I return below. Typical examples are representations of Russia as the top producer of viruses, Trojans, and spyware, ranking second in generating spam (RT, 19 February 2008); Russia as the second-largest host of malware according to Sophos (Megerisi, 22 March 2010); and Russia as a centre for selling private databases, for example, in the Savelovskii market (Stack, 17 March 2010).

Furthermore, reports on cybercrime gangs, exploits, and cyberattacks of various kinds frequently mention the Russian Business Network (RBN), which is described as capable of taking a whole country offline. NATO sees both the RBN and the Russian hacker community as a general threat (RT, 8 January 2010). Botnets (software that distributes malware) – one of the frequent tools of cyberattacks – are universally mentioned as a trademark technique of RBN and of Russian hackers in general. Botnets distributing spam and controlling millions of computers are also reported in coverage of the Estonian and Georgian cyberconflicts. In 2009, 75 per cent of business structures were reported to have been exposed to various cyberattacks, with Russia being among the top ten countries generating the threat (Secrest, 29 April 2010). The reporting of cyberattacks often mentions interviews with experts and the statistics of computer security firms such as Symantec, Sophos, and Kaspersky.

Russians are often described as being arrested for or linked to the most famous cybercrime incidents from 2005 to 2010, such as the Charles Schwab brokerage attack and the attack on the Royal Bank of Scotland (RBS), a robbery of six million pounds in 12 hours (Hawkins, 7 April 2010). And lastly, there is a recurrent reference to the Russian mafia's cybercapabilities. However, admittedly, the RBS robbery was not technically sophisticated: the gang hacked into the system cloning 44 debit cards, but it was the coordination of cashers (individuals draining ATMs) that helped pull the robbery off in different countries. Nevertheless, the impression is given that the hackers had super cybercapabilities, as they managed to 'blitz more than 2,000 machines in 28 cities worldwide' (Findlay, 14 March 2010).

Inevitably, these stories create a mythology surrounding the abilities of Russian hackers, whereby they emerge as superhackers with astonishing accomplishments. Russia itself appears as a nation of highly capable hackers, a nation that both nurtures its computer specialists (thanks to its reportedly high-quality technical education) and fails them by dooming them to unemployment and lack of opportunities, thus 'forcing' them to turn to cybercrime.

Another aspect of media coverage of Russian hacking is the alleged link between cybercrime networks, cyberespionage, and political hacking. The researcher and blogger Nart Villeneuve argues that there is a potential relationship there, as the boundaries between crimeware networks and cyberespionage 'appear to be blurring, making issues of attribution increasingly more complex. It may also indicate that there is an emerging market for sensitive information and/or politically motivated attacks, as crimeware networks seek to monetise such information and capabilities' (Villeneuve, 10 April 2010). More importantly, this prompts Villenueve to believe that such attacks demonstrate that botnets involved with criminal activity are being used to conduct both political and apolitical distributed denial-of-service (DDoS) attacks (ibid.).

Examples of this type of activity abound in the Russian and post-Soviet landscape. For instance, the website of the Russian newspaper *Novaya Gazeta* (New Newspaper), critical of Russian authorities, experienced six days of downtime due to a hacker attack in 2003 (Periscopeit, 3 February 2003). In 2010, *The Guardian* reported a more recent attack on *Novaya Gazeta*, in which the newspaper staff described the scale of the attack as comprising more than a million hits a second on the server. This report suggested that the attack was carried out by a 'highly sophisticated' state agency displeased with the newspaper's editorial direction (Harding, 27 January 2010). Other incidents include attacks on the Polish government system, which coincided with the 70th anniversary of the outbreak of World War II and a visit by Russian Prime Minister Vladimir Putin (Leyden, 13 October 2009). In Kyrgyzstan in 2009, two of the country's main Internet service providers, ns.kg and domain.kg, came under a massive denial-of-service attack. Some reports stated the assault had shut down 80 per cent of the country's bandwidth. Media descriptions presented this as a case of suspected Russian influence (Weinberger, 14 May 2010).

The linking of cybercrime to cyberconflict is explicit in media reports that one of the botnets drafted for the Georgian cyberattack was 'Black Energy', a Trojan horse-hijacked army of PCs thought to have been used to hit Citibank, while 'Black Energy 2' was being used to launch DDoS attacks against Russian banks (Keizer, 7 April 2010). The Georgian press also made the link to cyberconflict explicit by suggesting the involvement of the Russian intelligence service, the Federal Security Service (FSB). According to these reports, the FSB attacked the National Bolshevik Party and moderate opposition groups like 'The Marc of Those Who Disagree', and mainstream media outlets such as *Kommersant* and *Ekho Moskvy*. The reports quote Andrei Soldatov's piece in *Novaya Gazeta*, where he suggests that the FSB did not have to use their own in-house resources but could simply point the growing community of 'hacker-patriots' in the right direction (Goble, 31 May 2007).

In the case of the Georgian cyberconflict, the circumstances were different, but here, too, patriotic hacking was the main element. It was reported as a 'virtual war' in cyberspace accompanying the brief war in the summer of 2008 between Georgia and Russia. Once again, the media accused Russia of orchestrating the cyberattacks, even though it appeared to be due to patriotic hacking by individuals or groups of hackers.

Diplomacy, espionage, and security in cyberspace were frequently discussed in media narratives of Russia and Russian hackers implicated in cyberconflicts. These issues form part of the narrative that consistently blames Russian hackers for any type of activity involving the use of computers. What emerges here is a new Cold War discourse, often used to discuss together the geopolitics in the region, the role of NATO in maintaining cybersecurity, and the specific cases linked to Russian hackers.

One telling example is the discussion in the global media of cyberespionage perpetrated by Russia and China. It is worth noting here that cyberespionage is not currently a crime under international law and not usually a grounds for war. In a report in the UK's *Telegraph*, Jonathan Evans, the head of MI5, has warned that Britain faces 'unreconstructed attempts by Russia, China and others' who were using 'sophisticated technical attacks' to try and steal sensitive technology on civilian and military projects, along with political and economic intelligence (Gardham, 4 December 2009). In the *Times*, Evans is mentioned once again, writing to 300 businesses in 2007 to warn them of Chinese hacking attacks and data theft (Loyd, 8 March 2010). Anthony Loyd links the interests of hostile state intelligence agencies and cybercriminal syndicates known as *partnerka* (syndicate, partnership), claiming they lead 'commercial espionage in Europe and are known to have links with Harry and his comrades in the FSB' (Loyd, 8 March 2010).

Such narratives regarding global security espionage and cybersecurity are linked in the media to questions about Russia and the participation of countries previously within the Soviet sphere of influence in NATO. This is particularly prevalent in the media debates around the coverage of Estonian and Georgian cyberconflicts, as well as around NATO's cybersecurity capabilities, doctrine, and general regulation of cyberconflict. The problem is viewed in the mainstream media as NATO's need to develop an agreed-upon concept of what constitutes worldwide cybersecurity (Austin, 10 January 2010). Most of the coverage related to Russia and NATO makes extensive use of the Cold War framework. For example, NATO Secretary-General Anders Fogh Rasmussen is reported to have understood the special security concerns of East Europeans 'who chafed under Moscow's decades-long domination during the Cold War, and criticised Russia's new military doctrine' (Reuters, 12 March 2010).

Questions of cybersecurity are also embedded in international politics of secession and recognition. For example, then U.S. Secretary of State Hilary Clinton stated that the United States supported Georgia and would recognize neither Abkhazia nor South Ossetia. South Ossetia was the reason for the war between Russia and Georgia, with Russia recognizing South Ossetia and Abkhazia's quest for independence. Besides the international relations aspects of the Russian-Georgian war, there are regional media issues linked to this case. 'The only war we can win against Russia is an information war, so we shouldn't miss our chance', argued the Georgian political analyst Tornike Sharashenidze (Kiguradze, 13 November 2009). The Georgian media environment is described as highly politicized, with broadcasters providing either an intensely progovernment or pro-opposition view (UNCHR, 16 February 2009).

The actual Georgia-South Ossetia cyberconflict started the same day as the military offensive on 8 August 2008, although attacks were also registered in July. The websites of the president of Georgia, the Georgian Parliament, the ministries of defence and foreign affairs, the National Bank of Georgia, and online news agencies were attacked, with the cyberconflict becoming more intense as the real conflict escalated. Images of Hitler were manipulated and juxtaposed on the Georgian president. The Georgian response involved using filters to block Russian IP addresses, moving websites elsewhere, and appealing to Estonia and other countries for help. Estonia dispatched specialists, and Poland provided websites for Georgian use (Heickero, March 2010).

Possibly the most fascinating discussion on the Georgian cyberconflict comes in the form of a journal article written by Stephen Korns and Josua Kastenberg and published in *Parameters*. In their article, they reaffirm the view that most security experts have attributed the 2008 DDoS attacks to 'an amalgam of government-incentivised agents, hackers and citizen protestors' (Korns and Kastenberg, 2009, 66). They give the example of an Internet journalist who accessed a website and downloaded prepackaged software that would have enabled him to join in the attacks, had he chosen to do so (Morozov, 2008, cited in Korns and Kastenberg, 2009, 65).

In fact, Korns and Kastenberg make very interesting observations about this cyberconflict. First, they bring up the issue of cyber neutrality: in contrast to Estonia, which experienced cyberattacks but essentially defended in place, Georgia manoeuvred by relocating strategic IP-based cybercapabilities to a private company in the United States (Korns and Kastenberg, 2009, 68). Korns and Kastenberg believe that Georgia's unconventional response to the August 2008 DDoS attacks, supported by U.S. private industry, adds a new element of complication for cyber-strategists (ibid., 61). Secondly, they show that since the 2001 Council of Europe Convention on Cybercrime, to which the United States is a party, omits any reference to the terms 'cyberattack' or 'cyberweapons', cyberattacks are currently part of cyber*crime* and not cyber*war*, as such. From that perspective it would have been Interpol, rather than NATO, that would have to respond to Estonia and Georgia (ibid., 64–65).

To push Korns' and Kastenberg's argumentation further, any cyberat-tack could be framed as cybercrime and prosecuted as such, unless it is part of an armed conflict. This implies that any political hacking could be prosecuted as a (cyber) crime. Indeed, one of the patriotic hackers (or a cultural protester, as he was portrayed by some) in the Estonian cyber-conflict discussed earlier was convicted and fined for his 'cybercrime' activities. The ethical debate on hacktivism notwithstanding, this shift could potentially mean that electronic disobedience or hacktivism as we know them could also be prosecuted as criminal activities, despite their mostly symbolic effects. An additional problem here is the difficulty in determining with certainty the origin of cyberattacks or establishing whether an attack is a state-sponsored mission or an ad hoc initiative. As Korns and Kastenberg put it, 'cyber conflict between nations is a serious concern, but as the Georgian DDoS attacks demonstrate, perhaps of even greater concern is the growing trend of cyber conflict between nations and ad hoc assemblages' (ibid., 70).

The Estonian cyberconflict led to the establishment of a Cooperative Cyber Defence Centre of Excellence by NATO in 2008 in Tallinn (Johnson, 16 April 2009). Furthermore, in May 2010, the secretary of defence Robert Gates announced the activation of the Pentagon's first comprehensive, multiservice cyber operation, the USA Cyber Command (CYBERCOM), with Keith Alexander as its commander. Talking about cyberspace as the fifth battle space, transferring soldiers from communications and elec-tronics to an Army Forces cyber command, and wondering how cyber-warriors should be trained confirms a trend toward militarization of what was previously a criminal and commercial matter (Rozoff, 26 May 2010). With Russia and China frequently depicted as the main suspects, the United States and its NATO allies have had to address cyberwarfare questions in its twenty-first century strategic concept. With 120 coun-tries developing cybercapabilities, NATO's director of policy planning Jamie Shea commented that 'there are people in the strategic commu-nity who say cyber attacks now will serve the same role in initiating hostilities as air campaigns played in the twentieth century' (Rozoff, 26 May 2010).

NATO will have to eventually create a coherent strategy for cyberwarfare. This problem has been addressed by various scholars of Internet security (Central European University, 7–8 June 2010). In June 2010, the *Sunday Times* reported that a team of NATO experts led by former U.S. secretary of state Madeleine Albright prepared a document stating that a cyberattack on the critical infrastructure of a NATO country could equate to an armed attack, justifying retaliation (Smith and Warren, 6 June 2010). The organization's lawyers were reported saying that since the effect of a cyberattack can be similar to an armed assault, there is no need to redraft existing treaties. If an attack on critical infrastructure resulted in casualties and destruction comparable to a military attack, then the mutual defence clause of Article 5 could be invoked. Still, the level of attack is not exactly clear, as the perception of the dangers of cyberwarfare continues to change.

To conclude the discussion of Russian hackers, let me now turn to the Climategate hack – an incident which was consistently attributed to Russia by the global media. This attribution became particularly clear after several key figures, such as Professor Jean-Pascal Ypersele, the vice chairman of the Intergovernmental Panel on Climate Change, supported the Russian hackers scenario. Here are some typical examples of the narratives that followed: 'Russian hackers illegally obtained 10 years of e-mails between the world's top climate change scientists' (Kolasinski, 4 December 2009); 'The British media and some U.N. scientists have suggested that the Russian secret service, the FSB, was complicit in the theft' (Snapple, 7 January 2010); 'The guiding hand behind the leaks, the allegation went, was that of the Russian secret services' (Walker, 7 December 2009); 'Russia, a major oil exporter, may be trying to undermine calls to reduce carbon emissions' (*Telegraph*, 6 December 2009); 'This is not the first time Russian hackers have created global Internet disarray' (MacNicol, 7 December 2009); 'Russian computer hackers are suspected of being behind the stolen e-mails' (McCarthy and Owen, 6 December 2009). A typical article in the *Times* by Tony Halpin sums up all the reasons why Russian hackers and Russia were immediately implicated: Russia's desire to discredit the summit; poor, talented, but unemployed hackers; the RBN and the use of patriotic hackers by the FSB. All these were connected together, fitting the overall move to blame Russian hackers – a move already built up by the global media (Halpin, 7 December 2009).

Most media representations of the Climategate hack linked the events to other incidents in the past, suggesting a consistent narrative frame that blames the attacks on Russian hackers. Russian hackers were ideal in this respect. Although the Climategate material was uploaded on various servers in Turkey and Saudi Arabia before ending up in Tomsk in Siberia, it was Tomsk that became the key factor in the Russian hackers story. Reporters interviewed students in Tomsk, where a computer school was located, and it was also stated that 'in 2002 Tomsk students launched a "denial of service" attack at the Kavkaz-Tsentr portal, a site whose reports about Chechnya angered Russian officials'. The FSB office in Tomsk put out a special press release stating that the students' actions had been a legitimate 'expression of their position as citizens, one worthy of respect' (Stewart and Delgado, 6 December 2009; also reported by Merchant, 7 December 2009). Around the same time, the media frequently linked the Georgian and Estonian cyberconflicts to the Russian security service and accused the Russian police of turning a blind eye to cybercrime (Judge, 7 December 2009).

Several reports, some from bloggers, however, began deviating from the general certainty and consensus that attributed the Climategate hack to the Russians. Since hackers used open proxies to mask their identities, they could have originated from anywhere in the world. And if Russian hackers where indeed involved, leaving the files at Tomsk would be too obvious. And yet most reports pointed a finger at Russian hackers. The media repeatedly mentioned Russian hackers' sophistication, linking it to earlier, equally skilful attacks. In the case of the Climategate hack, the impression was given that the hackers selected specific information implicating the scientists of the past 13 years. None of the media reports mentioned that the files titled after the Freedom of Information Act might have been collected by someone working at the University of East Anglia. Fred Pearce reported, for example, that a number of people claim to have stumbled on nonpublic files on the UEA server in the months prior to the hack. Among them was David Holland, a British engineer and an amateur climate sceptic, who in December 2008 notified the university that the search engine on their home page was broken and falling through to a directory. In November 2009, Charles Rotter, the moderator of the blog Watts Up With That (http://wattsupwiththat.com/), wrote that in July of that year he had discovered that the university had left station data versions from 2003 and 1996 on its server, and that those who knew where to look could find the files available in public access (Pearce, 9 February 2010a; 2010b).

There are other reasons why the leak version might be more plausible than an attack by Russia or Russian hackers. Lance Levsen, for example, has argued that if the file was not already collected and stolen, the actual collection of the material and cracking meant a super sophisticated operation. A reasonable explanation for the archive being in such a state is that the FOI officer at the university was practicing due diligence and that someone at UEA found the file and released it into the wild. The release of FOIA2009.zip could have occurred not because of a hacker, but because of a leak from UEA by a person with scruples (Levsen, 7 December 2009). Also, notably, the 'hackers' made several efforts at disseminating the material before succeeding; this, once again, is not consistent with the pattern of how Russian hackers would operate. Paul Hudson, a weatherman and climate change sceptic, was sent a sample a month before the documents were leaked, but he did not use it (Leigh, Arthur, and Evans, 4 February 2010b). Matthew Taylor and Charles Arthur explain that a month after Hudson received his sample, someone hacked into the RealClimate website using a computer in Turkey and uploaded a zip file containing all 4,000 e-mails and documents. At that point, the website's cofounder shut down the site. Then hackers used a computer in Saudi Arabia to post a fresh copy of the zip file, this time stored on the Tomsk server. Then the incident was picked up by blogs and organizations all over the world (Taylor and Arthur, 27 November 2009). Eventually the story spread through climate change sceptic sites and then found its way into the mainstream media (Hurlbut, 20 November 2009).

And lastly, the fact that the documents were on a server due to a computer security failure at UEA and then 'magically' found their way to climate change bloggers (Pearce, 9 February 2010a; 2010b) provides another competing explanation to the Russian hacking scenario. *The Guardian* reported that Norfolk police interviewed climate researcher Paul Dennis, who heads an adjacent laboratory at UEA and had e-mail contact with American bloggers such as McIntyre of the Climategate Audit, Patrick Condon of the Air Vent, and Anthony Watts of Watts Up With That. All these bloggers were sent the leaked material. A connection to Russian hackers indeed was not proven. Moreover, according to *The Guardian*, Norfolk police have discounted tabloid stories of links to Russian intelligence in this incident (Leigh, Arthur, and Evans, 4 February 2010a).

The way Russian cybercrime gangs and incidents are narrated by global mainstream media, alternative media, and bloggers shapes a very specific portrayal of Russian hackers and their superior abilities in relation to hacking and cybercrime. There is no significant difference between mainstream and independent media and blogs, except that in blogs the bias against Russians is often far more explicit. The hackers are consistently portrayed as having 'incredible' powers to support criminal activities and to attack opposition groups' virtual presence or hack for the benefit of the state in time of need. This stereotypical depiction of Russian hackers is reminiscent of Cold War imagery, such as that of the incredibly intelligent Russian spies who are forced to work for their government to survive poor living conditions. At the same time, this depiction creates a consistent narrative frame to explain any international incident as one carried out by this specific ethnic and cultural group. This narrative frame helps explain the certainty with which the 'Climategate hack' was attributed to Russian hackers without any valid proof and based solely on speculation.

The ammunition for blaming Russian hackers for the Climategate hack is to be found in the public discourse that portrays Russians as superhackers and links cybercrime to patriotic hacking, international espionage, and global politics. This explains media stories of Russia's government and politico-economic elite allegedly intermingling with the Russian mafia and cybercrime gangs to get support during cyber-conflicts, in which the Russian state is opposed (cyberattacks against opponents), implicated (Estonia), or engaged in a brief war, as was the case with Georgia.

The global media have portrayed Russian hackers in a consistent manner, playing up their capabilities (such as, for example, their sophistication) and linking them to cybercrime gangs, robberies, and identity theft. Even if there are indeed individuals from Russia or elsewhere in the post-Soviet space who are engaged in cybercrime, the assumption of Russian guilt in all cases reinforces the older Cold War portrayal of Russians in the Western world. There is a demonstrated tendency for the global media to look for a Russian hand and geopolitical implications in stories relating to former Soviet countries or countries under Soviet influence in the past. Also, there has been an exaggeration of the sophistication of Russian hackers, primarily because of their use of botnets to conduct attacks previous to the Climategate hack, particularly in patriotic hacking in the cases of Estonia and Georgia. By the time the Climategate hack appeared with a huge impact just before the Copenhagen Summit, the scene was set for Russian hackers to be blamed for what under a calmer mind-set might have been more plausibly explained differently or at least reported alongside another, competing explanation.

This is a significant case study, which can enable us to understand the similar complexity of other incidents, such as the Sony hack in December 2014, where North Korean hackers were accused of the attacks.

2.2 China-related cyberconflicts, dissidents, and nationalist hackers

This is a case study we researched with Andrew Robinson, titled 'A Cyberconflict Analysis of Chinese Dissidents Focusing on Civil Society, Mass Incidents and Labour Resistance' for the *Routledge Research China Handbook*, edited Ming-Yeh and Gary Ransley (2015). Some of the events and incidents we discuss spill over to the fourth phase of digital activism (2010–2014); however, for the interest of consistency in our original argument, I include it here in this phase in its entirety so I can focus exclusively on WikiLeaks, the Arab Spring, and Snowden in the fourth phase.

This cyberconflict analysis of Chinese dissidents in the People's Republic of China (PRC) focuses on the last decade. A distinction is drawn between sociopolitical (or active) social movement uses of the Internet – which focus on organization, mobilization, and the networked form of the medium itself – and ethnoreligious (or reactive) social movement uses, which subordinate the medium to vertical logics. These are often expressed in terms of ad hoc mobilizations and tit-for-tat defacements and cyberattacks adhering to closed and fixed identities, such as nationality, religion, and ethnicity.

Cyberconflict is a synthesis of three overlapping domains of social movement theory (for sociopolitical movements), conflict theory (for ethnoreligious movements), and media theory (the intersection of cyberconflict, capitalism, and the state). This theory is applied in the context of a systemic structural analysis of capitalist power in a context in which neoliberalism and regime maintenance are both mutually reproducing and undermining. While the Internet, as a network technology, is most appropriate for network forms of power, it exists in a dynamic field in which hierarchies, and hierarchy-network hybrids, also proliferate, containing and channelling its emancipatory potential through strategies of recuperation, repression, inclusion, and exclusion.

More specifically, cyberconflict theory examines how politico-economic reforms, the media environment, and e-governance have affected dissent in China (e.g., communist party ideology, constructions of social and political identities, representations of and by dissidents, and the link to e-governance; control of information, level of censorship; alternative sources; media effects on policy; political contests). The second cluster of elements of concern are the effect of ICTs on mobilization structures, organizational forms, participation, recruitment, tactics, and goals of dissidents, as well as changes in framing processes and the impact of the political opportunity structure on resistances in China. Third, in relation to ethnic, religious, and cultural dissent, cyberconflict theory examines how the Communist Party state and dissident group identities are constructed in relation to ethnic/religious/cultural difference and the construction of competing national identities. Also, hacktivism (or variably termed digital activism, tech activism, and cyberactivism) and information warfare in China are discussed in a variety of settings, especially in relation to social networking media and contemporary dissent.

The first part discusses the political environment in China to provide the context for dissent and involves a broad stroke on neoliberalism in China with a further discussion on censorship and control in this environment. A second section maps networked dissent in terms of the impact and use of information communication technologies (ICTs) in relation to civil society, mass incidents, and labour resistance and shows how it links to broader resistance in the global mediascape. The final section concentrates on nationalism and the symptomatic repression of ethnic and religious minorities, as well as nationalism, which fuels and links to cybercrime and patriotic hacking.

Hypercapitalism and its discontents

Critics such as He Qinglian have suggested that neoliberalism in China has led to growing inequality and corruption (Arrighi, 2007, 15–16). In effect, the transnationally led growth strategy has transferred resources en masse to private capital in coastal cities, so as to provide incentives to lure transnational capital (Wei and Leung, 2005; Yusuf and Wu, 2002), an approach known in China as 'building nests to attract birds' (Zweig, 2002, 60). Changes in the urban landscape, for example, show the replacement of corporatist and traditional spaces with spaces of information-economy capitalism (Fu, 2002, 114). Transnational capital dominates urban areas both symbolically and economically, expressing itself in orthogonal growth (Gaubatz, 1999). The arrangement of spaces along a functional capitalist level, with a clustering of economic functions, is particularly apparent (Rimmer, 2002). Finance capital and landlords, aided by technocratic political leaders, become dominant classes within local power structures (Jessop and Sum, 2000, 2288; Yusuf and Wu, 2002, 1224; Chen, 1998). Transnational capitalist projects are unrestricted by state power (Wu, 2000, 1363). The state is able to extract rents on transnational flows (Zweig, 2002, 23–24) but suffers from increased dependency, as well as from the growing power of those on whom it depends to resist rent extraction. As in all global cities, local elites maintain rent extraction mainly through immobile infrastructure such as real estate (Brenner, 1998, 15), which functions as the source of monopolistic superprofit nexuses, allowing the extraction of above-market profits through nonreproducible conditions (Taylor, 2000). In China, such rent extraction runs against traditional rights of state tenants, whom local elites dispossess at will in order to accumulate revenue from corporate rents (Zhou and Logan, 2002, 141).

Furthermore, there is a discontinuity in global city emergence, with connectivity but not command-and-control functions (i.e., maintaining authority but with a distributive style of decision making) spreading to peripheral locations. Beijing for instance has much higher quantitative scores for connectivity than command and control (Taylor et al., 2009, 231, 238), while Hong Kong scores third in the world for connectivity but lacks global command functions (Taylor et al., 2009, 234, 237–238). Chinese global cities, as with others in the global South, differ from their Northern counterparts in being focused on attracting foreign investment (Wei and Leung, 2005, 19–20; Shi and Hamnett, 2002, 128). It can thus be argued that (coastal urban) China has become a dependent peripheral state within neoliberal capitalism, rather than an emergent hegemonic contender. This regime of accumulation is partly sustained in classic Southern fashion (Wolpe, 1972) by the persistence of a largely non- or semicapitalist agrarian sector, which underpins sub-reproduction-cost wages and resultant comparative advantage. This dual economy allows the hyperexploitation of undocumented migrants from rural to urban areas, with rural areas effectively treated as an internal periphery. Like other such models, it is destabilized by its simultaneous reliance on, and accumulation-by-dispossession at the expense of, the non- or semi-capitalist sectors. In addition, cities continue to rely on rural hinterlands (Lin, 2002, 302).

Some scholars write of a crisis of governance, with the regime seeing the effects of neoliberalism as introducing instability that threatens to produce 'chaos' (*luan*) (Kluver, 2005, 78). Along with other means such as nationalism, e-governance initiatives have been introduced as an attempt to restabilize Chinese society. Part of the difficulty with the position of the Internet in China is that it is simultaneously useful for neoliberalism and harmful to authoritarianism (hence to the specific form of neoliberalism prevalent in China). Rawnsley (2007) argues that the Internet's horizontal, networked structure is appropriate to 'economic modernization', and hence necessary for China, but clashes sharply with a centralized, hierarchical governance system. Regime integration depends on mainly vertical structures. Hence, Qiu (2004, 10–11) suggests that the path dependency of institutional legacies is the main reason for Internet censorship. However, there are also real dangers. The regime is highly fearful of 'linking-up' (*chuanlian*), the formation of horizontal connections and solidarities between different sites, which was central to the Cultural Revolution and is seen as prefiguring society-wide mobilization. The widely observed result is a self-contradictory relationship in which China both embraces the Internet and fears and seeks to control it (Taubman, 1998; Qiu, 2004, 101; Kalathil and Boas, 2003; Endeshaw, 2004).

Less widely noted is the basis of this contradictory policy in divisions between factions of the Chinese elite, with growth-oriented technocrats pitted against state-control interests in the army, propaganda system, and security agencies. The former care more about developmental-state concerns, the latter about keeping power and winning any emerging cyberwars (Qiu, 2004, 110). The latter institute policies that are unjustifiably costly in developmentalist or neoliberal economic terms, but which also serve as job-creation and import-substitution initiatives inside China (ibid., 112). China's attitude to global information flows is thus self-contradictory. The regime both wishes for such flows for economic reasons, and fears that they could be its downfall (Bennett, 2010). In particular, the regime is afraid of prodemocracy messages coming out of the global mediascape (Appadurai, 1990, 305).

Moreover, it has been noted that '[t]he Chinese government has chosen to address through information technology, problems of corruption, transparency and local government reform, and the development of poor areas' (Kalathil and Boas, 2003, 13). In effect, a controlled Internet provides the possibility for feedback mechanisms, which fall short of accountability, and therefore fall within the regime's view of stability. In part, this is an attempt to combat the culture of dissimulation by allowing a direct connection between the centre and individual citizens, bypassing local officials and allowing their surveillance by the centre (Kluver, 2005, 85). These are a recent, computer-mediated variance of a wider reliance on 'limited bottom-up citizen participation' as an accountability mechanism to control local officials, a practice which is dangerous for the regime, as participants often take up politicized issues (Minzer, 2009, 82–83). Such mobilization is aided by the fact that many local governments have been slow to take up computer technologies (Qiu, 2004, 107; Tong and Lei, 2010).

Further, the regime is making increasingly sophisticated use of control modalities that combine commercialization with government restriction, co-opting private actors to reinforce control. This process is creating a type of Internet openness that is restricted to entertainment functions (Weber and Lu, 2007; Qiu, 2004, 113–114). Despite the apparent softening, repression is never far below the surface and seems to be constructed to preempt and premediate dissent in advance through the logistical closure of space and the multiplication of both formal and informal regulations. For instance, in November 2012, the Communist Party congress was accompanied by at least 130 arrests of dissidents, with others placed under house arrest or exiled from Beijing; bans on pigeons, balloons, taxi door handles, ping-pong balls, and remote-control aircraft; restrictions on transport; and closures of NGOs such as the Beijing Aizhixing Institute of Health Education, which offers advice to migrant workers. At least half of the sex workers in the city were reportedly arrested and expelled from Beijing. The Ministry of Information Technology expressed the need to 'seal the network' (*fengwang*) during the Party Congress, and it was impossible to access the *New York Times* article exposing the financial operations of Premier Wen Jiabao (Barboza, 26 October 2012; Jacobs, 3 November 2012). 'Unlucky' words such as 'death', 'die' and 'down' were even banned from TV shows (*Economic Times*, 3 November 2012).

This general climate of repression – which is typical of major events in China – creates a generalized feeling of disempowerment, an inability to protest, and even an existential gap between the regime and any possible opposition. The *Economic Times* (3 November 2012) quotes a microblogger: 'In the face of these absurdities, we are powerless. It's a reminder that no matter how ridiculous and comical, this is an era that we can't laugh in'. Ai Weiwei, an international artist and famous dissident, who is discussed more extensively below, said his police minders allowed him to engage with anything, except the coming party congress. 'To be honest, it's O.K. because it's just an internal meeting for those people. It has nothing to do with me. Or with anyone else, really' (Jacobs, 1 November 2012b). Shao Jiang (1 November 2012), another leading dissident, summarizes in one paragraph the political climate in the country: 'Stability maintenance' has been bolstered as a way to strip the rights of human rights lawyers, activists, petitioners and digital activists. This is a departure from the reign of President Jiang in the 1990s, which was characterized by its suppression of members of the China Democracy Party and Falun Gong practitioners. Methods of suppression under the recent administration have become more calculating than before, with authorities making blatant and extensive use of diverse and often harsher techniques to retaliate against activists, including abduction, enforced disappearance, torture, illegal detention in 'black jails', soft detention, forced 'tourism' (a form of residential surveillance away from home), and trumped-up charges like 'disrupting public order' or 'tax evasion'.

Such intimidation is focused on activists, and its degree of visibility to the wider public is debatable. The regime relies on an array of 'deliberately vague and arbitrary regulations' to maintain control (Rawnsley, 2007; cf. Dickie, 2007). In this context, policies such as web censorship and news bias may serve to signal the limits to tolerated dissent at a particular time. Tuinstra (2009) suggests that Chinese users now rely on the Internet as their eyes and ears regarding government policy and practice, creating risks to the government in interfering too much with it. Pye (2001) suggests that Chinese leaders rely on informal decision making to maintain control. This echoes broader patterns of 'shadow power' typical of the global South.

China's cyberspace censorship regime has been deemed the most extensive in the world (see Walton, 2001; Chase and Mulvenon, 2002; Qiu, 2004; Dowell, 2006; Lum, 2006; Karatzogianni, 2006; Minzer, 2009; McKinnon, 2010; Zittrain and Palfrey, 2010; Cunningham and Wasserstrom, 2011). China seeks to control the Internet by funnelling connections 'through a small number of state-controlled backbone networks', which are in principle vulnerable to censorship and surveillance (Kalathil and Boas, 2003, 21). This is an attempt to combat the horizontal, rhizomatic architecture of the Internet. It is continuous with the Maoist ideal of vertical control of communication (ibid., 18).

Nevertheless, the viability of such strategies long term and on a wider scale is questionable in the current global communications environment. This has led to an emerging policy of 'not trying to control too much' (Dickie, 2007). It has been suggested that China is using its censorship systems 'sparingly since this prevents a new generation of Internet users from discovering the numerous ways netizens have figured out to thwart their efforts' (Tuinstra, 2009), in effect choosing a relatively lightly censored Internet over a more heavily censored, and therefore more widely resisted, control system. It has also been suggested that the 'great firewall' has been replaced or supplemented with second- and third-generation forms of control based on corporate censorship, the normalization of surveillance, and state-sponsored information campaigns (MacKinnon, 2010, 27). This makes the approach of simply enabling dissidents to circumvent first-generation blocking insufficient or even dangerous (ibid., 30). As a result of such measures, Yang (2009a) argues that China has moved from sovereign power based on 'hard control' such as Internet censorship, towards disciplinary and biopolitical power based on 'soft control' through using human actors' self-censorship and responsiveness to cues. On the other hand, the feeling of efficacy inspires online protests. Surveys also reveal that people both trust the Internet as a source of information and feel it to be an open space in which their discussions are not restricted (Yang, 2009a, 132). Tuinstra (2009) suggests that the Internet obtains trust as an information source in China because Western media are suspected of anti-Chinese bias and Chinese media are regarded as controlled. Information continues to reach Chinese Internet users through social media and other sources, leading to a credibility gap, which delegitimates the government (Rawnsley, 2007). However, scepticism is necessary regarding the effects of information flows. Quantitative research suggests that the credibility of official media is a much bigger correlate of political outlook than access to alternative information (Hu and Zhou, 2002). Similarly, Thornton (2009, 202–203) suggests that problems of astroturfing and difficulties assessing the scale of dissent render it difficult for online movements to gain trust. The regime is also trying to steer online discussions through the use of paid astroturfers, known in China as the '50 cent party'. It has been estimated that at least 280,000 astroturfers are paid by the Chinese regime, in addition to party members who do it for free and independent bloggers co-opted by regime patronage (Bandurski, 2010; MacKinnon, 2010, 23–24). There is also a system of hiring college students to work part time as Internet police and censors (Qiu, 2003, 11).

Transnational digital networks of dissent and protest

> The struggle is worthwhile, if it provides new ways to communicate with people and society.

> If someone is not free, I am not free. (Ai Weiwei)

> Overall we feel that every person has a right to express themselves and this right of expression is fundamentally linked to our happiness and even our existence. When a society constantly demands that everyone should abandon this right, then the society becomes a society without creativity. It can never become a happy society. (Ai Weiwei video interview, Lamborn, 25 October 2012)

khaoid @khaoid   30 Jul
@sdv_duras you have a point, many **Chinese dissidents** e.g. Ai
WeiWei seem to default to idealizing 'Western values' @_ludens

(Twitter Screenshot: Debating Chinese dissidents and Western Values on Twitter, 30 July 2012)

The above words and images show the global media literacy of celebrity dissident Ai Weiwei, which extends to the appropriation of the popular 'Gangnam Style' Internet meme. This suggests that Ai is an artist and dissident who understands social media activism and knows how to obtain and retain the attention of a global audience. Ai Weiwei here shows himself to be more attuned to the global mediascape than the Chinese regime, which persists in its scepticism toward cyberspace and global media culture. It is thus not entirely inaccurate to say that Ai has 'escaped' through YouTube: he is able to exist within an alternative sociopolitical community through a computer-mediated transition to a global scale.

This type of dissident is partly a product of immaterial labour development in China. Intellectuals and artists, involved in what has been termed immaterial affective labour (Hardt and Negri, 2000; Karatzogianni and Schandorf, 20 October 2012), are often expected to be dissidents, and the correlation of dissent and intellectual status are expressed in artistic and literary awards to Chinese dissidents. This expectation of dissent is transmitted from the West via global discourse and runs against a Chinese tradition expecting intellectuals to serve the state. Intellectuals in China move within a space in which limits to government tolerance constantly shift. China also has a division between *Tizhi* (official system) writers and *Minjian* (literally 'among the people', i.e., unofficial) authors. *Minjian* intellectuals often admit to being outsiders, but deny being dissidents or activists as they seek to stay just inside the margins of regime tolerance (Zhou, 2005). The Chinese regime is enthusiastic about the international recognition of intellectuals, but unhappy when they use their status to demand reforms. For instance, when Mo Yan won a Nobel Prize for Literature, Chinese Communist Party (CCP) propagandist Li Changchun observed that it 'reflects the prosperity and progress of Chinese literature, as well as the increasing influence of China' (Tatlow, 2012b), ignoring Mo's call for the release of Liu Xiaobo, a previous prize winner from 2010. Similarly, when Liao Yiwu won the German Book Trade's Peace Prize, he accepted his award with 'a scorching speech whose theme was: "This empire must break apart"' (Tatlow, 2012b).

The style of transnational dissent discussed here resonates with broader cases of scale jumping as a means to appeal to the global community to protect human rights. Wanning Sun (2010, 540) explains the usefulness for the scale-jumping concept:

> Chinese media within the context of two related social processes: a growing social-spatial stratification within China on the one hand, and the formation of widespread but uneven translocal linkages on the other. Additionally, it may help us gain a clearer appreciation of how communication technologies and media practices either assist or inhibit the activity of scale-fixing or scale-jumping, activities that are engaged in by various players: the state, capital, individuals, and of course, media institutions.

In other cases, such a rescaling has given considerable power to local actors whose political opportunities are blocked at a national level, through appeals using global human rights discourse (Sikkink, 1993). The Internet encourages such scale jumping. As Severo, Giraud, and Douay (2011), following Barabási, have argued, an Internet posting moves an issue from a local to a global scale. This is partially the case in China, as the regime is unable to control hacktivist groups located outside China (Qiu, 2004, 113). This allows dissident groups to promote what Thornton (2009, 187–188) calls a 'boomerang' effect, with activism curving around local repression and indifference to generate foreign pressure on local elites. For instance, Ai Weiwei stands out as particularly able to use the global mediascape, firstly in his use of social media to solicit funds, and secondly in conforming to the model of 'explicit' dissident which the Western press understands. He uses this media-constructed role to engage with an international audience. Ai has also attempted to articulate transnational dissident concerns with wider social unrest in China. In particular, he has taken part in campaigns over the government's handling of the 2008 Sichuan earthquake in which 90,000 people died.

Despite this repression, Ai, like many Chinese dissidents, stops short of a democratization agenda, instead calling for liberalization. In this, he is in continuity with many *Minjian* intellectuals. However, he is too explicit to be *Minjian* and is rather the style of dissident that the West understands and appreciates, as he is explicit and connected at the international level via social media and artist circles in major cities around the globe. For example, his art is exhibited internationally, and a movie made about his activism was screened at many international film festivals. Kelliher (1993, 380) has argued that to understand what was termed 'the democracy movement' (*minzhu yundong*, shortened as *minyun*) in its various phases (1987–1989, 1986–1987, and 1989) means to 'examine how Chinese intellectuals conceived of democracy; what political role...assigned for themselves; and what sort of elite-mass relations prevailed within the movement, between intellectuals, on the one hand, and workers and peasants, on the other'. In his analysis, Kelliher argues that mainstream activists who dominated the movement focused on liberalization, as in the establishment of rights to protect people's freedoms from government interference. It was only radical elements of the movement who pushed for democratization and popular sovereignty. The exile journal *China Spring* suggested that activists 'first strike for human rights and then for democracy'. It is worth diverting here to add that some of the biggest articulators of Chinese dissidence are political exiles and the diaspora in Western countries, Hong Kong, Macao, and Taiwan (for instance, see M.Y.T. Rawnsley, 2012).

Yet it is the historical context that can provide the answer to the up-until-now failure of protest, dissidents, and resistance groups to topple the 'communist' regime, effectuate reform, or engage in any sort of dialogue with the elites forming the hierarchies of the state apparatuses. When an opportunity seemed to present itself in the aftermath of the Arab Spring in 2011, dissident calls for mobilization seemed to meet with little popular response. This failure to construct an overarching, popular dissident project is partly a result of the authoritarian practices routinized in contemporary China, from Internet surveillance to detention in labour camps to the everyday presence of street wardens and police. Another partial explanation is provided in the assertion by Kelliher (1993) that one of the reasons has been dissidents' demand for liberalization instead of democratization.

However, there are also problems in that the multitude, a thousand plateaus of dissent and rebellion – celebrity dissent, rural and labour unrest, and separatism – remains unarticulated under a common frame. This pushes dissent back into the arms of the regime. The Kelliher argument is significant also in another sense. Intellectuals monopolized the debate, creating an idea that excluded mass supporters, and were unable to talk to peasants and workers in a language they understood, while the urban-rural divide devastated prospects for a mass democratic movement (Kelliher, 1993, 381). This democracy was limited in a sense to intellectuals to the extent that Kelliher argues that 'the notion of elite democracy was a close cousin to the new authoritarianism (*xin quanweizhuyi*) – the hard government/soft economy variety, the notion that democracy would have to wait until the economy developed' (ibid., 381).

Within China, moves toward contestation on the up-down axis can be seen in terms of the still more cautious emergence of a networked civil society. Guobin Yang's voluminous work in particular makes a strong case that the Internet is driving an emerging civil society or public sphere in China. Within China, tolerated civil society groups have emerged synergistically with the Internet, facilitating participation (Yang, 2003, 405). For example, the emergence of environmental NGOs 'coincided with the development of the internet in China' (Yang, 2005, 58). Yang goes as far as to suggest that China is undergoing 'a veritable associational revolution' fuelled by the Internet (Yang, 2009b). The incipient, dynamic nature of local civil society has rendered it particularly prone to adopt online methods (Yang, 2003, 406–407), with social uses emerging earlier than e-commerce and e-government (ibid., 411).

Guiheux (2009, 135–136) suggests that the Internet has contributed to an increase in the number and range of political voices in China. The emergence of Chinese civil society, effectively an included stratum in negotiation with market and state, is still severely constrained by the context, though this has not prevented it from negotiating the relationship (Yang, 2005, 66). In a study of online forum postings, Hang (2003) concludes that the Internet is creating a nascent virtual public space in China. Similarly, Reese and Dai (2009) observe that censorship now takes place against a background of global connectivity, with bloggers emerging as a media watchdog criticizing censorship.

In the 2009 Panyu anti-incinerator protest in Guangdong, Zhao (2011) shows the importance of modern technologies in generating pressure for protesters' aims. Suggesting that this is linked to the middle-class, upwardly mobile constituency of the protests, Zhou argues that the Internet was used to get around regime censorship. Methods such as blocking websites, censoring newspapers, and interfering with protesters' transport arrangements proved insufficient given that protesters are constantly evolving their use of ICTs. In addition, protesters were using modern technologies to disseminate live information, to research and present alternative information, to debunk government claims, and to deter repression by filming officials (ibid., 20). New technologies create a means to challenge regime framing in such a way that the 'rightfulness' of protest can be articulated. She also draws attention to the postrepresentational nature of the protest, in which, when told to select representatives for negotiation, the crowd chanted, 'We don't want to be represented' (ibid., 17). However, protest leaders seem in practice to have tried to keep the movement within nontransgressive bounds (ibid., 23). The Internet is crucial in allowing such environmental movements to succeed. Ma Yan, an environmentalist who won the Goldman Prize, pointed to social media as being responsible for the frequency of environmental protests in China: 'Social media is a game changer. People can educate themselves and share information' (Larson, 29 October 2012).

A recent example of how social media accelerate protest is the protest against the building of a petrochemical plant in Ningbo. According to news reports, the protest by mainly middle-class residents, organized through microblogging, smart phone apps, and social media, was successful in forcing the authorities to cancel the project within two days (Larson, 29 October 2012). A similar case occurred in 2007, when residents in Xiamen used the Internet and text messaging to coordinate a demonstration against the building of a chemical plant (Yang, 2009a, 129). Another such protest – which succeeded without much government opposition – was directed against the extension of a train line, which would reduce house values and pose a health risk (Cunningham and Wasserstrom, 2011, 17). The middle-class composition of the protest perhaps explains the widespread use of social media, but this protest also prefigures possible future mobilizations as the Internet spreads to working-class and rural populations. It seems likely that the Chinese regime will have increasing difficulty in its strategy of using information blocks to impede social movements.

Another successful example (there are obviously protests that do not succeed, and more research could be done into understanding impact factors), mainly involving students, another group of relative 'Internet haves', saw online protests rapidly diffuse around a murder at Beijing University in 2000. Protests on campus and online were closely coordinated, and the issue rapidly spread from the murder itself to issues of free speech online (Yang, 2003a, 469–472). Yang concludes that 'the internet facilitates if not completely satisfies the key conditions of the emergence of popular protest', overcoming information problems and offering speedy, low-risk means of communication (Yang, 2003, 472). Research on participants in pro-democracy protests in Hong Kong similarly suggest that the Internet was an important mobilizing channel, with 54 per cent listing the Internet or e-mails as important factors motivating them to join a march (Ma, 2009, 59). Protest organizer Ng Gene-bond first discerned widespread student concern about the 'Article 23' reform from web forums, then set up a website to promote the march (Ma, 2009, 58). Kuah-Pearce (2009, 112) terms this part of the emergence of a 'protest ideology' and 'protest space' in Hong Kong, with antiglobalization overtones. Another recent example of this was the Occupy camp in Hong Kong, which ironically was tolerated while sites in America and Europe were suppressed. The camp lasted nearly a year before finally being suppressed, making it the last major Occupy camp to survive (Bradsher, 2010). This was significant for the Umbrella Movement in Hong Kong in late September 2014 (not accounted for here as this book was in production).

'Mass incidents' and labour resistance

One recent phenomenon is the 'large-scale Internet mass incident', which is a form of online protest usually used to censure government failures and corruption. The government has been forced to react quickly to such campaigns and 'rush solutions to appease public opinion', as well as to channel them into e-government (Tong and Lei, 2010, i–ii). The mass unrest phenomenon in China is difficult to quantify as most incidents are unreported. According to official sources, there are around 80,000 'mass incidents' each year. The term 'mass incident' is regime-speak for a demonstration or revolt in which police repression or negotiation is attempted. Some of these cases involve 'serious clashes between the public and the police' (Li, 2008). Such incidents have increased sharply, from 8,700 per year in 1993 to 23,500 in 1999, 58,000 in 2003 (Keidel, 2005, 1), 80,000 in 2007, and 180,000 in 2010 (*The Atlantic*, 2012). China has apparently changed recording criteria since then to avoid further such publicity (Goldkorn, 6 January 2013). Commentators refer to the 'extraordinary scale of social unrest' shown by such clashes (Keidel, 2005, 1). The majority of incidents are almost certainly rural, with many focused on issues of land grabs, corruption, abuse by officials or police, or pollution.

Reflecting Internet use patterns, these campaigns tend to express the political orientations of the middle class and students, but these concerns can also focus on the mistreatment of vulnerable people by the elite. Indeed, according to Yang, the three main issues of online campaigns are nationalism, misconduct by the powerful, and harm to vulnerable individuals (Yang, 2009a, 127, 129). The trick with such mobilizations is to catch the attention and imagination of the mass of Internet users who are mostly online for entertainment purposes. 'The more outrageous the incident, the more likely it is to arouse the virtual crowd' (Yang, 2009a, 134).

Responding actively to the space opened by tolerance of localized protests, 'Internet mass incidents' have encouraged scrutiny at a local level. Local officials are put under mass surveillance for slips of the tongue, corruption, and so on (Tong and Lei, 2010, 5–6). Other campaigns target police abuse. Like street protests, it has been suggested that online protests of this kind serve as a means to vent frustration against wider problems (Tong and Lei, 2010, 10) and that they are at root about 'the dark side of economic transformation' (Yang, 2009a, 130).

The modalities of such protests have been hotly debated. In terms taken from new social movement theorists Poster and Melucci, Yang (2009a, 129) argues that such campaigns are 'symbolic challenges'. Their main significance is in allowing the public to reframe issues. In contrast, Minzer (2009, 105) argues that, in a system where performance targets matter more than formal laws or legal rights, 'disgruntled parties' have learnt that Internet campaigns and mass petitions or protests (which put local leaders in violation of targets) are more effective than formal processes. The success of such protests shows both the regime's fear of widespread dissent and its preparedness to make partial concessions to head it off. In a cautionary analysis, Zheng (2008) warns that the most effective campaigns have been those that do not challenge the regime itself, instead dividing different factions of the regime against each other. When regime legitimacy is at stake, a repressive response it still typical. Activism is thus typically complicit with the regime's use of the Internet as a regime feedback mechanism (2008, 165). Conceding on such issues can be a way to prolong CCP rule without enacting substantive reforms (MacKinnon, 2010, 11). Furthermore, Xi Chen argues that, while petitioners have become more effective and achieved 'impressive successes' using the Internet, regime censorship has made this channel inaccessible in many cases (2009, 456). The mechanism of scale jumping is also central to such protests, which often target local issues or problems but bypass local power blockages by operating on a national scale.

Such developments have led to hopes that democracy is slowly emerging through everyday networks. In contrast, Wang has concluded that 'the Internet is unlikely to offer democratic hope for China' (2009, viii). This is because most users do not take part in political activities, as they participate in government-sponsored activity due to nationalism (ibid., ix). He suggests that Chinese netizens are most likely to protest against foreign forces, in continuity with grassroots nationalism (ibid., 39–40). The regime seems to encourage this channelling of discontent by being relatively tolerant of such protests (ibid., 104). Internet use does not statistically predict protest participation (ibid., 112), though this is perhaps to be expected given the correlation of Internet use with high social status.

Western-based websites often act as redistributors of underground dissident material (Abbott, 2001, 103). For instance, the *Epoch Times*, a Falun Gong-linked newspaper, claims to have distributed one of its texts to 2.3 million Chinese users and drawn 15 million into its campaign to renounce CCP membership (Thornton, 2009, 179). Thornton also suggests that the *Epoch Times* acts as an amplifier of successful actions

(2009, 184). Hence, resistance to the Great Firewall continues to take subversive forms. According to Qiu, '[t]he global networked nature of such oppositional forces is the most fundamental source of frustration' for China (2003, 13). However, activists outside a closed political context have limited leverage over regimes (van Laer and van Aelst, 2009, 246). In related cases within China, students use media such as bulletin boards to repost controversial material in protest against its censorship (Zhou, 2006, 218). In 2009, Chinese users overran a German website called the 'Berlin Twitter Wall', using it to get around censorship (MacKinnon, 2010, 2). In addition, the fluidity of the Internet has proven useful to both sides, as in the case of the purported resignation of official Meng Weizai, in which resignations and denunciations were exchanged by the two sides (Thornton, 2009, 179–181).

Such contestation on the up-down axis seems particularly risky, however. There is something of an anomaly that mass workers' protests often occur without serious repression, but visible dissidents like Charter 08 can be sentenced to a decade in jail. Much depends on whether a protest can be framed in terms drawing on the regime's own heritage – for instance, strikes against foreign companies (Cunningham and Wasserstrom, 2011, 15–16). The regime also seems harsher on protests that 'have the potential to draw support across generations, across classes, and across the country' than on those focused on local issues (ibid., 18).

Further, Chinese workers continue to be subject to the hegemony of the market and of the state (Blecher, 2002, 287). Pun (2005) argues that global capital and market mechanisms have inflicted an unprecedented wound on society and that migrant workers have not become a new working class because the state has impeded their emergence: 'Dagongmei, as half peasants and half proletariat, are displaced subjects produced by the hybrid conjugation of state and market machines'. Lee (2007, 71) discusses a range of protests emerging from Chinese workers, differentiating them into a number of categories: protests against wage and pension arrears; neighbourhood protests over public services; bankruptcy and redundancy protests; protests against corruption and abuse.

Despite the diversity of issues, Lee suggests that there is an underlying continuity beneath workers' grievances. 'The common denominator underlying these incidents is a pervasive working class feeling of betrayal by the state and victimization by the market economy' (Lee, 2007, 71). In this sense, these are protests of desperation. Lee looks at how workers frame themselves in protests, including the 'masses' (*qunzhong*), 'weak and disadvantaged groups' (*ruoshi qunti*), 'working class' (*gongren jieji*), and 'citizens' (*gongmin*). He makes an argument that *class consciousness is muted* because of problems arising from the identification of working-class power with state socialism. Since new workers (particularly migrants) must confront the domination of the capitalist class while also being excluded from the traditional categories of state socialism, this causes difficulties (Lee, 2007, 195).

Uneven development provides the driving force behind such unrest. While some are not directly economic, they are generally 'reported as reflecting depressed economic conditions affecting the demonstrators' (Keidel, 2005, 1; cf. Hung, 2010, 336). Many protests are directly economic, focusing on issues such as pay, layoffs, and water rights. Others focus on forced displacement, for instance due to desertification. Even ethnic conflicts often have an economic subtext (Keidel, 2005, 2–3). Such problems arise from the shifts entailed by neoliberal reforms, and Chinese peasants and workers 'attribute their difficulties to injustice and government incompetence' (ibid., 6), an analysis brought to a crisis point by corruption and misconduct (ibid., 7–8). The usual modality is for protests to target local injustices and demand central government support to resolve them. According to Keidel's analysis, there are two layers to grievances. Most of their 'basic energy' comes from 'dissatisfaction over the impact of economic reforms', but this is often intensified by 'widespread enterprise and government corruption and malfeasance' (ibid., 1).

The role of the Internet is important in spreading information about such protests and making repression costly, because repression backfires, thus leading to larger protests. The Weng'an incident discussed by Li (2008) is a case in which the Internet enabled a rapid spread of information, bypassing regime disinformation and denial. It was reported that 10,000 people attacked official buildings as part of a revolt resulting from a suspicious death blamed on local officials. The spread of images from the revolt required the regime to back down from its initial position of denial and to admit the existence of the revolt. Li goes as far as to argue that the Dengist strategy of using state violence against protests to prevent public demands is no longer effective, as the public has become 'a power beyond law'. With incidents channelling bottled-up anger and information now more accessible than before due to the Internet, repression is no longer enough (Li, 2008). This creates a spectre of the possible spread of revolt: the potential for revolution created by the digital materialization of protest, theorized as the 'revolutionary virtual' during the Arab Spring uprisings (see Karatzogianni, 2012; 2013). When this risk occurs, the regime no longer resorts mainly to the suppression of dissent, but instead channels unrest against local officials. As a result, in the case of Weng'an, 'the primary target of official sanction was not the rioting townspeople but the local officials' (Li, 2008).

According to Elizabeth Economy, protests are usually 'local in nature and generally resolved with a combination of payoffs, arrests, and promises of future improvement', occasionally supplemented by 'action against local officials' (Economy, 2004). The regime relies on handling them 'like brush fires', treating each as an isolated case and containing any broader challenge. Economy suggests that this is being undermined by the growing scale of mobilizations, particularly against dam building, which now crosses local and provincial boundaries. Similarly, Lum (2006, 12) suggests that protests have become better organized due to Internet and cell phone technologies. Ecological protests are beginning to link Beijing-based NGOs, which employ virtual communication and lobby for central government support, with militant villagers, who use tactics such as taking officials hostage. In one case, an NGO took villagers to a previous resettlement site to expose inadequate provisions. In another, local students acted as bridging connectors to bring local issues to the Internet. Hence, growing connectedness is undermining the potential for control in the face of sociopolitical uses of the Internet. If business as usual proves insufficient, the regime's options seem to be more extreme repression or reform (Economy, 2004).

The modalities of Internet use within this type of activism are mainly sociopolitical. Huang and Yip (2012) examine the Panyu and Xiamen protests and suggest that the Internet had four main uses: as information-disclosure platform, site of discussion, mobilization structure, and means to find external allies. This typology is typical of sociopolitical uses of the Internet, which focus on mobilization and network building. Three sociopolitical uses of the Internet impacting the offline world are highlighted by Yang (2009a, 137–138): the instantaneous advertisement of offline protests, the dissemination of online content as posters, and the use of the Internet as an organizing space. Similarly, Cai (2008) suggests that the pervasiveness of mobile phones and recording devices makes it more difficult for the state to resort to repression. The pattern can be traced through a number of revolts.

Another example occurred in Guangxi Chuang autonomous region in 2007. Local officials launched a hard-line drive to enforce the one-child policy, including forced abortions and home demolitions, sparking local unrest in which official buildings were destroyed (Minzner, 2009, 55). This is another case in which policies were reversed due to unrest, although it is also notable that the harsh crackdown violated central instructions. Minzner argues that local officials were placed in an impossible position between hard targets and restricted methods, which led them to violate the latter (2009, 55–56). Similarly, in 2005, an attack by hired assailants on farmers protesting against a land grab, in which six villagers were killed, was captured on video and publicized on the Internet, leading the regime to fire two local leaders and reverse the land grab (Lum, 2006, 4–5). Even more spectacularly, in 2012 residents of Wukan successfully defeated a land grab by local politicians, seizing control of their village and expelling police. After five days, the government backed down and not only reversed the land grab, but also allowed villagers to elect their own local leaders (*The Atlantic*, 2012). In 2010, a strike at the Honda Lock car parts factory by undereducated migrant workers revealed strikers to be 'surprisingly tech-savvy'. Accounts were spread online within hours, action coordinated by website, videos of security guard brutality uploaded, and stories of a previous labour victory accessed online. Strikers stopped using the QQ text messaging service after it was infiltrated by guards but have gotten around censorship by using code words and alternative networks such as VOIP (Barboza and Bradsher, 2010). In another case, Severo, Giraud, and Douay (2011) study the Internet spread of a 'Bloody Map' showing patterns of violent evictions in China.

The relatively positive outcome of such conflicts is partly due to their recuperability. Because they are focused on the left-right axis and are mainly local in scope (even though they function as a synecdoche for wider discontent), they can often be defused through local concessions. Nevertheless, such protests can be seen as shifting power relations without rupturing the dominant transcript, a key modality of infrapolitics (Scott, 2012). Protests are usually theorized through O'Brien's (1996) model of 'rightful resistance' using dominant rhetoric and demands for realization of existing rights and policies. Hung (2010) suggests that the growth of 'mass incidents' in China suggests that people fighting for their rights – known as the *wei-quan* movement in Chinese – pose a greater threat to the regime than before, and that modern ICTs are part of the reason for this, with 'at least some coordination of action/movement' (Hung, 2010, 331). He suggests that citizens 'are now being awakened and empowered to set their own policy agendas both in cyberspace and physical life' (ibid., 337). However, he also notes that such movements typically do not question regime legitimacy, instead pursuing rights within the dominant frame (ibid., 333). Furthermore, the fact that even Western observers cannot establish the sites, causes, casualties, or outcomes of most 'mass incidents' points to a continuing information problem.

The impact of the Internet extends to labour movements, despite their arising mainly among the information 'have-less'. As Qiu (2009) observes, knowledge of ICTs is spreading 'to a greater portion of society', leading to 'the formation of grassroots urban networks among have-less youth'. This has an amplifying effect on dissent, partially overcoming information problems: 'The problems triggered by for-profit reform force angry youth to roar together – not only in Zhengzhou and Dalian but also online and in the blogosphere – to protest the unfair situations that they are thrown into. This time, their voices are heard' (Qiu, 2009, 140).

Another example discussed by Qiu (2009, 194) about the power of blogs in pre-social media period was the example of Uniden employees 2004 in a Japanese electronics plant in Shenzhen, where the workers used blogs to broadcast the progress of their collective action. Nevertheless, Qiu does not view working-class access to ICTs as constituting a sufficient condition for cultural and political empowerment: 'Given the early formative stage of the technosocial emergence, its still has to involve larger segments of the urban society, including elite members, mass media, and institutionalized forces, especially the state' (Qiu, 2009, 243).

However, a couple of limits have appeared to this type of dissent. There is substantial dissent among rural and labour groups, but their dissent does not overlap substantially with international celebrity dissidents. In general, popular groups are nostalgic for the Maoist period, and hence not necessarily critical of state authoritarianism. However, they tend to be sceptical of neoliberal economic reform and concerned about the problems (such as corruption and instability) that it has brought in its wake (Tang, 2001). Opinion surveys show declining satisfaction with neoliberal reforms, particularly among rural and working-class groups (Tang, 2001, 896, 904). In terms of the Political Compass, this locates them in the top left quadrant. Their grievance with the government runs mainly along the left–right axis, which places them diametrically opposite the celebrity dissidents. In Hu and Zhou's (2002) values mapping, communism shares with postmaterialism a spiritual rather than physical needs focus, which places both at odds with individualistic materialism but differentiates them along an individualism-collectivism axis. Public opinion research in China suggests that there is no significant critical mass for change. Pro-regime attitudes are strongest on issues of social control, with majority support for state authoritarianism but weaker support for neoliberalism. However, people also report feeling increasingly disempowered, more so than during the Maoist or Dengist eras, as survey results have indicated a declining sense of political efficacy (Tang, 2001).

Another limit is the relative inaccessibility of new technologies. Chinese Internet use has been historically concentrated in the areas (coastal cities) and strata (urban educated middle class) that benefited from neoliberalism (Abbott, 2001, 106). This stratification has been undermined as usage has spread, but nevertheless, rural and labour strata remain relative 'information have-less'. Today, around 29 per cent of the Chinese population has Internet access (Tong and Lei, 2010, i). However, 28.8 per cent of users are students, 28.5 per cent are white-collar and professional workers, and 7.5 per cent are government staff. Only 2.8 per cent are farmers, 4.4 per cent are documented workers, 2.4 per cent are migrant workers, and 9.8 per cent are unemployed (Tong and Lei, 2010, 3). Hence, 'those who may benefit the most from counter-hegemonic uses of the Net may be precisely those who have least access to it' (Warf and Grimes, 1997, 270). People in these groups tend to be digital 'have-nots' or 'have-less'. However, Qiu (2009) documents the spread of the Internet to the 'have-less', leading to a working-class network society used both for self-betterment and labour control. He also suggests that the spread of the Internet today is insufficient for labour empowerment, with Internet use still relying on alliances with other forces (Qiu, 2009, 243). Finally it is important to note that migrants are excluded from protest. A large portion of the population are migrants from rural areas who, lacking an urban *hukou* and corresponding right to live in the cities, are equivalent to undocumented migrants in other areas. Local migrants rarely develop a sense of community in their locality as they lack rights, and they are often blamed for social problems by other residents.

Nationalism, ethnic and religious minorities, and the cybercrime frame

Since the Tiananmen Square protests in 1989, the Chinese regime has constructed a new ideological basis in a nationalist narrative aggressively promoted through media, propaganda, and education (Zhao, 1998). Key aspects of this narrative include a golden age of national greatness, the 'Century of Humiliation' when greatness was destroyed by imperialists and internal division, and a current reemergence as a major power. Emergence is articulated somewhat anomalously with economic growth and seen as dependent on national unity and the prevention of *luan*. National division and disorder are seen as sources of misery and weakness, usually caused by foreigners (Zheng, 1999, 13–15). Nationalism in

China includes elements of pride about economic growth and a narrative blaming state weakness for earlier humiliations (ibid., 2, 17). The promotion of nationalism has allowed a relatively free cyberspace to nevertheless remain firmly under regime control. Nationalism is a powerful force in Chinese cyberspace, which includes the aggressive promotion of nationalist discourse throughout the Chinese diaspora and the crowd-sourced reproduction of a narrative of stolen greatness and revival (Wu, 2007). Chinese survey respondents were almost twice as likely to protest over foreign compared to domestic threats (Wang, 2009, 179). Nationalism is often seen as counteracting the tendency for cyberspace and indeed protest more broadly to become sites of dissent, with nationalistic netizens and protesters prone to follow the government line even when they have the power to counteract it (ibid.). Indeed, there are recurring rumours that the regime encourages protests targeting foreign countries as a safety valve (Sinclair, 2002, 26). Nationalism is used to encourage passivity and compliance in the face of unpopular reforms (Tang, 2011, 908). Indeed, authoritarian beliefs seem to be actually increasing in response to the apparent success of Chinese development (ibid., 899–900).

Although this is usually seen as reinforcing regime control of the Internet, it also creates spaces for autonomous political discussions through which users 'challenge the state monopoly over domestic nationalist discursive production' (Liu, 2006, 144) and in which the nationalism stoked by the regime spills over outside its control (Hughes, 2002). Wang's research suggests that nationalists are no less likely to protest against the Chinese government than others – the loyalty derived from nationalism seems to be offset by greater online political activity, with the Internet effectively weakening the 'taming effect' of nationalist discourse (Wang, 2009, 189–191). Hence, the Internet can function as a route around ideological blockages. On the whole, however, it seems that the power of nationalism as a form of reactive network formation allows the emancipatory potential of the Internet to be countered. Networked power emerges but takes increasingly reactive forms and is thereby plugged into dominant hierarchical power apparatuses.

It is this pervasive nationalism that allows the regime and its supporters to discredit transnational dissidents by portraying them as pro-Western and anti-Chinese. In the *Global Times*, which reflects the Chinese government's views, Shan Renping (16 October 2012) in a surreal twist *asks dissidents to overcome their hatred*, portraying them as irrationally hostile to the regime. He claims that dissidents are 'closing themselves off' to Chinese reform, that 'Chinese are used to Westerners using dissidents', and that prizes for dissidents will fail to undermine relations between China and the West, as he assumes they intend. The logic here is that dissidents are dangerous, because of their potential to use the global mediascape to pressure for reforms.

The major impact of the violence of nationalist discourses has been the repression of ethnic and religious minorities. The most extreme instances of repression have without a doubt occurred in Tibet (Xizang) and East Turkestan (Xinjiang), which are the locations of strong separatist movements. The Chinese media have framed conflicts in Tibet and Xinjiang as ethnic conflicts and have drawn on a powerful nationalist discourse in countering them. The repression of these protests and revolts has been particularly fierce, with hundreds rounded up and some protesters sentenced to death. Both movements, however, are highly active online, with networked online movements providing a context in which digital nationalisms are sustained in the face of repression.

The Tibetan cause is particularly well situated. Powers (2004, viii) conducted a web search on Tibet and found that, of the first 230 URLs, all but three were pro-Tibetan, the three being Chinese government sites. He observes that 'modern technology, including the advent of affordable desktop publishing and the Internet, allows a people that has lost the war militarily to continue the ideological struggle through the production and reproduction of its version of events' (ibid., 3–4). The Tibetan exile leadership, including the Dalai Lama, use the Internet to disseminate speeches and other material and have generated worldwide movements, such as the 10 March commemorative demonstrations (ibid., 143). This strategy is at once sociopolitical, using the Internet mainly to promote a particular view, and ethnoreligious, establishing a conflict frame between two contending accounts. However, the regime has managed to mobilize nationalist counterprotesters to target Tibetan protests abroad, particularly during the Olympic torch relay protests of 2008 (Wang, 2009, 158–159). In Australia, Chinese officials have also been caught sneaking copies of pro-regime works into bookshops (Powers, 2004, vii).

A similar process of survival through the Internet is observed in the persistence of various suppressed spiritual groups such as Falun Gong and *qigong* groups. Exiled leaders were able to continue to issue directives to followers. Aided by public relations professionals in the West, such sects converted into 'cybersects' able to maintain a network of believers while remaining anonymous (Thornton, 2009, 186). In the case of Falun Gong, Yuezhi Zhao refers to the group's media as 'rhizomatic', 'global', 'multilayered', 'interactive' and increasingly computer mediated, to the extent that 'the Internet has been instrumental to its more prominent emergence as a transnational global community' (Zhao, 1998, cited in Yang, 2009b). Furthermore, they are even able, through an exemplary case of scale jumping, to organize protests around the world whenever Chinese leaders visit (Tai, 2006, 106). In one case, they were even able to hack into and broadcast on a local radio station in China (Thornton, 2009, 198).

Uighur nationalism in Xinjiang, in common with similar movements worldwide, is a historical construct arising from the educational activities of intellectuals and took place prior to the rise of the CCP (Schluessel, 2009). Today, the Internet continues such educative activity. Indeed, research suggests that the modern mediascape and related consumption are causing Uighur culture to thrive and expand (Erkin, 2009). In this context, Uighur are turning to the Internet to construct narratives of national identity, a phenomenon referred to as cyber-separatism (Gladney, 2004, 229–259). Compared to Tibet, the Uighur cause has proven unattractive in the West due to associations with Islamism, but it has powerful resonance in Muslim countries, especially Turkey (Shan and Chen, 11 July 2009, 15–16). Chinese commentators, reluctant to admit a national dimension, chalk the conflicts down to economic inequalities, which persist in spite of affirmative action (Shan and Chen, 11 July 2009, 14). In particular, minorities face disadvantages from lack of contacts in the Han-dominated national market and tend to be outside the 'modern' capitalist economy. Local handicrafts and commerce are often decimated by Han-led modern industries, and Uighurs resultantly believe that economic growth benefits only Hans (Shan and Chen, 11 July 2009, 18–19). It has been suggested that the 2009 'Urumqi Riots' in Xinjiang were spread by a 'ripple effect' arising from 'the power of modern communications, such as cell phones and Internet', which explains for instance why an initial fight in Guangdong was so quickly translated into conflict in Xinjiang (Shan and Chen, 11 July 2009, 15). Shan and Chen (11 July 2009, 15) suggest that the regime had learnt from the Tibet unrest of 2008, rapidly shutting off cell phones and the Internet, but allowing access by foreign media.

Nationalism also leads to emerging forms of cyberconflict. Nationalist hacktivists react intensely to international conflicts, emerging quickly to coordinate mobilizations. Their 'collectivist tendencies and links to state and corporate establishments' set them aside from Western hacktivists (Qiu, 2004, 116) and also clearly mark them as an ethnoreligious cyberconflict group. It takes the form of a recurring 'short-term political spasm', which emerges quickly and aggressively and disperses quickly under state pressure (ibid., 116). In short, China is managing to contain the Internet not only through repression, but also through the constrained flourishing of forms of online self-activity which are marked by mimicry and conformity to the dominant discourse. This model is unstable, requiring both the continuation of Chinese economic growth (the absence of which would cause a legitimacy crisis) and a failure to obtain its goal (the achievement of which would lead to a postmaterialist culture and resultant antiauthoritarian movements similar to the 1960s in the North; cf. Skeldon, 1997, 267).

The successful use of nationalism allows China to rely on hackers to take part in cyberconflict from a progovernment perspective in the event of conflicts with America, Taiwan, Japan, and so on. This is considerably different from the basically hostile relationship between Western regimes and locally based hacker communities. China has taken part in crackdowns on piracy and hacking, but in an unenthusiastic way, reflecting the 'killing the chicken to scare the monkeys' principle. In 2010, China responded to international criticism by arresting three hackers, but the move was denounced as 'window dressing' by Canadian cybersecurity expert Ronald J. Deibert (Bradsher, 2010). China also claims to have arrested hundreds of domestic hackers, but focused this crackdown on the hacking of Chinese victims (Chao, 2010). There is an exception for anti-regime hacking, which on occasion has even been met with death sentences (Abbott, 2001, 103). On the whole, however, China continues to be a relatively welcoming environment for hacking, and also for commercial cybercrime activities, compared to most Western countries. In effect, China seems to be adopting an approach of predominantly seeking to tolerate and recuperate hackers, in contrast to the Western response of seeking suppression. This situation potentially serves to locate China at the cutting edge of technological development, as well as providing military advantages. It allows China to draw on local hackers to gain advantages in asymmetrical warfare and to carry out interstate cyberconflict.

It also serves to keep hackers out of the dissident milieu, keeping them focused on ethnoreligious forms of cyberconflict that are useful to the regime. Hacking as a form of asymmetrical warfare is encouraged by Chinese military strategists (Qiao and Wang, 2002; Karatzogianni, 2010, 4). The Chinese government uses hackers to attack the records and accounts of dissidents based outside China (Chase and Mulveron, 2002, 71). For instance, after the 1999 organization of a demonstration online by Falun Gong, the regime engaged in cyberattacks against related websites abroad, 'transform[ing] cyberspace into something of an electronic battlefield' (Wacker, 2003, 66). The best-known incident, announced in January 2010, was massive hacking of Google from inside China targeting both dissident Gmail accounts and Google's source code (Karatzogianni, 2010, 1). China also appears to be using hackers to 'steal' American software (ibid., 5), aiding technological leapfrogging and breaking superprofit monopolies.

If China has an emerging sector to power its rise to hegemonic status, it may well turn out to be the quasi-black-market mass production of virtual and real-world goods in an environment of loose enforcement of copyright laws – an environment which is already allowing Chinese companies to leapfrog technological and immaterial gaps and undercut monopolistic Western prices with generic versions of consumer goods. Similarly, despite crackdowns, China remains particularly prone to piracy, which was crucial to the transfer of Internet technologies to China in a context of global quasi-monopolies (Qiu, 2004, 107–108). China reportedly has one of the highest piracy rates in the world, with a 95 per cent piracy rate for movies, far exceeding U.S. and EU levels, and the United States claiming significant trade losses as a result (Eschenfelder et al., 2005). Another example of overlaps between illicit Internet activities and the regime was the story revealed in 2011 that prisoners in labour camps were being forced to play online games as part of the vast 'gold farming' industry run out of China (users play online games in a repetitive way so as to generate in-game currency, which companies sell for real-world money). If China is able to emerge from dependency, it may be that it takes the form of a particularly large, and correspondingly difficult to control, 'island in the net', ironically creating a climate for the new forms of virtual productivity which have long been theorized by cyber-libertarians, under the nose of one of the most authoritarian censorship regimes in the world. Cyber-libertarianism plays a significant role in the fourth phase of digital activism in relation to the WikiLeaks and Snowden affairs. This is where we turn to next.

3
The Fourth Phase (2010–2014): Digital Activism Invades Mainstream Politics

3.1 WikiLeaks: ideological and organizational tensions

The WikiLeaks revelations in my view became the symbol of the mainstreaming and popularization of digital activism in the public sphere, and this is why I view this as the start of a fourth phase in digital activism. WikiLeaks was in a sense a continuity for online collaborative communities, such as the FLOSS movement, as was explained in the first chapter. I started thinking about how affect theory could contribute to the study of the first reactions to the WikiLeaks revelations when I was preparing a chapter for the edited volume we published with Adi Kunstman in 2012. I am reusing material from that chapter here (Karatzogianni, 2012). By using affect theory, which I explain in depth in Section 4.4, I sought to enrich cyberconflict theory beyond the identity, media representations, discourse, conflict analysis, and resource mobilization elements I utilized in previous studies.

WikiLeaks is a continuation of a tradition of an overall information age ideology adhering to 'information wants to be free', wanting to change the world through making government open and accountable, through fostering some kind of alternative to capitalist relations, and through peer-production and collaborative networks. There are dozens of groups, some political and others less so. The peer-production and open-source groups have given us an array of beautiful products and have proven that human collaboration outside and in parallel with the capitalist system is both possible and sustainable. Indeed, there is a longer tradition of civil disobedience, political dissidence, and social movements in the historical narrative that various hacktivist groups might be drawing from as well, which were present already in the very first phase of digital activism (1994–2001). The criminalization of protest and hacktivism, cracking down on freedom of expression, their portrayal as threats to global security and as terrorism is a tactic that was a backlash from the second phase due to 9/11 (2001–2007).

The reactions to WikiLeaks in terms of content, but more importantly I think in terms of what the organization itself stands for, are swamped by strong feelings and by intense flows of affect, which eventually overspilled to cause revolutionary change in countries in the Middle East and the potential for more change elsewhere. If you are to discuss the psycho-political formations that digital movements and antagonistic organizations tap into, you only have to look at the reactions to the WikiLeaks saga: authoritarian leaders urging their subjects not to listen to Assange, portraying him as a Western stooge; liberal democratic governments talking of threats to national security and fear for soldiers' lives; the call by mainstream conservatives in the United States for Assange to be trialled as a traitor and executed; in left-wing and radical quarters, treated as a hero and an icon for the digital revolution by some, and criticized regarding his leadership style, for not being accountable, decentralized, or rhizomatic enough, by others.

In Assange's case, the mainstream media narrative followed a spectrum that coincided with the initial portrayal of Assange by his chosen partners in leaking Cablegate to the world (*The Guardian, New York Times,* and *Der Spiegel*), only to shift like a pendulum in the opposite direction, with criticism of his personality and personal life, when mainstream media and governments around the world, especially the United States, began attempting his demonization. This shift in the narrative produced even stronger affective reactions, polarizing the feelings around Assange and creating instant enemies and supporters, some of whom demonstrated their feeling with a wide variety of actions, from asking for his death to hacking banks and online outlets for not enabling Assange's financial support. Undoubtedly, it is difficult to tell whether affect creates the events and the subsequent media coverage, or if it is the original media coverage of WikiLeaks and the Cablegate scandal that created the feelings which impacted on the digital virtual and enabled the upsetting of the status quo around the world, thereby acting not as a cause, but as an accelerating factor along with social media to the Middle East revolutions. It is these affective flows toward WikiLeaks and Assange played out by individuals, governments, and organizations, both in the actual and the digital virtual, which when they overflowed, accelerated the overthrow of authoritarian leaders in Tunisia, Egypt, Libya, Yemen, Syria, and elsewhere in the Middle East.

Julian Assange, the founder of WikiLeaks, in various interviews and on the WikiLeaks site has expressed the ideology behind WikiLeaks as an amalgam of principles, those underlying the Founding Fathers and the American Revolution, freedom of expression, open government, and the right of the people to hold accountable their leaders in a democracy. In his own words, 'So as far as markets are concerned I'm a libertarian, but I have enough expertise in politics and history to understand that a free market ends up as monopoly unless you force them to be free. WikiLeaks is designed to make capitalism more free and ethical' (Greenberg, 19 November 2010). Assange himself is arguing that there is 'a deliberate attempt to redefine what we're doing not as publishing, which is protected in many countries, or the journalist activities, which is protected in other ways, as something which doesn't have a protection, like computer hacking, and to therefore split us off from the rest of the press and from these legal protections' (ibid.). Despite Assange's effort to distance WikiLeaks from the hacker movement in order to promote it as a publishing outlet with the legal cover that it provides, it is obvious that it has had a wide influence on Assange's own ideology. Therefore, add to libertarianism the baggage of free culture, hacker culture where Assange is coming from, and you have the ideology of many plateaus and systems of thought ranging from liberal to libertarian to elements of anarchist thought and free culture all really comfortably attuned to what has been called information age ideologies.

The free culture movement and hacker culture encompass different types of ideology: some political, others apolitical, some truly revolutionary in both philosophy and practice and others less so, which have been examined extensively especially over the last decade (Castells, 2001; Weber, 2004; Lovink, 2007; Taylor and Jordan, 2004; Raymond, 2001; Williams, 2002). There seems to be an issue with attaching any online collaborative project, whether it would be a software project, a free culture offering, or a social media-enabled protest movement, to a specific ideology. One the one hand, there are ideologues who deliberately seek to realize the revolutionary potential of technology and enhance the effects in the political economic, social, and cultural process to change the system as a whole, such as the ideology of the free/libre software movement (Stallman, 2009). Nevertheless, often the commercial viability of a project means that the ideology of activism is played down to create focus on the value of the product offered. In this sense, free software was revamped as open source to dissociate from the ideological components (ibid.). Currently, ideology is often mixed with activism, with activist entrepreneurs and entrepreneurial activists; an obvious example would be China and social activism mixing with Internet companies and riding the bandwagon of activism to attract more hits on commercial sites for profit purposes (Yang, 2009b), as explained already in the previous chapter on Chinese dissent.

There is a wide ideological spectrum in information age ideologies, ranging from neoliberalism to cybercommunism, to libertarianism and to anarchist thought. In a way, ideology is almost transferred through the old lenses of traditional political thought and applied to the political economy, culture, and society of the digital virtual. In many ways, although the medium is postmodern, the aims and desires are still of the modernist variety. The groups engaging in cyberconflicts are still fighting for power, participation, and democracy, but they are using an accelerated process and a postmodern medium that enables asymmetries, empowering the previously marginalized or repressed, causing shifts in our understanding of identity and community, accelerating feelings and political attachments to foster unprecedented social and political change. The Internet encourages networked organization and mobilization, a version of the commons that is ungoverned and ungovernable, either by corporate interests or by leaders and parties. We have seen the empirical confirmation of this trend to include social networking in the revolutions that took place in the Middle East. Some of these groups, which are informed by a more postmodern reading of ideology are calling for the transfer of some of the features of the digital virtual to the actual world, and they are doing this by mixing and matching several elements of traditional political thought to express this affect for change. It seems that WikiLeaks is part of that creed.

In close proximity to problems stemming from the ideological platform are organizational problems in FLOSS communities, which have been discussed extensively (Dyer-Witherford, 1999; Weber, 2004, Benkler, 2006; Karatzogianni and Michaelides, 2009). Assange admitted that the growth of WikiLeaks was too rapid to allow for adjustments in organizational terms. This is where the initial failure to support Manning with funds, or to respond to global attacks, actual, mediated, or digital, can be partially explained.

We know from social movement theory (Snow, Zurcher, and Olson, 1980, 790–797) that the fewer and weaker the social ties to alternative networks, the greater the structural availability for movement participation, and movements that are linked to other groups expand at a more rapid rate than more isolated and closed movements (Snow, Zurcher, and Olson, 1980, 790–797). This is why the network effect is responsible for WikiLeaks and Assange being supported by such diverse actors. Various celebrities helped pay his bail in the sexual assault case, a former soldier offered him residence in the United Kingdom, and Daniel Ellsberg, a whistleblower of international status, spoke in his defence. Journalists and media organizations, politicians, and academics from various fields reacted almost emotionally to Assange and his organization, as did social movements, NGOs, human rights protesters, hacktivist groups such as Anonymous, various file-sharing communities, and information age pioneers and ideologues. All these individuals and groups adhere to different ideologies and have a wide range of race, class, gender, and nationality backgrounds. They are, in a bizarre way, the multitude in Hardt and Negri's sense (2004) of players, which nevertheless have to express their particular affect drawing from their individual causes and systems of belief. Through diametric opposite flows of affects, they either render Assange a hero or villain and his organization a revolution in the media ecology or an anathema to global security. In a way, Assange and his organization are this empty signifier filled ideologically to reflect the discursive mood of the movement or the individual, supported by different forces which outpour their feelings onto different facets of the WikiLeaks story, be it digital rights, freedom of expression, Internet censorship, international legal issues, national security, civil rights, privacy, whistleblowing against multinational corporations and governments, and on and on.

This was the difficulty of adhering to an organizational model for WikiLeaks that would satisfy the image and ideology of such disparate forces. Assange has called himself the 'boss' that fired Daniel Domscheit-Berg, although it is obvious that WikiLeaks started with an information age philosophy, which according to some was compromised when it all went global and mainstream, with mainstream media given leaks and deals made by the 'leader', often without consent or knowledge from his WikiLeaks base.

The leadership and organizational tensions evident in WikiLeaks are witnessed since the advent of the digital. In other groups, the threat of forks forced organization choices to be made to solve structural chaos and force sustainability by either forking or creating cryptohierarchies or open hierarchies. Recall that this problem already appeared in the first chapter of this book. An Icelandic parliamentarian and former WikiLeaks spokeswoman Brigitta Jonsdottir – the United States subpoenaed Twitter to hand over her personal details – has tellingly described the organizational problems thus, and notice how her affect and emotion pour from that account:

> There is not enough transparency within the organization about decisions and not good enough communication flow, and in order for a good communication flow, you have to have good structure and know whose role is appointed to each other. I just wanted to have a debate about this with sort of the core group of volunteers and I couldn't. I tried for a long time and it didn't happen. One of the biggest criticisms on WikiLeaks, just like WikiLeaks criticizes government for their lack of transparency, there was a big criticism of WikiLeaks for not being transparent enough about their financial system, their donations. It would have just been so easy to make that just completely open instead of defending it all the time and having these speculations. (McMahon, 15 January 2011)

The OpenLeaks fork was caused by disagreements over Assange's leadership style and the centralization of the organization, although his trouble with Swedish authorities over sexual assault allegations did not help either. It is often a charismatic leader who can inspire the community involved, and we have seen the failure to inspire positive affect in forks across software communities with threatened forks in Linux and actual forks elsewhere. OpenLeaks is in fact very close ideologically to the open-source movement, in that it keeps the traditional ideological constraints out of the picture to concentrate on improving the process and the product. It is projected as a neutral conduit of people interested in exposing injustices: 'Our intention is to function, as much as possible, as a mere conduit (akin to the telephone exchange and the post) between the whistleblower and an organization of their choice. This means that OpenLeaks does not accept submissions or publish leaked material directly' (openleaks.org).

In the WikiLeaks case, Assange has a broad spectrum of ideological influences, and he is very careful not to alienate by alluding to more radical systems of thought, even if his hacker culture background might mean he has certain beliefs that point to nonmainstream influences. Nevertheless, it is partly the concentration of leadership in his hands that caused the OpenLeaks fork: 'OpenLeaks is based on a more decentralized concept. We do not seek to publish information ourselves, but rather to enable third parties to do so' (openleaks.org). Smári McCarthy has been involved in various sociotechnical initiatives (for more, see http://www.smarimccarthy.com and http://planet.fabfolk.com) and was a candidate for the Icelandic parliament. He was initially involved in WikiLeaks and in his own words had to spend 'a lot of time trying to clear up the unfortunate aspects of my erstwhile connection to them'. He had this to say about the ideological issues: 'The stated ideology of WikiLeaks has very little in common with its organization. One of the reasons the Openleaks fork is important is because it allows the localization of the information politics, where WikiLeaks has been attempting to amplify itself and go for global impact, but falling very short of that due to the fact that their group's skillset is very western-biased' (e-mail interview with the author, 15 February 2011).

So far, the focus has been on WikiLeaks ideological and organizational tensions which caused difficulties in the perception of WikiLeaks in terms of what it was officially meant to be representing and with its dealings with other protagonists and its base of supporters; its inability to address the issues as they were arising due to organizational tensions; a too broad and confused ideological platform that could not reconcile the ideology, philosophy, and organization of the founding organization with a more centralized approach, which focused on its leader, Julian Assange, his personal life story, and his trouble with sexual assault charges in Sweden. The next section looks at the impact of the WikiLeaks phenomenon on scholarship.

3.2   WikiLeaks: impact on communication and International Relations scholarship

Subsequent to this work exploring the affect, ideological, and organizational tensions in WikiLeaks, I teamed up with my longtime coauthor Andrew Robinson to look at the impact of WikiLeaks on academic scholarship in 'Digital Prometheus: WikiLeaks, the State-Network Dichotomy, and the Antinomies of Academic Reason' (a shorter version of this work was published at the *Journal of International Communication*; see Karatzogianni and Robinson, 2014). We focused on the academic reinscription of the WikiLeaks affair, examining the different receptions received within different literatures and fields.

The WikiLeaks affair – with or without its hypothesized connections to the Anonymous collective and the Arab Spring – has had massive ruptural effects on aspects of the global political system. A small, movement-based website has inflicted a tremendous informational defeat on the world's last superpower, revealing the possible emergence of a global networked counterpower able to mount effective resistance against the world system, possibly even the emergence of a state–network conflict as the new great power bipolarity after the Cold War. Therefore, in many respects, and notwithstanding WikiLeaks' relatively closed political structures, the WikiLeaks affair expresses the power of networked, decentred social movements to disrupt hierarchical arrangements of state and capitalist power. WikiLeaks has struck a tremendous blow for the power of transnational activist networks against the power of states. How this blow – and the corresponding redistribution of global power – is perceived will depend fundamentally on how the commentator feels about the current distribution of global power in favour of states. Perspectives can thus be divided, not only by discipline, but also by the author's position on the state–network dichotomy. Furthermore, different academic disciplines can be mapped in terms of their relative closeness to the statist or network side of the controversy.

As we saw from the previous section, diverse affects and subject positions were mobilized by WikiLeaks through the 'Revolutionary Virtual' – the field of construction in which zones of affect are selected and actualized. As a creation of new zones or assemblages of affect, the WikiLeaks affair can be seen as an event, and like all events, it is controversial. From a Badiousian perspective, one might divide scholars' responses into those who are in line with the WikiLeaks event, and those who react against it as representatives of the established situation. The study of the academic reception of WikiLeaks is thus a study of the reverberation of an event through the social field.

WikiLeaks can be viewed through the figure of Prometheus – the archetypal Internet troll of Greek mythology. Prometheus is a trickster figure, bringing life to clay (to create humans) and fire to humanity (to create civilization), in defiance of the fatalistic order of the Gods. Tricksters in mythology are typically on the side of creativity and chance, and, crucially, aligned with the rebel who defies and escapes the order of Fate: 'the hero – for example, Prometheus – challenges fate with dignified courage, fights it with varying fortunes, and is not left by the legend without hope of one day bringing a new law to men' (Benjamin, 1995, 294). WikiLeaks here stands for exactly such a gesture: within the world of neoliberalism, the fatalistic advancement of global capital and of the state as the bearer of Fate (ibid., 285–286) has been interrupted by a technological 'progress' long forecast by the fatalists but detourned decisively from their fatalistic narrative of progression. Instead, this Promethean flame is an uncontrollable force of networked power, which seems chaotic from within the statist order of Fate. Hence the attempts of the state to punish Prometheus, to sentence him to eternal punishment, as did Zeus, for rupturing the divine order. But here the accounts of the myth diverge: did Heracles free Prometheus from his enchainment? Perhaps digital social movements are the Heracles in this scenario, flexing their own muscle (such as the Anonymous DDoS attacks) to protect Prometheus from the order of Fate. It remains an open question whether Zeus will have his revenge, or whether Heracles will ultimately prevail.

In discursive terms, these two stances can be mapped along two axes of intellectual controversy that arise in the literature. In International Relations (IR) and related disciplines, including foreign policy studies, comparative politics, and law, the main focus is on *transparency* versus *secrecy*: the ethics of whistleblowing versus national security, the impact of leaks on the 'war on terror' and American foreign policy, and so on. In disciplines more closely aligned to the social, such as cultural studies, media studies, and sociology, the major debate is between *openness* and *control*. Issues include the relationship between WikiLeaks and the hacker ethic, the constraint of overwhelming state power, the emergence of a global public sphere, the changing relationships between old and new media, and the emergence of shifts in social relationships marked by the current wave of social movements. These differences emerge for a particular reason: the framing of the state– (social-movement–) network conflict through the gaze of the state, or from an interpretive standpoint framed by the attempt to understand the social.

Furthermore, they express the anxieties and orientations of particular authors. As Foucault (1977) rightly argues, power and knowledge directly imply one another, and the success and survival of different academic schools and disciplines may hinge on the balance of global power (27). Advocates of disciplines threatened by a diffusion of information are likely to be far more alarmed at the WikiLeaks affair than those working in disciplines that flourish on networked methods. We see in some accounts the voice of Zeus seeking to silence and torture the digital Prometheus, in some the voice of a Promethean force, and in some the voices of those who would draw on the Promethean force to revitalize the order of Fate.

Methodologically, we analyse the ideology in academic scholarship by mapping along two axes of the intellectual controversy that arose in the academic literature immediately after the *Collateral Damage* video in July 2010. We used Google Scholar to capture academic scholarship and opinion from the summer of 2010 to December 2012, with an original sample of 40 articles, which then extended to snowball sampling stemming from the original sample. Of these, we chose to focus only on the two disciplines. Moreover, we chose that specific time frame for sampling and did not include the years 2013 and 2014, an effect of the journal review timeline process, and further, it would take the scope of the study to another level altogether, considering the academic literature involving several subfields. Unfortunately, this means we left out the most significant academic contribution in relation to the WikiLeaks phenomenon thus far by Brevini, Hintz, and McCurdy (2013) and other important works from 2013 and 2014, which could be examined in future studies. Thus, the work, reflexive of its limitations, presents a broad meta-analysis of the debates surrounding academic scholarship within a specific time frame and does not pose itself as an overall meta-analysis of all fields affected by the WikiLeaks phenomenon to this day.

International Relations scholarship: the right to a cover-up?

The first standpoint to examine here is that of the state, or Zeus. Like any good trickster, Prometheus is a prolific troll. He has successfully trolled Zeus, who is now, in online terminology, 'butthurt'. This is a source of endless schadenfreude, or 'lulz', for Prometheus and his allies. But the state's reactive affects, directed against the trickster, take the horrifying form of divine vengeance. In academia, the standpoint of the state, and the order of Fate, is borne mainly by mainstream scholars within International Relations and security studies. These scholars are bearers of the desire to chain and torture Prometheus – variously manifested as declaring WikiLeaks a terrorist group and arguing in favour of assassinating Assange or jailing him as a spy, torturing Chelsea Manning, and rounding up Anonymous and other hacktivists as 'criminals' or even 'enemies'.

Statists generally minimize the benefits provided by WikiLeaks to maximize its alleged harms. From the statist point of view, the events exposed in the WikiLeaks cables are unsurprising. Anarchy is theorized by realist IR scholars as the absence of a global centralized government, which views the state – despite its evils – as a necessary guarantee of a worthwhile life. Further, for realists, it is normal for states to use Realpolitik to achieve their objectives. Indeed, the content of the cables may strengthen realists against rivals such as liberals and constructivists, who maintain that states can be constrained by norms and ethics. The realist objection to WikiLeaks is not, therefore, to the information revealed, but to the violation of a state privilege, which is taken to amount to an anarchist destruction of the state (Lim, 2010). Steinmetz (2012) explains the American state's responses – such as threatening to prosecute Julian

Assange for espionage, labelling WikiLeaks a terrorist group, and calling for the execution of whistleblowers – the following way:

> Realpolitik explains why those events – and others – may have occurred and why the government became so upset when revealed. It is posited here that the United States was largely not concerned with maintaining foreign policy relations for ethical or moralistic reasons. Rather, these relationships were manipulated and maintained for the state's own interests. (Steinmetz, 2012, 22)

Steinmetz admits a real danger that the government can use secrecy to cover up wrongdoing (ibid., 23–24). Steinmetz demonstrates through his analysis of secondary data sources that the government officials' public statements 'attempt to manipulate public opinion in a manner conducive to realpolitik governance' (ibid., 27). His analysis points to the arbitrary U.S. rhetoric of supporting government transparency and whistleblowing but considering WikiLeaks an organization seeking to undermine national security. In this way 'the U.S. reserves the right to define who is and who is not a whistle-blower and seeks ways to prosecute those who are not categorized as such' (ibid., 35), while this 'process of employing arbitrary rhetoric then deciding who is covered is a result of intense realpolitik' (ibid., 36). Realism simultaneously exposes and condones the double standard whereby America attacks WikiLeaks while condemning China for its actions against Internet dissidents (Karatzogianni, 2010) and while operating its own cyberwar capabilities, including arguably the networks that DDoS'ed WikiLeaks.

There are two views of cyberspace and its relationship to society: a view that cyberspace must conform to existing institutions and a view that cyberspace is reordering society and unleashing new possibilities for human freedom (Sterner, 2011, 1). These two views can be summarized as a state and a network perspective, respectively. Not surprisingly, Sterner is broadly sympathetic to the former view, maintaining that WikiLeaks has harmed American national security and typifying Internet freedom advocates as 'expansionists' (ibid., 3). This follows a long tradition in IR of accusing new political formations of aggression and revisionism, of disrupting the stable balance of world peace. So-called expansionists ostensibly believe that 'large institutions and organizations, such as governments, are not entitled to privacy or secrecy' (ibid., 4). On the other side, proponents of imposed conformity are typified as instrumental, seeing cyberspace as a 'tool of society' which 'should conform to established relationships, values and laws' (ibid.). Despite this assessment, Sterner also sees WikiLeaks as part of a trend that is here to stay, based in the culture of the Internet, and which will 'undermine the long-term utility of the Internet for commerce and governance' (ibid., 3). He sees the two sides engaged in an intensifying conflict that is playing out in courts and legislatures across fields such as Internet neutrality and intellectual property (ibid.). Nevertheless, this idea of expansionism is seriously problematic.

Sterner's criticisms of so-called expansionists are twofold. Firstly, attacks on the 'instrumental view of cyberspace' are taken to undermine 'trust', which makes cyberspace less useful for 'conducting activities'. Secondly, if large institutions and corporations 'step back from the use of cyberspace because they lose trust', its revolutionary potential is also diminished (ibid., 7). The subtext here is blatant: cyberspace is valuable, only if global elites can still exploit it, without which, it becomes useless. By an act of verbal acrobatics, Sterner thus portrays a process of corporate and state enclosure of an autonomous zone as a status quo threatened by aggressive attacks. The scenario of complete decommodification of the Internet, he posits, is unlikely, unless accompanied by a thoroughgoing move toward networked, peer-to-peer production structures. Outside such a context, a less corporate-friendly Internet would see capitalists forced to reach compromises and conform to Internet culture, rather than altering it. It would take more than a reduction in trust to prevent their exploitation of whatever profit opportunities they can find, since as we know from the subprime mortgages affair, capitalists are not necessarily averse to risk. In any case, the biggest threat to the trustworthiness of online transactions is doubtless the state's attempts to break encryption systems through means such as quantum computing, a process that poses very real risks of rendering e-banking and secure purchasing obsolete.

The idea of 'expansionism' is seriously problematic. As suggested by various scholars (Christofoletti and Oliveira, 2011; Flew and Liu, 2011; Ludlow, 2010), WikiLeaks has its ideological origins in the hacker ethic. Since the hacker ethic is as old as the Internet and arguably provides the constitutive power generating the Internet's emergence and evolution, claims of 'expansionism' are poorly directed. Rather, it is the state's attempts to striate or encroach on the Internet as an autonomous networked terrain, largely due to the expansion of corporate and conformist assemblages online, that entails 'expansion' and the revision of the status quo.

It is worth contrasting Sterner's work with another work from a similar angle. From a cybersecurity perspective, Betz and Stevens (2012) argue for a less repressive approach to the governance of cyberspace. The state must accept the autonomy of cyberspace in order to benefit from its economic potential. The division among statist scholars shows a key dilemma of state power, between the addition of axioms and tolerance of autonomy so as to exploit it, and the subtraction of axioms and repression of autonomy so as to suppress lines of flight (Karatzogianni and Robinson, 2010, 50–52). The expansion of capital, and thus of state power, depends on the exploitation of flows of creativity, but tolerating or enabling these flows requires a relaxation of the pervasive desire for control. In seeking to make cyberspace 'safe' for itself, the state risks killing the goose that lays the golden eggs. Ultimately the Promethean fire of constitutive power underpins the order of Fate, and Zeus is at risk of destroying himself along with his 'enemy'.

The WikiLeaks phenomenon is a line of flight, or as put by Saunders (2011), a hacktivist challenge to the diplomatic system. Saunders argued that the cables on the whole revealed little more than gossip – such as the scandalous leaks about Berlusconi, Qaddafi, and Putin – or else affirmed unsurprising facts about American foreign policy, such as Yemen's collusion in drone strikes, NATO plans to defend the Baltic States and Poland, and American anger at Armenian arms sales to Iran. A few leaks, he admits, were genuinely revealing, such as American complicity in Ukrainian tank sales to South Sudanese militias, and Hillary Clinton's orders to spy on key UN officials (ibid., 6). More broadly, he sees the WikiLeaks affair as a 'crisis' that threatens 'traditional forms of diplomatic power in the international system, particularly those that are dependent on closed networks, reliable distinctions between public/private information and established geopolitical narratives' (ibid., 2). This challenge comes from emergent structures of digitized global communication: 'Perhaps at no time in history have ordinary citizens possessed so much power in the field of global politics' (ibid., 9).

Overall, however, Saunders' verdict rules out the participation of new political formations in global diplomacy. 'While Julian Assange & Co. proved that even the most clandestine exchanges might be plastered across the front page of the *New York Times*, no member of the WikiLeaks will ever be called upon to solve the Israeli-Palestinian crisis, negotiate trade agreements between Ajerbaijan and Russia, or set environmental policy for the G-20' (ibid., 9). This importance is not only ethical, but strategic; since diplomatic elites can shape mainstream media discourse, they will continue to rule the roost (ibid.). What this account misses is that social movements and networks *do* seek to act on all these issues, from mass resistance to unequal trade agreements in Korea and Bolivia;

to ecological protests, which have forced strong concessions in regions such as Uttarakhand and the Penan territories; to grassroots conflict transformation initiatives such as those of La Ruta Pacifica. States are, of course, more effective in finding statist solutions that benefit elites, but social movements are very much players in all of these fields, often in a highly public way. The transfer of power from states to networks may alter the balance of power toward social movements in many of these fields, ensuring more socially just and sustainable outcomes than statist diplomacy would have realized. In addition, the revelation of what is already known or suspected is itself significant, in that it removes the deniability behind which power can otherwise hide.

And yet Bronk (2011) emphasizes the rise of 'cyber-enabled diplomacy', in which cyberspace is itself used for diplomatic purposes by the U.S. government. He suggests that the WikiLeaks affair triggered the United States' decision to install a 'cyber coordinator' (ibid., 4), but also suggests that the incident is ultimately unimportant, since similar information breaches are unlikely to be repeated in similar ways (ibid., 13). The Edward Snowden leaks in the summer of 2013 have spectacularly refuted this argument. In Bronk's case, it is the technical, tactical, and operational emphasis that creates the chain connecting scholar to state: by seeing the WikiLeaks saga solely in terms of a technical failure to prevent a 'breach' (defined as such from the state's point of view), Bronk is a typical 'problem-solving theorist', bracketing out the broader frames within which technical problems are embedded. The WikiLeaks 'event' in effect becomes invisible, reduced to a failure of the coordination of elements in the existing situation.

On a similar note, Erbacher (2011) uses the WikiLeaks affair as the basis for a discussion of technical means for preventing further leaks – deemed in the usual fear-inflated language as 'insider threats'. He proposes the use of procedures that will expose 'significant irregularities' so as to identify threats (ibid., 1). As Erbacher admits, such profiling has traditionally been avoided because it both fails to detect actual threats and accuses too many innocent people. In the authoritarian drive for a threat-free, totally controlled world, Erbacher glorifies the use of data-mining techniques, which effectively can breach both privacy and encryption and criminalize difference. The NSA and GCHQ surveillance operations as revealed by Edward Snowden are a case in point of the pitfalls of such an approach and the potential for abuse.

French critical scholars Devin and Törnquist-Chesnier (2010) argue that diplomacy is evolving into a new configuration in which the public-versus-secret dichotomy no longer operates, and the relation to nonstate actors becomes more important. This 'opens up new fields for research by questioning the intra-systemic relations of a "diplomatic community" conceived in expanded terms, examining networks of diplomacy in terms of vertical and horizontal connections' (ibid., 73). They call for a move toward a 'new diplomacy' that is multilateral, public, and itinerant instead of secretive, sedentary, and individualized, a transition arguably aided by WikiLeaks, which is a symptom of the newfound vulnerability of states to nonstate actors (ibid., 71).

Diplomacy discussions also involve fears that diplomacy, as currently constituted, is at risk. According to its advocates, the diplomatic privilege and the confidentiality of diplomatic communications are supposed to allow 'states to communicate with each other in open and candid ways, and also for important figures to say things they think true, but too politically damaging or physically dangerous for publication' (Page and Spence, 2011, 237). Page and Spence argue that the system is flawed and requires change. The leaks should inspire caution in America's sources, as well as raising concern over the boundaries between diplomacy and espionage. Nevertheless, they feel that in the longer term, diplomacy will not change and, if anything, will become more secretive rather than less (ibid.). Governments are more likely to respond to the risk of leaks through increasing self-censorship, secrecy, and the use of oral briefings, which 'will lead to worse decisions and less accountability for the decisions that are made. It seems a high price to pay for gossip' (Chesterman, 2011, 4). One can perhaps revisit the irony of such visions of diplomacy, with Assange living under diplomatic asylum in the Ecuadorian embassy since 19 June 2012, and with the British government threatening to violate diplomatic norms to get him out.

On the basis of the WikiLeaks phenomenon, Rosenzweig (2011) argues that the United States needs an online counterinsurgency strategy. He sees WikiLeaks as 'launching an assault on state authority' (ibid., 1–2), expressing an enemy ideology that is shared by groups such as Anonymous. He also suggests that Anonymous' vulnerability to counterattack is likely temporary. He calls for attacks to 'isolate fringe actors from the general populace and deny them support and refuge' (ibid.,. 5). Though differentiated from a purely technical response, this approach still fails to engage with the adversary on anything other than an operational level. The technical means used are simply broader (and more dangerous to civil liberties). The possibility that actions against a secretive and repressive state might be justified is simply framed out of this kind of analysis, which takes the legitimacy of the global system for granted and sees any means that preserve it as justified.

Strong statist positions have also appeared in the ethical theory litera-ture. For instance, Somerville (2010) has argued that leaking is a wrong means, which is not outweighed by good ends, as well as arguing that it poses large risks such as global war. She argues that it poses such a threat to America's 'social capital' – such as trust in the government – as to be considered harmful. In other words, government wrongdoing should be covered up so as to maintain the basis for social support for the dominant system. Responding to Somerville's view, media and prop-aganda theorist Marlin (2011) argues that WikiLeaks is on the whole a good thing for media ethics. This does not simply mean that ends justify means, but a higher ethical good negates the wrongness of the means. Hence, Marlin maintains that WikiLeaks is deontologically – not only consequentially – defensible. WikiLeaks is a counterforce against antidemocratic forces in the contemporary world, providing 'the raw material that the public often needs to form sound judgements' (ibid., 5). WikiLeaks could also lead to great goods, such as making it harder to fabricate the basis for going to war (ibid.). He concludes that 'some drastic means are needed to push back against the increasing inequali-ties favouring the very rich' (ibid., 6). Marlin thus embraces power redistribution from concentrated to diffuse forces, which WikiLeaks entails, whereas Somerville construes it as a threat. There is a signifi-cant irony here. In other contexts, the state is all for what Virilio (1997) terms 'telepresence', supporting surveillance with the duplicitous claim 'nothing to hide = nothing to fear'. The inversion of telepresence, the sudden exposure of the state to the ease of visibility in the information age, thus exposes the hypocrisy of its own reactions, seeking a special exception from the vulnerability to visibility it imposes on others.

In this logic, Radó (2011) argues that WikiLeaks opens up questions of the inside and outside of the public and private spheres in a digit-ally networked world. Using concepts such as sense/nonsense, mate-riality/simulation, state/nonstate, and participation/spectatorship, she asks whether the current system should fear the collapse of the public sphere and dominant forms of diplomacy, or whether WikiLeaks instead portends the expansion of the public sphere. Her position is that 'WikiLeaks presents an in-between phenomenon, in which case its appearance on the stage of world politics already signifies that there is a move from a traditionally conceptualized "public sphere" towards the operation of the sphere of "publicity" in the terrain of politics' (Radó, 2011, 6). WikiLeaks thus portends, not an apocalyptic scenario of uncon-trolled harm, but a rebalancing of the relationship between society and state toward a more participatory regime of power.

Overall, critical IR scholars emphasize the outpouring of violent rhetoric and repressive actions by the American regime, from threats to assassinate Assange or designate WikiLeaks a terrorist group, to attempts to have Assange extradited. Such responses are taken to show the worst about sovereign power, as they 'amount to a profound showing of authoritarianism' (Springer et al., 2012). The broader context of WikiLeaks is one in which the United States is attempting to reproduce a climate of global war. Strategic analysts such as Miskimmon, O'Loughlin, and Roselle (n.d.) offer a constructivist account of the situation. These authors suggest that strategic narratives are 'a means for political actors to construct a shared meaning of international politics to shape behaviour of domestic and international actors' (ibid., 8). The argument that 'American identities are deeply embedded and remain heavily imbued with racial, religious and imperial features' also challenges any transformational claims of the Obama national security strategy (Parmar, 2011, 153). To put it bluntly, the U.S. state is seeking to keep alive the 'war on terror' strategic narrative, even while seeking multilateral engagement (Gray, 2011).

Between human rights and sovereign exception: legal scholarship

Also broadly within the state domain, but more alert than most to the abuse of power and concerned to protect the professional niche of law from the expansionist national security apparatus, legal scholars have responded by focusing on the ambiguities thrown up by the affair. In the American literature, the WikiLeaks affair reignited ongoing debates between the liberal commitment to transparency – enshrined in the First Amendment and the Freedom of Information Act (FOIA) – and the nationalist obsession with preserving security at any cost. Legal scholars have called for clarification or reform of existing laws to determine what information is protected and what is prohibited (Opper, 2011, 240–241), though in the current climate this is likely to lead to a securitarian outcome. American regime commentators have been quick to distance WikiLeaks from First Amendment precedents such as the Pentagon Papers case, instead seeking to frame WikiLeaks within the 'global war on terror', as espionage, terrorism, or a security threat. This expresses a contradiction within law, which is becoming increasingly salient in the context of securitization, and which is highlighted especially by Agamben: the contradiction between the claim to legal inclusion, such as human and civil rights, and the 'sovereign exception' on which law is secretly based, the arbitrary decision to divide the world into bare life and politically recognized life, that is between the state as orderly life and as divine vengeance. Pro-regime commentators have been quick to seek to portray WikiLeaks as 'bare life', unprotected by media freedom, whistleblowing precedents, or the American First Amendment, whereas supporters of WikiLeaks emphasize its fundamental continuity with other cases of whistleblowing and the arbitrariness of the sovereign exception. As Wall (2011) suggests in relation to the Anonymous collective, the defence of human rights in a contemporary period is 'anti-sovereign', occurring across the boundary between liberal rights and a radical theory of the multitude. It involves the enforcement of human rights by networks, against states.

Legal scholars have generated a backlash against the militarization of the WikiLeaks affair which stands somewhere between a strong statist perspective and a pro-network position, as one might expect from the position of lawyers as part of the included stratum, seeking to constrain but not undermine the state. Criticizing the expansion of sovereign power to cyberconflict, military legal specialist Dunlap (2011) argues against the common view that there is a lack of international law governing cyberconflict, suggesting that the difficulty is, rather, in establishing the facts necessary to apply the law. He suggests that a less tolerant 'national security' framework is being used, in which force is used to eliminate perceived threats and is 'intolerant of any injury', instead of a 'law enforcement' framework, which uses force to detain suspects for trial (ibid., 84). Dunlap suggests that online incidents such as the WikiLeaks affair are insufficient to qualify as use of force or to justify acts of war, both because the harm caused is insufficiently great, and because the actors involved are not representatives of states. This places the issue within the field of law enforcement. Such an approach would certainly pare back discourses of national security, but still seems to suggest an ultimate primacy of states over social movements. He fails to see the social factors – that is, the emerging power of networks and their ability to act autonomously from states – which repressive 'national security' regimes seek to suppress.

In Australia, while political responses have been conflictual as to what international whistleblowing might entail, there is a developing pressure 'for a new whistle-blowing framework, so that current unworkable presumptions against any disclosure are removed, and conflicts are more manageable' (Brown, 2011). Such apparent legal ambiguities arise from the conflict between the state's expansive demand for logistical control of territory and the restrictions placed on this demand by other social forces in the course of history. The difficulty is in fact an effect of the dual structure of neoliberal law, in which a regime of rights coexists with expansive sovereign exceptions grounded on security. Since the twin dynamics of movement-led opening and state-led closure construct the material field in which the conflict of values occurs, it seems utopian and dangerous to trust to one of the contenders – the state – to arrive at a fair 'balance'.

Another legal scholar, Fenster (2011), suggests that WikiLeaks calls into question the meaning and effect of the suppression and disclosure of government information on a level more about power than law. With networked technologies creating an age of transparency, the relationship between government and citizens is changing. Fenster suggests that the information revealed by WikiLeaks is less important than the fact that government officials can no longer assume that their communications will remain confidential.

> The WikiLeaks disclosures both represent and portend enormous changes in how secret documents become public, and in the meaning and extent of transparency in a wired, digital age. The celebrity suggests that disclosure matters – that, in some combination, the documents have enlightened the public, affected the ability of state actors to perform their jobs, and created risks for the ongoing efforts that the documents revealed. (Fenster, 2011, 15)

In short, the rise of disclosability in a wired age portends changes in the balance of power between states and other actors – a recurring claim across all perspectives.

A particularly strong counterpoint to security perspectives in legal scholarship comes from those seeking to protect transparency, free speech, and media inquiry from what they see as government censorship. For Benkler (2011b), there is no constitutional basis to prosecute Assange in America. The U.S. government has overstated the dangers of the leaks, and the media has been complicit in this, engaging in self-censorship. Benkler likens the case to the Pentagon Papers release. He suggests that the attempt to single out WikiLeaks as a singularly irresponsible media actor distinct from mainstream media is simply government rhetoric. He cites WikiLeaks' activities and media commentary on them as evidence that it is an instance of exemplary investigative journalism. In contrast, he calls for prohibitions of private operators' withdrawal of service to a target of government or public outcry, on the grounds that the present arrangement of privately run communication provision leaves dissidents vulnerable to what he terms 'vigilante responses' by allies of the government.

'We told you so': sociology, media, and communication studies

What is for statists a matter of loss of control in the project of protecting national security is for social scholars a matter of potentially emancipatory change. Scholars of diplomacy have a vested interest in the preservation of diplomatic records necessary to the pursuit of their own craft and, hence, in the availability of untainted records in 30 years, rather than instant records now and a risk of no records tomorrow. Scholars in other fields, in contrast, have found the WikiLeaks cables an invaluable source of data. Social scientists, particularly scholars in media studies and 'Internet and society', start from similar observations to other scholars: WikiLeaks emerges from digital social networks and expresses a growing power of, and emerging culture of, digital networks counterposed to (certain forms of) state power. However, they are generally either sanguine or excited about the prospects for change, which this redistribution entails. To be sure, few of these scholars write purely from the side of Prometheus. Many are liberal democrats, seeking to insert greater accountability, transparency, and responsiveness to popular power into the existing system, or to bring it in line with new technologies. Nevertheless, their closeness to the Promethean flame, and ambivalence regarding the Order of Fate, are clear markers of their closeness to the networked, societal side of the WikiLeaks divide.

For instance, human geographers find the data revealed to be a treasure trove for mapping contemporary conflicts (O'Loughlin et al., 2010). Similarly, el-Said (2012, 1) suggests that the leaked cables show a 'bleak picture' of American imposition of intellectual property laws on the global South. He uses the WikiLeaks cables on the American-Jordanian Free Trade Agreement negotiations to reveal America's manoeuvres and agenda, with the United States pushing on behalf of pharmaceutical lobbyists to impose their patents on Jordan, to the detriment of the Jordanian health system. El-Said's research on Jordan is echoed by Sarikakis (2012, 16), who shows that WikiLeaks exposed American lobbying for repressive antipiracy laws in France and Spain. WikiLeaks has provided a valuable trove of data, which, due to its publicity, can be mined by academics as well as journalists and activists.

At the core of the media-communication debate, the broader issue of transparency versus privacy is a recurring theme. Citizen journalist Heather Brooke (2011) frames the WikiLeaks phenomenon as part of a wider information war in which grassroots activists challenge the control over information exercised by the ruling establishment. She suggests that this movement could determine whether the Internet empowers people or ushers in a new age of surveillance. Ludlow (2010) emphasizes the role of hacker ethics in WikiLeaks, particularly the idea of sharing information, and ridicules the posture of statists who seek an evil mastermind behind the organization. In contrast, Rosen (2011) frames the issue in terms of the death of privacy in an era of enforced visibility. Arguably, this debate about values is something of a smoke-screen for the real stakes, which are about diffuse versus concentrated power. It might be suggested that the values of transparency or secrecy are actually split: neither state secrecy nor the transparency of social action to state surveillance are positive phenomena. Correspondingly, both individual anonymity, or small-group invisibility, and 'sousveil-lance' against the powerful are liberatory. The dispute's real stakes are not between two generic values applied in a classless way but rather in a conflict between concentrated and diffuse forms of power.

Although many social scholars are interested in the revolutionary potential of new technologies, some are more interested in how this potential can be recuperated. From a citizenship and participation perspective, Bruns (2012) suggests that the 'self-organizing community responses' shown by the Anonymous actions and WikiLeaks' mirroring project show the ability for networked groups to 'bypass or leapfrog, at least temporarily, most organisational or administrative hurdles' (35). WikiLeaks is itself sustained by citizen-to-citizen connections, drawing on a sense of directly 'fighting the system' (ibid., 46). As befits someone interested in citizen integration, however, he is also concerned that the dynamic is 'too decentralized', 'outside the social compact of society', and lacking means for citizen–government negotiation (ibid., 47).

A key contribution to this debate comes from Benkler (2011a), who argues that the Internet renders media more censorship resistant, altering the power distribution among actors in an actor network (723). He suggests that the Internet makes actors such as WikiLeaks freer than they would otherwise be, which in turn constrains actors such as the U.S. government:

> WikiLeaks can be said to be an exercise in counter-power, because it disrupts the organizational-technical form in which governments and large companies habitually control the flow of information about their behavior in ways that constrain the capacity of others to criti-cize them. (ibid., 728)

The Internet provided Chelsea Manning with information about the army and a means to disseminate information, which gave her increased power (Benkler, 2011, 722). Alleyne's (2011) discussion emphasizes that WikiLeaks acted as a focal point for a global community of hackers and open-source activists, using methods that Alleyne emphasizes are hardly new and not at all reducible to the personality of Assange.

Furthermore, WikiLeaks can be 'seen as the pilot phase in the evolution toward a far more generalized culture of anarchic exposure beyond the traditional politics of openness and transparency' (Lovink, 2011, 177). Lovink views WikiLeaks as a small player in global affairs, which is nevertheless able to exercise power through media attention and spectacular revelations, bypassing the formal 'one-world' structures that bind most civil society groups into existing forms of state power (ibid., 178). He also suggests that the U.S. state is a relatively soft target, compared to more authoritarian or culturally diverse states, or to corporations. In retrospect, his argument holds considerable weight in light of the Snowden revelations in the summer of 2013. The structural difficulties with WikiLeaks stem from its position somewhere between a mere conduit for data and a media agency selecting and publicizing content. Lovink also emphasizes the impact of 1980s hacker culture and problems with Assange's 'sovereign' role in the organization (ibid.). Against the image of Internet expansionists, Lovink suggests that statists are seceding from a previous libertarian consensus that kept regulation at arm's length. This is occurring because the outcomes of growing social networking are not what corporate rulers wanted (ibid.).

Network power now escapes the apparatus of power, much more than does traditional journalism (Castells, 2010). Attempts to shut down WikiLeaks by cutting its connections have failed because of the proliferation of mirror sites, showing the structural prevalence of freedom of information today. 'No security is at stake for states. At issue is the right of citizens to know what their governments are doing and thinking. Hence, the WikiLeaks affair is an instance of cyberwar between states and civil society' (ibid., paras 6–7). In a later work, Castells (2012) embeds WikiLeaks in a broader account of technologically mediated social change. Observing that Internet use increases people's valuation of autonomy and also discussing the Arab Spring, Castells suggests that WikiLeaks is part of a broader 'mass insurrection against secret information'. What is important about WikiLeaks is the reaction against it, not WikiLeaks itself. This reaction is so excessive because WikiLeaks attacks the heart of contemporary power: control over information. The state–network conflict exemplified by WikiLeaks is what Balász Bodó (2011) understands as a manifestation of the counterpower of networks. 'The ability to place the state under surveillance limits and ultimately renders present day sovereignty obsolete. It can also be argued that WikiLeaks (or rather the logic of it) is a new sovereign in the global political/economic sphere'. Bodó suggests that the repressive response to WikiLeaks raises questions about how networked power can sustain itself when states attack. WikiLeaks was attacked through its connections to a world system vulnerable to statist and corporate intervention – its access to the global payment system, web hosting, and use of the domain name system. This happened without any legal charges or due process. Network power still suffers from vulnerabilities relative to the state, and to state uses of networked power to their own advantage. Such vulnerabilities are already being addressed through projects such as the PirateBay plan to operate servers from mobile drones, the emergence of Bitcoin, and the creation of radio-based Internet transmission to combat state blackouts. Bodó also repeats the criticisms of WikiLeaks' organizational model, which is clandestine and far from transparent, suggesting that it shares too much of its social logic with its adversaries and could become a new sovereign. This reveals a possible tension between the hacker ethic and the goal of a public, networked world.

Despite this tension, Christofoletti and Oliveira (2011) view WikiLeaks as the most potentially transforming journalism since the rise of Twitter and a part of a growing and irreversible trend. Analysing it as a cross-over between journalistic ethics and hacker ethics, they argue that it is a positive force for uncovering information in the public interest (ibid.). Chadwick (2011) uses WikiLeaks as a case study of an emerging hybridity between old and new media, which throws into question the separation of the two within media studies. WikiLeaks is part of 'broader networks of affinity' defined by 'libertarian hacker culture' (ibid., 17) and is best defined as a 'sociotechnical assemblage' (ibid., 21). Further, collaboration with old-media partners is used as a way to increase impact and recognition (ibid., 24–25), leading to a 'symbiotic' relationship with traditional media (ibid., 26). On the other side, traditional media used a custom search engine to mine the massive trove of data provided by WikiLeaks (ibid.). Chadwick also refers to constant attempts by journalists to boundary-police their relationship to WikiLeaks, falsely claiming to be more responsible or that WikiLeaks was 'just a source' (ibid., 35), claims that leave WikiLeaks vulnerable, in violation of older precedents of media rights (ibid.). In contrast, he argues that WikiLeaks 'occupies an important boundary space between old and new media' (ibid., 36).

WikiLeaks has also been cautiously welcomed in postcolonial studies. Yamaguchi (2012) argues that, before WikiLeaks, few scholars exposed the functioning of American state decision making relative to its spaces of exception, suggesting that this is an effect of a pervasive Orientalism, which reinforces the construction of exception. It has also been noted, however, that the value of transparency is culturally relative (Southern Perspectives, 2011), while some leftist commentators have questioned the valuation of transparency over secrecy (Birchall, 2011). Discussing the impact on the Middle East, al-Karoui argues that the WikiLeaks phenomenon could only happen in societies that place a high value on transparency. Nevertheless, it was framed through a false dichotomy of 'a tradeoff between the security of citizens and society on the one hand, and sacrificing transparency on the other' (ibid., 1). However, it should be noted that similar hacktivist methods *are* used in countries such as China and Iran as ways to fight censorship. The similarities between these movements and the Western campaign for WikiLeaks is shown by the support offered by hacktivist collective Anonymous to the Iranian 'Green Revolution' and the Arab Spring. Ironically, it was WikiLeaks that exposed Chinese hacking against the Dalai Lama (Simmons, 2011, 592), while another group, the Hong Kong Blondes, similarly disrupted Chinese networks in the 1990s (Ludlow, 2010). In short, the relationship between WikiLeaks, Western values, and 'transparency' is not as easily linked. The empowering effects of diffuse technologies for otherwise weak social actors are obviously not exclusively observed in Western liberal democratic societies.

Conclusion

The receptions of the WikiLeaks phenomenon across (and on the margins of) academia are thus diverse and reflect different subject positions in relation to the eventual effects, both of the WikiLeaks phenomenon itself and of the broader redistribution of social power that it expresses and portends. The WikiLeaks phenomenon is a characteristic instance of an irruptive event that disrupts an existing power order. The reactionary response of statists seeking to preserve or restore a status quo ante manifests itself in a series of panicked outpourings calling for the restoration of order. In contrast, scholars sympathetic to emerging social networks – whether as a source of a revolutionary, peer-to-peer social alternative, a source of constraint on overempowered elites, or a source of energies and innovation to be exploited by capital – have embraced WikiLeaks as an expression of fundamentally positive changes. Internet and network scholars have been unsurprised at the phenomenon, which demonstrates the validity of their existing work on emerging forms of networked power, while media scholars have welcomed the new informational openness enabled by digital media.

Overall, then, what are the prospects that the digital Prometheus can be unchained from the law of Zeus? Ultimately, the persistence and expansion of networked power does not come down to the contributions of scholars. It is an effect of the innovations made by social movements and dissidents on the one hand and logistical controllers on the other. It can be questioned whether scholarly commentary can really do much more than interpret the forces at play, arguably aiding their recuperation. Nevertheless, different streams of scholarship are feeding rather differently into the balance of forces. While securitarian statist scholars provide a veneer of respectability to the repressive backlash, social researchers frequently contribute to the comprehensibility of the WikiLeaks phenomenon, inserting it in a wider social context and showing its wider social effects. By rebutting the statists' hysteria, helping the transmissibility of emergent forces to new domains, reducing fear of the unknown, and showing the enormous positive potential of networked social forces, it is hoped that scholars can play a role in the process of unchaining Prometheus.

To conclude, this section was researched during 2010–2012 in order to understand the immediate impact of WikiLeaks in the relevant academic fields. Since then, Edward Snowden, by revealing the massive surveillance operations of the U.S. government, has opened further, and in a spectacular manner, the debate about ethics and privacy in cybersecurity and Internet governance, which earlier WikiLeaks had inevitably forced on academe. It is our view that this is healthy and vital, however many antinomies it generates, for academics involved in the debates explored here and elsewhere to engage in debates with practitioners that could still unleash creative energies to a new world, where individual privacy is protected and where social justice, solidarity, and transparency are enmeshed in free, open, and inclusive social networks.

3.3 The 'Arab Spring' uprisings

Gillian Youngs asked me to offer a critical analysis of the Arab Spring uprisings in 2011, which situates its digital elements within a historical, geosociopolitical, and communications context for her book *Digital World Connectivity, Creativity, and Rights* (2013). I revisited my cyberconflict framework to seek support for such an analysis.

At the first instance, a cyberconflict perspective on the Arab Spring discusses the environment of cyberconflict. This would include situating the different countries 'swept' by the 'Arab Spring' in the world-systemic, *geopolitical and International Relations context,* and the regional and national sociopolitical and economic positions and relationships these countries have historically held. To put it simply, then, I seek to understand the impact of the similarities and differences and to identify the common threads in the diffusion and spread of the uprisings across so many different settings, outside of the obvious social media acceleration, diffusion, and transnationalism hypotheses, which are offered relentlessly in the global mediascape.

A second cluster of issues involves the *political economy of communications* in each country, and particularly e-governance issues and digital infrastructure development. Arab Spring countries were in different stages of digital development. The regimes involved took different steps to cut the digital lifelines from the protesters. Digital networked everyday media and social media networks were used in creative ways to connect the protest both internally and externally to international players, media actors, and global opinion, and to plan and accelerate protest mobilizations, in line with previous empirical evidence from a long decade of academic scholarship on ICTs in social movements and activism. And yet the role of social media and digital networks was mediatized in the global public sphere as an unprecedented phenomenon. Here established *mainstream media coverage* of the events, the protesters, and the governments involved are still relevant. For example, what ideologies, constructions of social and political identities, representations of and by protesters can be located? What is the level of regime censorship, alternative sources, and media effects on policy? Who is winning the political contest – the international buy-in – and how this is accomplished?

A major component of new media theory in conjunction with Internet studies would also have to be employed to situate the tech/digital/online/cyber activism of the Arab Spring in the wider *history of protest, resistance, and digital activism.* Here, there is need to place this Arab 'digital' resistance within wider networks of discontent and protest against the neoliberal capitalist order in a time of global financial crisis, for example, the use of social media and media movements/protests in Europe against austerity in Greece, Italy, Spain, and Portugal, and the Occupy movement assemblage). Inevitably, we want to ask questions about what type of democratization can occur in such a context. Indeed, the debate over whether digital media was a cause or just a tool in the Arab Spring is a superficial one, considering a long history of online activism starting with the Zapatistas in the mid-1990s against neoliberal capitalist expansions and accumulation by dispossession in an alienating hierarchical order operating on the social logic of state and capital. It is therefore critical to probe deeper.

Further, a cyberconflict analysis would involve a third cluster of issues employing social movement and resource mobilization theories: *the effect of ICTs on mobilization structures, organizational forms*, participation, recruitment, tactics, and goals of protesters, as well as changes in framing processes and the impact of the political opportunity structure on resistances (the latter being critical because of the 'wave' character of the diffusion of protests in different countries resembling Europe in 1989, where the window in the structure opened with the collapse of the USSR). Also, digital media and social networking as enabling resistance through *hacktivism* (or invariably termed digital, tech, cyber, or network activism) and information warfare would have to be discussed in a variety of settings, especially in relation to media movements, ad hoc assemblages, and collectives engaging during the Arab Spring (e.g., Anonymous cyberattacks in support for the uprisings). Lastly, in relation to *ethnic, ethnoreligious, and cultural conflicts* occurring simultaneously with the uprisings, we can ask how group identities are constructed in relation to ethnic/religious/cultural difference or in this case also *gender difference* and structural mapping discussed in the first instance above. This section concentrates only on a few of what are, in my view, the critical issues found in these clusters of cyberconflict analysis that might prove relevant to future theorizations of the Arab Spring. Some of the threads left out can be equally critical; for example, there was no space to delve into the Palestinian issue, which is at the heart of Arab concerns. Before getting into the analysis, a very brief description of the Arab Spring is required.

This so-called Arab 'awakening' is the third of its kind, with the first occurring in the late 1800s with Christians, parliamentarians, and lawyers seeking to reform politics and separate religion and state, while 'the second occurred in 1950s and gathered force in the decade following. This was the era of Gamal Abdel Nasser in Egypt, Habib Bourguiba in Tunisia, and the early leaders of the Baath Party in Iraq and Syria' (Ajami, 1 March 2012). As Ajami describes it, the political environment in the Arab world before the revolutions materialized was sterile and miserable, with consent drained out of public life and the only glue between ruler and ruled being suspicion and fear:

There was no public project to bequeath to a generation coming into its own and this the largest and youngest population yet. And then it happened. In December, a despairing Tunisian fruit vendor named Mohamed Bouazizi took one way out, setting himself on fire to protest the injustices of the status quo. Soon, millions of his unnamed fellows took another, pouring into the streets. Suddenly, the despots, seemingly secure in their dominion, deities in all but name, were on the run.

Tunisians took central squares in Tunisian cities, and Ben Ali fled into exile on 14 January, ending 23 years in power. His extravagant lifestyle and that of his family were documented in cables leaked earlier that year by WikiLeaks and were made available through media partners to a worldwide audience (prompting the 'WikiLeaks revolutions' mediatization). The summer of 2010 is when what I have called the Revolutionary Virtual began its rapid materialization. On 25 January, protesters in Egypt took to the streets enraged by the death of a blogger in a mobilization organized by a Facebook site:

> On 6 June 2010 Khaled Said, an Egyptian blogger, was dragged out of a cybercafé and beaten to death by policemen in Alexandria, Egypt. The café owner, Mr Hassan Mosbah, gave the details of this murder in a filmed interview, which was posted online, and pictures of Mr Said's shattered face appeared on social networking sites. On 14 June 2010 Issandr El Amrani posted the details on the blog site Global Voices Advocacy (Global Voices Advocacy, accessed on 24 June 2011). A young Google executive Wael Ghonim created a Facebook page, 'We Are All Khaled Said', which enlisted 350,000 members before 14 January 2011 (Giglio, 2011, p. 15). (Khondker, 2011)

Protesters took to removing Mubarak from office in sustained action for 18 days and concentrated in Tahrir Square:

> On February 11, Mubarak stepped down and turned power over to the army. Waves of protest continued to develop throughout the Middle East. After Tunisia and Egypt, protest emerged in Bahrain, Algeria, Libya and then Morocco, Yemen, Jordan, Syria as well as Lebanon, Oman and Saudi Arabia. Protest is still in motion in most of these countries ... In addition, this succession of unpredictable revolutionary episodes took place in what Migdal (1988) would label 'strong states and weak societies'. (Dupont and Passy, 2011)

The different regimes and the support and opposition they faced were not similar, and so the results of the uprisings were also diverse. In

Tunisia an Islamist party took over, while in Egypt Mubarak was toppled and the military took over, with protests continuing until in turn democratic elections occurred, with renewed occupations of Tahrir in late November 2012:

> Democracy is all very well, but how do you cope when the judges belong to the old regime, the army protects its privileged position, society is deeply divided, the Christian Coptic minority are up in arms, the more extreme Salafists are snapping at your heels and a constitution has still to be written? (Hamilton, 29 November 2012)

In Libya foreign interventions helped in the overthrow of Qaddafi. Unrest continues in various countries in the Arab world. Syria continues at the time of writing (late November 2012) to be in civil war – China and Russia will not approve intervention, while Israelis and Palestinians have had a week of war exchanging rocket attacks with dozens of people dead and the diplomatic community visiting Gaza eventually managed to negotiate a cease-fire. Remarkably, Palestine was also recognized by the United Nations as a non-member observer state.

Further, most countries saw Islamist parties take over. This in part can be explained by the loss of the population's trust in secular parties and the belief that religious parties are more ethical and less corrupt. The Islamic version of democracy is imported without Western liberal values and rests on Islamic values (interview with Cohen-Almagor, 19 November 2012). Islam and politics are seen as historically inseparable by those framing nonreligious rule as illegitimate: 'The challenge of political Islam to secular modes of government is a recent phenomenon although it is presented by its advocates as a prolongation of an extended tradition in Islamic political thought' (Al Otaibi and Thomas, 2011, 138).

Consequently, it is counterproductive thinking about democratization and rights in Western terms and the debates on liberalism, republicanism, and deliberative democracy in contemporary political thought (for examples of these debates, see Benhabib's 1996 volume on *Democracy and Difference*). In this sense, it is arguable that the Arab Spring that brought procedural democracy with popular sovereignty, but with Islamic values, which continues for example to place women in the home and not welcomed in politics (more about this below), can be really thought of as similar to what is understood *normatively* as a Western style of liberal democratic politics. It is worth keeping this in mind for the subsequent analyses.

World-systemic, geopolitical, and International Relations context

A first question regarding the uprisings in the Arab world concerns 'the sudden surge and stiff resistance and demonstrations' in societies where there was fragmentation of grievances with multiple salient cleavages and the fact that the regimes concerned were supported economically, politically, and militarily by important allies, such as the United States, the EU, Russia, and China (Dupont and Passy, 2011). Western governments reacted according to a prescribed protocol to deal with upheavals in repressive regimes they were backing up. Dixon (2011, 309) describes it like this:

> With the US at the helm, high-level government officials urge 'restraint on both sides'. When the revolts appear to be not so easily thwarted, they then call for reform. Tensions escalate and international media attention grows, the call for reform turns to an acknowledgement of the need for a new government.

As any Arab democracy is an unknown quantity (the concern being especially with the popular vote going to extreme Islamist parties and the link to the war on terror), Western governments are reluctant to risk security interests (Springborg, 2011, 6). In the European Union policy sphere, there is a struggle between being a relevant actor in the MENA region and being a simple spectator, due to the trained relationship between a particular country and common interests, subregionalism and bilateralism versus interregionalism, and so on (Schumacher, 2011, 108). Perthes argues for the importance of the political signal sent through these uprisings for Europe's democratic market-economy model in relation to China and also points out that EU policies 'betrayed the professed European values of freedom, democracy and the rule of law rather than exporting them' (2011, 82).

However, when Western governments eventually accepted this new reality, this is where the appropriation of Arab revolutions began by the Euro-Atlantic axis (Africa, 2011, quoted in Dixon, 2011). Examples of such discourse are Obama's address to Egyptians attributing the success of the revolution to their 'ingenuity and entrepreneurial spirit', while at the same time a more neoconservative discourse even credits George W. Bush, claiming that it was his policy that helped the region's democratic movements to flourish (Dixon, 2011, 311). A U.S. assistance package with expertise to help involves the following:

> (1) Microsoft will work with civil society groups to improve information and communications capacity; (2) the US Overseas Private

Investment Corporation (OPIC) will support private equity firms and US–Arab business partnerships; (3) the administration is asking Congress to establish a Tunisian–American enterprise fund; and (4) business leaders and young entrepreneurs will connect through the US–North Africa Partnership for Economic Opportunity. (Kaufman, 2011, quoted in Dixon, 2011, 311)

Further, both Egypt and Tunisia were considered as examples of the neoliberal reform agenda, and there is a direct link of the revolutions occurring against regimes that were following that agenda (Armbrust, 2011, cited in Dixon, 2011, 314). In the 1990s, the IMF led a bulk of structural adjustment programmes (Mackell, 25 May 2011). It is obviously myopic to think that the uprisings occurred just against corrupted elites: 'Corruption is more than the personal wealth "stolen", but rather is those in power and with connections enriching themselves through legalised processes of privatisation' (ibid.).

It is tempting to think of the commonalities of the countries involved and treat the uprisings as a single movement, due to the diffusion and the domino effect of revolts against strong states by weak civil societies. It is worth entertaining this argumentation in this section to then be able to identify how the differences impacted the diversity of revolutionary outcomes. There are various examples of such analysis. Way (2011) for example compares the Arab uprisings to the revolutions and regime transitions after the collapse of communism in Eastern Europe. The conclusion drawn by Way in this comparison is that more autocrats will hang on in 2011, while where authoritarian collapse occurs, they will be less likely to democratize than their European counterparts were: 'authoritarian retrenchment in Bahrain, massive repression in Syria, and instability in Libya and Yemen – illustrate the paradoxical influence of diffusion in the absence of other structural changes' (Way, 2011, 17). Byman (2011), analysing what the revolutions mean for the Israeli state, quotes an Israeli official as saying, 'When some people in the West see what's happening in Egypt, they see Europe 1989. We see it as Tehran 1979'. And it is not just Israelis, who have played the democratic card against their neighbours, who think that; it is also a view held by feminist movements and women political participation activists in the region. Women have been excluded from major decision-making bodies since the fall of Mubarak, and Isobel Coleman warns, 'Arab women might soon be channeling their Iranian sisters, who have complained that Iran's Islamic Revolution has brought them little but poverty and polygamy' (Coleman, 20 December 2011). It is well known also that electoral authoritarian regimes establish multiparty elections to institute the principle of popular consent, while they keep subverting it in political life (Schedler, 2006).

Another factor beyond the obvious commonalities in the Arab countries where revolts were experienced, beyond political repression, social media, youth unemployment, and the domino effect (the opening in the political opportunity structure), is the matter of domestic food prices. Harrigan (24 May 2012) argues that the timing can be explained by the rising food crisis and food security in the Arab world. This is also supported by Way (2011) in that high unemployment and the rise of food prices fed mass-level discontent. And yet Way argues that in Tunisia and Egypt, the countries experienced growth and were robust enough to pay the police and soldiers. It is the nonmaterial values and ties which made these regimes robust. This shared ethnicity or ideology in a context of deep ethnic or ideological cleavage was not there to boost the legitimacy of the regimes (ibid., 20), and this is particularly interesting in terms of the globalization of values (more below).

In the next section, the media context of the Arab uprisings is discussed in order to situate the discussion on the extent of the role of social media activism within the digital development and e-governance environment specific to each. Social media activism is looked at here in relation to the history of digital activism and resistance: 'digital' resistance within wider networks of discontent and protest against a neoliberal capitalist order in a time of a global financial crisis; the effect of ICTs on mobilization structures, organizational forms, participation, recruitment, tactics, and goals of protesters; changes in framing processes; the impact of the political opportunity structure on resistances; and hacktivism, cyberattacks in support of the protesters or against crackdowns by government authorities over Internet dissent.

Digital development and social media use: does technology guarantee revolution?

A second edition of the Arab Social Media Report released by the Dubai School of Government (http://www.arabsocialmediareport.com) offers empirical evidence on the importance of ICTs and their political economy as a deciding factor in the Arab Spring uprisings. Facebook usage between January and April swelled in the Arab region and sometimes more than doubled, with the exception of Libya. These are some snapshots of important findings of that report to set the platform for this part of the discussion. Peak usage of Twitter and Facebook in the Arab region, the consumption of news through social media more than other outlets, the online acting as a barometer of the offline and vice versa, and efforts at censorship are the significant aspects here (Huang, 6 June 2011).

The most popular Twitter hash tags in the Arab region in the first three months of this year were 'Egypt', 'Jan25', 'Libya', 'Bahrain', and 'protest'. Nearly nine in ten Egyptians and Tunisians surveyed in March said they were using Facebook to organize protests or spread awareness about them. All but one of the protests called for on Facebook ended up coming to life on the streets.

During the protests in Egypt and Tunisia, the vast majority of 200-plus people surveyed over three weeks in March said they were getting their information from social media sites (88 per cent in Egypt and 94 per cent in Tunisia). This outnumbered those who turned to nongovernment local media (63 per cent in Egypt and 86 per cent in Tunisia) and to foreign media (57 per cent in Egypt and 48 per cent in Tunisia). The flurry of tweets spiralled during the turning points of the uprisings. In Tunisia they peaked around the 14 January protest start date. In Egypt they spiked around 11 February, when longtime president Hosni Mubarak stepped down. And in Bahrain they jumped in the days after the demonstrations began on 14 February. The authorities' efforts to block out information, the report said, ended up 'spurring people to be more active, decisive and to find ways to be more *creative* about communicating and organising'.

Nevertheless, and rightly so in my view, other analysts of the Arab Spring do not see ICTs as a major catalyst for protest, even where multiple underlying causes are present (Stepanova, 2011, 2). Underdeveloped countries would be excluded from social media activism by default owing to underdevelopment and the lack of Internet access, such as Iraq and Afghanistan or other countries such as Myanmar and Somalia. Stepanova also found that no direct regional correlation can be traced between levels of Internet penetration and other IT indicators (such as the spread of social media networks) and the proclivity for and intensity of social protest: 'States with some of the highest levels of internet usage (such as Bahrain with 88 percent of its population online, a level higher than that of the United States) and states with some of the lowest levels of Internet exposure (like Yemen and Libya) both experienced mass protests' (ibid.). In cases with low levels of exposure, cell phones, tweets, e-mails, and video clips were used to connect and transmit protests to the world. Different ICTs were used in different ways, and social media did not outmatch satellite or mobile communications:

> While the media utilized the term 'Twitter revolutions' for the developments in the Middle East, identifiable Twitter users in Egypt and

Tunisia numbered just a few thousand, and the mobilization role of micro-blogging as a driver of protests has been somewhat overemphasized, as compared to other ICTs, including cell phones, video clip messaging (such as YouTube), and satellite television. (ibid., 3)

Khondker (2011, 677) also thinks that to overstate the role of the new media may not be helpful: 'Certainly, social network sites and the Internet were useful tools, but conventional media played a crucial role in presenting the uprisings to the larger global community who in turn supported the transformations. The new media, triggering mass protests'. Still, the difference that the images and films put on Facebook of two million users made to protests in Tunisia was great in contrast to protests in 2008 (then with only 28,000 Facebook users), which were not publicized and never reached a global audience. In the Tunisian case, there were only 2,000 registered tweeters, and only 200 were active (ibid.).

Saletan (18 January 2011) does an excellent job in posing certain crucial issues in a report on the Future Tense Forum sponsored by Slate, Arizona State University, and the New America Foundation, where bloggers and activists from countries in turmoil, particularly in the Middle East, gathered to talk about how interactive media and social networks are influencing events on the ground. The main points of his account are summarized here and are worth exploring further:

1. Technology doesn't guarantee revolution. Sometimes poverty impedes revolution by impeding access to technology.
2. The medium can lead to the message. Young people went online to keep up with their friends and youth culture. In doing so, they became politicized.
3. Online crowd dynamics mimic offline crowd dynamics.
4. The Internet facilitates repression, too.
5. Pressure causes adaptation; censorship creates activists who know how to circumvent control.
6. Geography matters, even offline (i.e., the use of neighbour countries' systems to circumvent censorships).
7. Think small (cell phones, text messages, CDs, flash drives, and Twitter are critical to circumventing totalitarianism).
8. Beware Animal Farm (i.e., who replaces the regimes and what type of democratization occurs).
9. Regimes can use the Internet to keep power the right way (how the government can identify grievances online and address them).

On the first point, on technology and revolution, in terms of the stage of digital development and the impacts of use in varied political contexts and the issue of high or low use, Stepanova (2011, 3) argues that ICTs can have a more critical impact in countries where the regime has little or no social base. In the case where the regime has partial social support or legitimacy, there are limitations on what social media can achieve. Stepanova also believes that 'for ICT networks to succeed, the younger, relatively educated generation, which represents the most active Internet-users, should make up not only the bulk of activists, but also a sizeable percentage of the population at large'. In this analysis the critical pattern with high social media use is the likelihood to have less violent protests, while where there is low or minimal social media use, this corresponds with more violent escalations (ibid., 6).

On the second point of the medium influencing the message: when a young educated mass *prodused* themselves to the point of organizing a revolution, while social media brought together groups that would not collaborate in the offline world, and where there was no strong civil society, it was social media that created a common thread (Howard and Hussain, 2011, 41). This coming together in organized protests through Internetted movements in rhizomatically organized sociopolitical networks has been historically a frequent occurrence in mass mobilizations since 1999 in Seattle with the antiglobalization movement. The use of social media and ICTs during the Arab Spring was not a surprise for scholars of digital activism, hacktivism, and cyberconflict. It is a well known empirically proven fact that ICTs and especially networked media have transformed organizational forms, enable the acceleration of mobilization, force transformation on framing, and allow a much faster grasp of an opening in the political opportunity structure.

It is not wise to look at the Arab uprisings in a homogenous manner, but since they were mediatized in the global public sphere as sudden, spontaneous, unpredictable events, it is worth asking whether they were sudden and whether the usual 'elements usually associated with revolutionary processes (pre-existing networks, power fragmentation, cross-class coalitions, etc.)' were present. Another issue frequently brought up is how groups with such different values and contradictory ideologies, identities, and strategies come together in a short period of time. Again this was the case with both the global justice movement and especially relevant to the antiwar mobilizations in 2002–2003, where diverse groups joined in protests without obvious ideological coherence or leadership (ibid.). Again, this is not new, and it is observed with the Occupy movement and other social media-enabled protest movements. It is also known that 'the use of interactivity and networking on the websites contributes to micro-mobilization, and also to enhancing internal cohesion and bonding, rather than to building dialogic communication and solidarity online' (Moussa, 2011, 48). Different platforms accomplished different functions and were suited for countries and societies in diverse digital infrastructures. During the anti-Mubarak protests, an Egyptian activist put it succinctly in a tweet: 'we use Facebook to schedule the protests, Twitter to coordinate, and YouTube to tell the world' (Global Voice Advocacy, 2010, cited in Khondker, 2011).

In certain respects, whether social media were a crucial factor or just a facilitating factor is not a question worth posing. For anyone paying half attention, it is obviously a key factor in transforming how social movements operate, and it has been so for over a decade now. To be posing this question again only means that commentators will be asking it every time there is a revolution or a social media movement of any description, especially in the developing countries, and it is not meaningful as such for media policy or e-governance or for advancing theory in the various literatures. Obviously suddenly knowing that others feel the same as you in their thousands and are willing to mobilize, having access to the information that the regime is weak, and trusting the leaders of the protest to know that a potential mobilization will be successful is all bound to the use of social media to exorcise fear and uncertainty that a protest will be met violently by the regime. This is the reason certain uprisings succeeded and others did not, and this is the reason why in Iran and China the regimes are still able to hold on to power.

Further, political opportunity and diffusion questions for future research in relation to social movement and resource mobilization theory in the cyberconflict framework include:

Did ruling elites play a crucial role in opening up this window of opportunity? Were ruling elites divided and split into rival factions as was the case in communist East Germany? For example, Tunisia, Egypt and Libya were initiating power transition processes. Relatives of the strong men in power had been groomed for succession … Did these succession plans fissure the unity of powerholders and open up a breach for contenders? And what was the role of the army in these authoritarian countries? Did revolutionary episodes follow patterns of diffusion, and if this is the case what are the channels of this diffusion: networks and ties binding protestors across countries, traditional media such as Al Jazira, social and virtual networks such as Facebook or Twitter, or still other channels allowing for the spread of

protest throughout the region? And what was diffused: action strategies, tactics to avoid repression, organizational models, symbolic
action frames, or still other elements? (Dupont and Passy, 2011)

Another factor in the success of the protesters is that activists and their
innovative use of technology and social media 'increased the potential
political costs that the military would incur if it sided with the regime
and violently attacked civil resisters. Since the whole world was watching,
this type of crackdown would surely have elicited international condem-
nation and the potential end to diplomatic relations, trade agreements,
and aid' (Nepstad, 2011, 490). Nevertheless, one problem with overre-
lying on social media and ICTs as the crucial factor is ignoring other
factors, such as the role of the military in influencing the outcome of
a revolt. In fact, Nepstad (2011) argues that the military and its decision to remain loyal to the regime or to side with civil resisters played
a critical role in shaping the outcomes of these Arab Spring uprisings.
In the case of Tunisia and Egypt, the nonviolent movement won the
support of the regime's military and achieved regime change. In the case
of Syria, this was not so, and on top of that, Nepstad argues that 'if military personnel are comprised of different ethnic or religious groups that
have unequal power relations to the regime, the likelihood that the military as a whole will side with the opposition movement is low', while
when military defectors take up armed struggle against the state, 'the
nonviolent aspect of the struggle will dissipate and the nation will likely
slide into civil war (Libya and potentially Syria)'. Nonviolent disruption
and discipline meant that the military was more likely to side with the
protesters, making it difficult to shoot reasonable civilians with reasonable demands. Treating social media as the cause or the main factor
in the uprisings, by terming them the Twitter, Facebook, or WikiLeaks
revolutions, misses important elements and treats them as homogenous
protests bound together by the common thread of networked everyday
digital technology. On this, intersectional conflicts and a far more
specific quest for rights are examined below.

Intersectional conflicts and the demands for rights

In this last section, it is worth posing the question of how group identities are constructed in relation to ethnic/religious/cultural difference
and also gender and class difference in intersectional conflicts occurring
during the uprisings. For instance the already mentioned Goneim, one
of the leaders of the Egyptian uprising, a Google executive for the MENA
region, left his home and swimming pool in an affluent neighbourhood

in the Emirates to join the revolution. There are various class issues to be explored in terms of who was leading the protests using social media and the digital gap between the have-mores and have-lesses, for example. Although this and the religious and minority factions and conflicts are worth exploring in the Arab uprisings, the focus in this chapter is unsurprisingly on women, pointing to the debate generated about women and social change and women's parliamentary participation (Al Otaibi and Thomas, 2011, 139).

However repugnant, the cases of female reporters raped in Tahrir Square from United Kingdom, French, and American media are obviously not the only reason to be concerned about the role of women during and after the uprisings. Examples include the military in Egypt carrying 'virginity tests' during a demonstration on 8 March, International Women's Day, which 'attracted a few hundred women but was marred by angry men shoving the protesters and yelling at them to go home, saying their demands for rights are against Islam' (Coleman, 20 December 2011).

As mentioned earlier (Cohen-Almagor, 19 November 2012), Islamic parties are proving to be the winners in postrevolutionary countries, as they are seen as less corrupt, which means that it is Islamic values with a certain view on the place of women in political life that will inform the new Arab democracies. Over the last decade, prejudice and discrimination are more pronounced among the younger generation of the voter sample. Al Otaibi (2008, quoted in Al Otaibi and Thomas, 2011, 139) found in the case of Bahrain, 'This may be due to their being impressionable and thus easily influenced by religious extremists. It is noteworthy that an Islamic fundamentalist trend in terms of segregation and sectarianism has recently re-emerged in Bahrain'.

Ebadi has also argued strongly on this case questioning the term 'Spring': 'I do not agree with the phrase "Arab Spring". The overthrow of dictatorships is not sufficient in itself. Only when repressive governments are replaced by democracies can we consider the popular uprisings in the Middle East to be a meaningful "spring"' (12 March 2012). A proliferation of Islamic parties might mean Islamic values informing Arab democracy in a way that will not necessarily improve the social and legal status of women in the Arab world. Ebadi encourages interpretations of Sharia law toward a conception of being a Muslim and enjoying equal gender rights, which can be exercised while participating in a genuine democratic political system (ibid.). She also recommends using legal tools such as the International Covenant on Civil and Political Rights, so in the case of Iran 'the international community can play an important role in urging Iran to ratify the Convention on the Elimination of All Forms of Discrimination Against Women', while her recommendation is that 'Arab women familiarize themselves with religious discourse, so they can demonstrate that leaders who rely on religious dogma that sets women's rights back are doing so to consolidate power' (ibid.).

A lot of hope is placed on how the political changes across the Arab world in 2011 might result in a radical social change of fortunes for women in politics and the role of social media as tools of liberation: 'The future prospects for women's representation in politics in Bahrain as elsewhere in the Arab world lie with such social media in the masterful hands of a younger politically-astute generation' (Al Otaibi and Thomas, 2011, 152). Nevertheless, Mohamed Ben Moussa, who looked at websites used as tools of liberation in the Arab world, points out what is also true about digital activism in the rest of the world: its potential is always embedded within local and transnational power relations. The discourses and power relations are in turn always reproduced in the digital virtual environment. 'In traditional conventional religious cultures, women are perceived to be less qualified than men to run for, achieve and hold public office' ... 'The reasons for women's disempowerment and male dominance are in his view three-fold: economic looting; sexual looting; and ideological looting' (ibid., 145). No matter how social media are mobilized and connect demands for rights in incredibly creative ways across the Arab world, these are residual structural factors and will remain hard to change, the fact that women 'score high as mothers and very low as political participants' (Mustapha Higazi, cited in ibid.).

The short-term picture is that this 'Facebook generation' has yet to create a political platform, and indeed there is resistance in getting involved in institutional politics, with activists divided as to whether they should even be seeking to form or support institutionalized political parties. Springborg argues that 2011 will be more like the 1948 failed revolutions than 1989 and captures the critical issues. It is worth quoting in full here:

> How the globalised Facebook generation can convince large numbers of struggling Egyptians that their economic needs and demands can be addressed more effectively through democratic institutions than through access to patronage in an authoritarian system, remains to be seen ... The poster children of the Arab Spring, Tunisia and Egypt, do not seem well equipped to imitate the success of Eastern European

countries following the collapse of communism. The context in which Egyptian reformers are seeking to democratise their country is not nearly as conducive as was that in say Poland, largely because the security concerns of global and regional powers are thought by them to be better served by at best a very cautious, tentative democratic transition. (2011, 12)

More optimistically, in what is a groundbreaking account using Deleuzo-Guattarian logic to theorize the interplay of digitality, orality, and cultural diversity, Alakhdar (2012) argues that the kind of connectivity of the online world does not have to reduce cultures into one singular form. Rather, the Internet has the potential to promote traditional cultures as much as it promotes market culture. Reinventing spaces, these *produsing* e-immigrants and e-nomads 'take energy and flow from their real lives, expand and negotiate their cultures online then borrow from it to re-assemble their real worlds'. And elsewhere: 'Islamic cultural interaction online revitalizes the goal of global connectivity known of Islamic traditional culture' (ibid., 221). And still the questions remain what happens to cultures that are not *prodused* online and 'how far are traditional cultures themselves rhizomically open for development across speed and mobility?' (ibid.).

This perspective and these questions are critical in understanding the long term of networked everyday media in the Arab world and their importance, not as a trendy tool that overtook the MENA region like a storm, as the mainstream media would have it, and premediating not only in manipulating populations (Grusin, 2010), but also as creating spaces of peace enabling political and social transformation in these societies, initiating a creative discourse that links, for example, Islam to civil, human, and gender equality rights discourses.

The Arab uprisings are occurring at the same time as protests and massive mobilizations against austerity measures in Southern Europe (Greece, Italy, Spain, Portugal), in which digital media and activism are recognized as a key facilitating factor and have been recognized as such (but not as the cause of mobilization) since 1999 with cyberactivism in Seattle, the anti-Iraq War mobilizations, and now the Occupy movement that has spread around the globe in a postnational demand for reform in radical opposition to transnational corporate control of politics, economics, and society. The so-called Arab Spring and accompanying media movement is part of this story, even if the demands had a 'patriotic' and nationalist character (i.e., 'We are not traitors financed by foreign governments, we want to save country from corrupt elites' type of discourse), which mostly did not link directly to anticapitalist movements and resistances.

In the next section, I examine digital surveillance ideology in relation to the Snowden leaks in order to nuance the politics, traditions, ethics, values, and affects mobilized by governments and corporate elites to justify the collect-it-all practices by a *ménage à trois of 'trusted' global networks*. These trusted global networks comprising governments, corporations, and international organizations seem to have the mandate, or simply the monopoly of planning power, to represent the interests of citizens/consumers in the global networked public sphere. I argue that there is an ideology of the centre of the political spectrum, in combination with elements of a centralized network surveillance complex 'collect-it-all' ideology, that forms a *quasi-totalitarian ideology* at work in societies of liquid surveillance and control, by examining specific empirical examples directly drawn from media reports of the Snowden revelations. This study was prepared for a special issue of the Journal *New Formations* (the final journal-published version was later coauthored with Martin Gak. I only include here my first original version, as it was prepared for this book).

3.4   The Snowden affair

'Who has the info on you? It's the commercial companies, not us, who know everything – a massive sharing of data'. Sir Iain Lobban, Former Director of Director of the Government Communications Headquarters (GCHQ), UK. (Moore, 11 October 2014)

While public concern is continuously rising over surveillance and control (Associated Press-NORC Center for Public Affairs Research, 2013), governments and tech elites blame each other for the loss of trust by the public in relation to their handling of privacy and surveillance of network communications. The NSA programmes were put in place for seven years without any public debate of any kind. The Obama administration justified the agency's programmes by claiming they have been crucial to 'successes' in counterterrorism. The debate is happening for the first time since 9/11, and it is a debate on what affects rights/ liberties and freedoms in the digital age, and which subsequently has become a crusade in defence of democracy and constitutions in place to protect people from unreasonable searches and seizures unless there is a warrant. This was the frame offered by *The Guardian*, which led the media reporting of the Snowden leaks, starting with the famous Laura

Potras/Glenn Greenwald video interview with Snowden in Hong Kong. In the trade-off between privacy and security, governments argue for the need for secrecy to protect the public against terrorist and criminal networks, while civil society organizations advocate transparency and open access-enabled deliberation and oversight of the processes involved. Meanwhile, tech elites pronounce exasperation with their own relationship to governments and project their own need to protect their customers' privacy in order to guarantee their own income flows and their reputation as socially responsible corporate actors.

Within this disastrous ménage à trois of 'trusted' global networks, which have the mandate, or simply the planning power, to represent a bastardized citizen/consumer, it is still the individual who has to solve his or her information communication problems in relation to privacy and surveillance. It is the individual who has to buy digital equipment, access, and literacy in the form of consumption, education, and training. And, it is the individual who has to acquire skills and software to protect his or her privacy in digital homes built by tech elites and surveilled by governments (for security) and corporations (for profit). This paradoxical conundrum places the individual citizen/consumer in the impossible situation of 'hack or be hacked', which inspires the rationale for this analysis.

If individuals are controlled in their digital pursuits by monopolized and centralized surveillance, they will always be controlled, unless their purpose of communication is always declared in a specific manner. And yet the global middle classes mostly believe that digital communication matters only affect personal or professional enterprise and that they do not interfere with basic values of life. Nevertheless, Wacquant points to the 'desolidarizing' impacts of 'synoptic' surveillance (where the many observe the few) and 'lateral' surveillance (where people and neighbours watch each other) (Wacquant, 2008, cited in McCahill and Finn, 2014).

Against this background, I am inclined to follow Hayek's argument on economic control and totalitarianism. Only in this case, I argue that it is digital control and *the assumption that it does not affect freedom* that mirrors his argument about economic control. To demonstrate this point, I shall resort to crude sensational measures by replacing his *economic* (freedom) with *digital* (freedom) and in all other instances:

> The so called *digital* freedom which the planners promise us means precisely that we are to be relieved of the necessity of solving our own *digital* problems and the bitter choices which this often involves are to be made for us. Since under modern life we are for almost everything

dependent on means, which our fellow men provide, *digital* planning would involve direction of almost our whole life. There is hardly an aspect of it, form our preliminary needs to our relations with our family and friends, from the nature of our work to the use of our leisure, over which the planner would not exercise his 'conscious' control. (Hayek, 2007, 127)

Further, it is the unchecked power of 'digital planners', the tech corporate, and deep state digital order that is really the crux of the matter in the discussion of societies of control. The recent Snowden leaks and Assange's WikiLeaks provide significant evidence in hundreds of thousands of documents that there is what resembles a *U.S.-led transnational authority composed of global trusted networks* presently directing surveillance of digital networks almost in their entirety, and that it does involve the collaboration, albeit protestant, of transnational corporate tech elites. The power over information and communication this authority can master, due to monopolized surveillance, is nothing less than *control over both digital consumption and production, and this at a global level* (Shirky, 2011; Fuchs, 2011; Castells, 2012; Harvey, 2012; Lovink, 2012). Currently, the global citizenry is at the mercy of these digital planners.

Nevertheless, I would argue, what is of interest is not just the power and resistance to these digital planners, but *the specific type of ideology* used to justify both the power and the source of this power over information and communication via surveillance, as well as the relentless governmental crackdown on movements in favour of transparency and advocacy of new alternatives. The reason I think this is an urgent discussion to be had is that academic debates over surveillance are restricted to worthy but often isolated disciplinary areas, which do not nuance specifically the ideology of digital surveillance. For instance, McCahill and Finn (2014) examined surveillance in settings as diverse as migrants, protesters, schoolchildren, and individuals under probation and pointed to *surveillance capital*: subjects utilizing everyday tacit knowledge developed through their engagement in power relations to challenge this power, which provides subjects with enhanced agency in local contexts and settings. These authors argue that targeted individuals and groups in surveillant assemblages

have the police knock on their door after they have been seen 'out and about' on camera in areas where crimes have been reported that fit the surveillance profile; they are followed by security guards who ask to see their money before granting them permission to enter the shopping mall; they have their emails read by the police and telephone calls intercepted by the authorities; they are regularly pulled out of the queue at the airport and questioned by the authorities; and they have their performance monitored by the management as they work 'on camera' when patrolling the shopping mall. (ibid., 9)

There is nothing new about that. Surveillance might prove empowering by this use of surveillance capital, whereby 'long-term activists utilized economic, social and cultural capital to evade or contest surveillance in various ways…the subjective experience of surveillance was often expressed in positive terms with many protesters describing their experiences in terms of "play", "excitement", and as "identity affirming", rather than "oppression" or "coercion"' (ibid., 80). This is consistent with Foucauldian notions of resistance against the microphysics of power in the everyday (McNay, 1994).

Although McCahill and Finn provide via Bourdieu (2005) a new theoretical frame termed surveillance capital, there is demand to understand technosocial agency in broader theoretical and philosophical discussions. New materialist accounts drawing from recent theories of affect and embodiment, posthuman-influenced materialisms, accelerationism, postmodern critical theory, and critiques of network theory explain individual human agency as a nexus of overlapping and often competing subjectivities within the context of technologically distributed agency (Karatzogianni and Scandorf, 2014). This is a significant philosophical and theoretical development that cannot be left out in discussions of surveillance and privacy in digital networks. Indeed, Berardi, in his doctoral defence, recently spoke of 'neuro-totalitarianism' as an explanatory frame of a new species in the societies of control (Lovink, 24 October 2014).

I introduce the term 'quasi-totalitarianism' to explain how technosocial transformations of agency should enhance a civil type of association inspired by radical democratic politics to counter enterprise association dedicated to profit making and securitization in the digital public sphere. I then proceed to support this frame with specific empirical examples from the Snowden documents, reports of those documents by diverse media, and opinion expressed regarding the balancing act over privacy and surveillance in the digital public sphere.

Quasi-totalitarianism of the centre

Despite ethereal and postmodern conceptualizations of a digitality of utopian and dystopian creeds, the old modernist demands for power, participation, and democracy still hold currency, while race, gender, class, and other hierarchizations are produced and reproduced in digital networks. It is therefore poignant to identify the 'older' more traditional ideologies driving the surveillance complexes in the United States, the United Kingdom, and elsewhere, as well as countries where different political systems are in place, for example, in China, Iran, or Russia. In that sense, my argument is that as far as tech corporate and government elites are concerned, there is an indication of an emergent *quasi-totalitarianism* in relation to digital surveillance that resembles certain elements of historical totalitarianism, but that cannot be called 'totalitarian' as defined by leading scholars in the field of totalitarianism and the intricate matrices of debates therein. Nevertheless, I am using the term 'quasi-totalitarianism of the centre' as a concept within a genealogical continuum to historical academic and political discussions about the totalitarian left and the totalitarian right, as well as authoritarianism and despotism (Fascism, Nazism, the Soviet regimes, semi-peripheral dictatorships in Latin America and the MENA region, post-totalitarianism, and so on) (Arendt, 1951; Friedrich and Brzezinski, 1956; Talmon, 1961; Rupnik, 1988; Siegel, 1998; Žižek, 2011).

Within the context of these debates, the term 'quasi-totalitarian' I introduce here fits better with the surveillance ideology in contemporary times, because it explains the resemblance of the collect-it-all practices of the governments and corporate actors to historical practices of the past, without trivializing the horrific historical experiences of totalitarianism, which ranged from mass murder to totalistic control of the thoughts and actions of a country's population under specific historical regimes.

Moreover, on another level, the quasi-totalitarianism of the centre points to the 'centre' of the ideological spectrum. Traditionally, the centre has been occupied by liberals and social democrats of some description or another in democratic systems. Nevertheless, I would argue that the ideological centre in nondemocratic states is in turn the ideological centre in the specific spectrum of the political culture in country-specific contexts. The quasi-totalitarianism of the centre refers here to a second layer in relation to centralized hierarchical organizations, even if they are networked, as the sociopolitical logic remains hierarchical despite the use of network communications. The centres of digital planning and of surveillance networks are steeped in an ideology that is quasi-totalitarian in character, but obviously not the historical totalitarian left (communism) or totalitarian right (fascism) instantly recognizable as historical events, regimes, political practices, or ways of the total politicization of everyday life.

This is exactly why liberals and social democrats, parliamentarians, and others in the Western ideological centre find it preposterous to suggest that ubiquitous surveillance (the digital planners' control over global networks) is a totalitarian practice. It is because the ideological centre is blind to this simple fact: *the ideology of the planners, whoever they happen to be, is directly drawn from the ideological centre of the political system they have emerged from and which they now operate.* In this sense, surveillance complexes are the direct genealogical offsprings of and mirror the political ideology dominant in any given political system.

However, the paradox in the present case scenario is that neither neoliberalism nor social democracy, which are the two dominant ideologies in contemporary liberal democratic states, are the ideologies by which digital control is exercised in practice. Who can believe Chris Hune, secretary of state for energy and climate change from 2010 to 2012, and his exasperation about having no idea about GCHQ activities? 'Cabinet was told nothing about this' (Hopkins, 6 October 2013). I argue that there is a new form of ideology emerging: that of the *collect-it-all centre*, a hybrid of the traditional ideological centre infected by the centre in the form of centralized networks of surveillance complexes. This ideological hybrid relies on a type of enterprise association to flourish, in contrast to civil association, which was until recently the most common ideal type of association in traditional representative politics and fed in favour of or in opposition to the totalitarianism of the left, the right, and the liberal and social-democratic varieties of the past.

Zóon politikon: Edward Snowden and human conduct as civil association

In the context of intensely networked societies, it is no longer enough to mobilize constitutionalism and representative democratic politics against the control of big data and digital network infrastructures by state and corporate actors. It is obvious that the digital network war machine is entangled within both state and corporate-controlled network environments. This type of contemporary critique (e.g., Terranova, 2003; Wark, 2004; Benkler, 2011) traces back to authors such as Deleuze and Guattari (1987), Foucault, Marx, or the situationists. It is also a critique, which is widely accepted by key actors in the antisurveillance, freedom of information, and transparency-related movements. For a 'Network res publica' to function without resorting to closed, fixed, surveilled, and censored networks based on the reactive affect of biopolitically controlling/ed subjects and the microtargeted commodification of desire, it is critical to understand how human conduct is affected by the network form.

To that effect, I use these modes of civil versus enterprise association to differentiate human conduct in network societies by reconsidering Oakeshott's ideas in *On Human Conduct* (1981), because I think that association in the digital public sphere is taking place mostly within the confines of corporate platforms (geared toward enterprise), even when the association involves civil functions such as political participation and dialogue. *Civil association*, as a self-authenticating practice of practices, has no corporate aggregate purpose except to keep politics open and the discussion going and can serve both as a response to the above critique and as a powerful new vision for the network res publica, which is presently dominated by human conduct primarily geared toward forms of enterprise association. As Terry Nardin (2001) explains, 'The idea of civil association as association on the basis of agreed laws addresses this problem. The state as a legal order provides a procedure for adjudicating interpretive disputes, and in a state that is understood to be a civil association that procedure is concerned with legal rights and duties, not with promoting substantive goals'.

In other words, whereas the market is about economic growth, civil association is about restraints on arbitrary power. The danger as Noel O'Sullivan (2012, 310) explains does exist, because of 'a tension between the rule of law to which civil association is committed and the subordination of it to the administrative powers of governments bent on imposing substantive conceptions of the good society'. Despite extensive criticism from all ideological sides on Oakeshott's political heritage, O'Sullivan also points to how radical thinkers like 'Chantal Mouffe, a sympathetic critic, has suggested that Oakeshott's narrowly conceived concern with civil association might be overcome by *relocating the civil model within a radical democratic framework* that would encourage active participation in politics, thereby removing Oakeshott's reliance on what may prove to be a minority consensus about forms and procedures' (ibid., 306). Significantly, the danger of not recognizing the transformation of a civil into an enterprise state is a crucial problem in present politics: 'Even though the transformation of a civil into an enterprise state may be acceptable on occasion, insofar as it is necessary to defend or maintain civil association itself, the price to be paid must be clearly recognized: it is that the rule of law ceases to be the bond of citizens, and thus the state, for the time being, is no longer a free one' (ibid., 296).

Commensurate with this argument, I argue here that Edward Snowden in his leaks of hundreds of thousands of National Security Agency documents conducted himself specifically against enterprise association in the form of complete structural acquisition of data from private individuals and organizations both by governments and also tech elites and international organizations, the disastrous ménage à trois of 'trusted' global networks. The affective response to Snowden's 'Let us put surveillance to public scrutiny' from Anonymous – a new vigilante formation in global politics fighting against surveillance, censorship, injustice, and resistance in favour of solidarity with movements fighting against repressive and authoritarian governments – shows quite poignantly how Snowden's revelations were received by movements working against quasi-totalitarian models of the digital public sphere:

> Your privacy and freedoms are slowly being taken from you, in closed door meetings, in laws buried in bills, and by people who are supposed to be protecting you…. Download these documents, share them, mirror them, don't allow them to make them disappear. Spread them wide and far. Let these people know, that we will not be silenced, that we will not be taken advantage of, and that we are not happy about this unwarranted, unnecessary, unethical spying of our private lives, for the monetary gain of the 1%. (http://revolution-news.com/anonymous-releases-private-nsa-documents)

According to one of the main media organizations Snowden collaborated with, *The Guardian*, Snowden revealed NSA's Prism, which, according to the Snowden documents, is the biggest single contributor to its intelligence reports. It is a 'downstream' programme, which means the agency collects the data from Google, Facebook, Apple, Yahoo, and other U.S. Internet giants. One slide claims the agency has 'direct access' to their servers, but this has been hotly disputed by the companies, who say they only comply with lawful requests for user data (*The Guardian*, 1 November 2013). Snowden also leaked the existence of Tempora, a programme established in 2011 by the UK's GCHQ that gathers masses of phone and Internet traffic by tapping into fibre-optic cables. GCHQ shares most of its information with the NSA. The documents, which are reportedly marked top secret, come in the wake of other high-profile disclosures attributed to Snowden since he first started collaborating with the paper for articles published beginning 6 June 2013. The U.S. government has since indicted Snowden under the Espionage Act, he requested asylum from no fewer than 20 foreign nations, and ended up in Moscow, as the Putin regime ironically obliged to provide him with asylum.

The relationship between the NSA and tech giants is a paradoxical one indeed. Again according to *The Guardian*, from June to July 2010, data from Yahoo generated by far the most NSA intelligence reports, followed by Microsoft, and then Google. All three companies are fighting through the courts to be allowed to release more detailed figures for the numbers of data requests they handle from U.S. intelligence agencies. The agency is allowed to travel 'three hops' from its targets – who could be people who talk to people who talk to people who talk to you. Facebook, where the typical user has 190 friends, shows how three degrees of separation gets you to a network bigger than the population of Colorado. According to internal documents cited by journalists, Microsoft 'developed a surveillance capability' that was launched 'to deal' with the feds' concerns that they'd be unable to wiretap encrypted communications conducted over the web in real time. The response from Microsoft vice president John Frank was, 'We continue to believe that what we are permitted to publish continues to fall short of what is needed to help the community understand and debate these issues' (RT, 11 July 2013).

Two French human rights groups filed a legal complaint targeting the U.S. National Security Agency, the FBI, and seven technology companies they say may have helped the United States snoop on French citizens' e-mails and phone calls. The complaint denounced U.S. spying methods as revealed by Snowden and filed against 'persons unknown' but named Microsoft, Yahoo, Google, Paltalk, Facebook, AOL, and Apple as 'potential accomplices' of the NSA and FBI. The International Federation for Human Rights (FIDH) and the French Human Rights League (LDH) argued that 'This blatant intrusion into individuals' lives represents a serious threat to individual liberties and, if not stopped, may lead to the end of the rule of law' (Huet, 11 July 2013). Reports also point to '"alliances with over 80 major global corporations supporting both missions". In NSA jargon, "both missions" refers to defending networks in the US, on the one hand, and monitoring networks abroad, on the other. The companies involved include telecommunications firms, producers of network infrastructure, software companies and security firms' (Poitras et al., 1 July 2013).

Mark Zuckerberg, CEO of Facebook, and Marissa Mayer, CEO of Yahoo, defended their companies against critics who charged tech companies with doing too little to fight off NSA surveillance. Mayer said executives faced jail if they revealed government secrets. Yahoo unsuccessfully sued the foreign intelligence surveillance (FISA) court, which provides the legal framework for NSA surveillance. In 2007, it asked to be allowed to publish details of requests it receives from the spy agency. Mayer reportedly said that 'When you lose and you don't comply, it's treason. We think it makes more sense to work within the system', while Zuckerberg said the government had done a 'bad job' of balancing people's privacy and its duty to protect with his now famous quote: 'Frankly I think the government blew it' (Rushe, 12 September 2013).

The public appearance of tension, whether this is actually real or presented as such in the public sphere, either way points to decision making outside democratic politics, because it involves back-channel negotiations between state and corporate elites, under secrecy, as the tech corporations are not allowed to divulge information about requests made by the NSA. That would be treason, which makes Mayer's quote all the more important. Stop Watching Us campaigns and the 11 February global campaign against surveillance, as well as privacy groups such as the Electronic Privacy Information Center and the Electronic Frontier Foundation launched lawsuits that have led to the disclosure of hundreds of pages of FISA rulings on Section 215. GCHQ and NSA surveillance is facing a legal challenge at the European Court of Human Rights from Big Brother Watch, English PEN, and the Open Rights Group. Google, Microsoft, and Yahoo, facing a backlash from their users in the United States and overseas over mass surveillance, are fighting to be allowed to be more transparent about their dealings with the intelligence agencies. These companies, along with Facebook, Apple, and AOL, have also written an open letter to the Senate demanding reform. In fact the review by the Obama administration was conducted as a response and did little to satisfy critics.

There are two more areas that point to quasi-totalitarianism beyond this bizarre relationship between state and corporate elites. The first is at the level of International Relations and global politics, and the second involves the role of investigative journalism in holding governments accountable. Let us take these in turn.

There is a matrix whereby governments are not allowed to spy on their own populations, but they can spy on another nations' as they are defined as foreign nationals. The United States views as second parties the United Kingdom, Australia, Canada, and New Zealand (the five eyes), and other countries such as Germany and France as third parties, which it can spy upon. This included the EU and notoriously Angela Merkel's mobile phone:

On an average day, the NSA monitored about 20 million German phone connections and 10 million internet data sets, rising to 60 million phone connections on busy days, the report said. In France, Der Spiegel reported, the United States taps about 2 million connection data a day. Only Canada, Australia, Britain and New Zealand were explicitly exempted from spy attacks. (Reuters, 30 June 2013).

The reaction in European capitals to U.S. and UK spy activities has been underwhelming. French president François Hollande condemned the practice, saying, 'We cannot accept this type of behavior between partners and allies' and the hacking was not necessary for anti-terrorism efforts. 'I do not think that this is in our embassies or in the EU that this risks exist' (Schow, 1 July 2013). Germans watched as their chancellor barely seemed to protest at the revelations. In a *Der Spiegel* article, 'The Chancellor and the NSA: Merkel Has Abandoned the Germans', the author argues, 'And this about our loyalty to America. Or international terrorism. Or even the role of intelligence services. Everyone has their own opinion about that. This is about our rights being violated without us being able to resist it. We stop being citizens and turn into subjects' (Augstein, 16 July 2013). An explanatory analysis of why this might be the case points to a division of duties and at times extensive cooperation among the intelligence agencies in the Western world: 'Britain's GCHQ intelligence agency can spy on anyone but British nationals, the NSA can conduct surveillance on anyone but Americans, and Germany's BND foreign intelligence agency can spy on anyone but Germans. That's how a matrix is created of boundless surveillance in which each partner aids in a division of roles' (Poitras et al., 1 July 2013).

In contrast to European reactions, Brazil's Rousseff cancelled an official meeting with Obama and at the UN's General Assembly called on other countries to disconnect from U.S. Internet hegemony and develop their own sovereign Internet and governance structures, because NSA rules also impose geo-locational-based jurisdictional mandates (based on the route of your Internet traffic or the location of the data services and databases you use). This would infringe on 'Article 19 of the Universal Declaration of Human Rights – protecting the right to freedom of opinion, expression, and the opportunity to participate in the information society – is at risk' (Meinrath, October 2013).

Besides the lukewarm reaction to the revelations in Europe, based on the Western intelligence argument – governments and populations between allies will be spied upon routinely, justified by 'war on terror' requirements – another critique is truly relevant to the quasi-totalitarianism frame I am proposing. This involves the Iraq War legacy in the American deep state. Greenwald, one of the journalists who brought the Snowden story to public attention, discusses here a profile on the former director of the NSA, Gen. Keith B. Alexander, by the *Washington Post*:

> The Post explains how Alexander took a 'collect it all' surveillance approach originally directed at Iraqis in the middle of a war, and thereafter transferred it so that it is now directed at the US domestic population as well as the global one: 'At the time, more than 100 teams of US analysts were scouring Iraq for snippets of electronic data that might lead to the bomb-makers and their hidden factories. But the NSA director, Gen. Keith B. Alexander, wanted more than mere snippets. *He wanted everything: Every Iraqi text message, phone call and e-mail that could be vacuumed up by the agency's powerful computers.*' Rather than look for a single needle in the haystack, his approach was, '*Let's collect the whole haystack,*' said one former senior US intelligence official who tracked the plan's implementation. '*Collect it all, tag it, store it. ... And whatever it is you want, you go searching for it. ...* ' ... And, as he did in Iraq, Alexander has pushed hard for everything he can get: tools, resources and the legal authority to collect and store vast quantities of raw information on American and foreign communications'. (Greenwald, 15 July 2013)

McCoy, writing about the making of the American surveillance state, similarly writes about the operational mentality of Keith Alexander in the following way:

> During a visit to a GCHQ facility for high-altitude intercepts at Menwith Hill in June 2008, NSA Director General Keith Alexander asked, 'Why can't we collect all the signals all the time? Sounds like a good summer project for Menwith.' In the process, GCHQ's Operation Tempora achieved the 'biggest Internet access' of any partner in a 'Five Eyes' signals-intercept coalition that, in addition to Great Britain and the U.S., includes Australia, Canada, and New Zealand. When the project went online in 2011, the GCHQ sank probes into 200 Internet cables and was soon collecting 600 million telephone messages daily, which were, in turn, made accessible to 850,000 NSA employees. (McCoy, 15 July 2013)

Houston writing at *The Economist*, which is not of the Popular Resistance ideological variety as is the origin of the previous quote, nevertheless again similarly writes,

> What kind of message are we sending about the viability these democratic ideals – about openness, transparency, public participation, public collaboration? How hollow must American exhortations to democracy sound to foreign ears? Mr Snowden may be responsible for having exposed this hypocrisy, for having betrayed the thug *omertà* at the heart of America's domestic democracy-suppression programme, but the hypocrisy is America's. I'd very much like to know what led Mr Obama to change his mind, to conclude that America is not after all safe for democracy, though I know he's not about to tell us. The matter is settled. It has been decided, and not by us. We can't handle the truth. (Houston, 9 July 2013)

The *Atlantic* responded to Obama's surveillance speech with equal frustration about his justification of NSA activities, which included references to open debate and democratic process:

> Obama '...I called for a review of our surveillance programs. Unfortunately, rather than an orderly and lawful process to debate these issues and come up with appropriate reforms, repeated leaks of classified information have initiated the debate in a very passionate but not always fully informed way...I'm also mindful of how these issues are viewed overseas because American leadership around the world depends upon the example of American democracy and American openness, because what makes us different from other countries is not simply our ability to secure our nation. It's the way we do it, with open debate and democratic process'. (Friedersdorf, 12 August 2013)

The third area pointing to quasi-totalitarianism, beyond the collaboration/conflict relationship with tech companies and the Western matrix of intelligence that enables the collect-it-all targeting of millions of records of data of various countries' populations, is the impact of the Snowden revelations on journalism overall. It is rather obvious that smashed servers in *The Guardian*'s basement is not the flagship product of a democratic state, and it rather *resembles* historical totalitarian practices (in Nazi Germany it started with the burning of books and it finished with the burning of people). The detention of Greenwald's partner by the authorities was yet another melodramatic knee-jerk reaction by the

UK government, which needs to appear to pull its weight in the special relationship.

The most significant support for the quasi-totalitarianism frame I developed in the first part of this section is the explanation offered by Edward Snowden himself. Snowden's flight to Hong Kong and then Russia and his subsequent asylum there to be joined by his awesome pole-dancer girlfriend does seem to be a story line taken out of a James Bond movie or a Hitchcock plot behind the Iron Curtain during the Cold War. And yet it is worth examining the target of his conduct and his professed ideological enemy. This is how his statement at Moscow's Sheremetyevo International Airport was reported:

> On 12 July 2013 Edward Snowden met with a number of human rights organizations at his temporary refuge in Moscow's Sheremetyevo International Airport. Here are a few of the points he made: – Through his working connection to the National Security Agency, Snowden found that he 'had the capability without any warrant to search for, seize, and read your communications. Anyone's communications at any time. That is the power to change people's fates.' – Snowden also concluded that the daily use of this capacity by the NSA was a 'serious violation of the law. The 4th and 5th Amendments to the Constitution of my country, Article 12 of the Universal Declaration of Human Rights, and numerous statutes and treaties forbid such systems of massive, pervasive surveillance.' – 'My government [U.S.] argues that secret court rulings, which the world is not permitted to see, somehow legitimize an illegal affair.... The immoral cannot be made moral through the use of secret law.' – Appalled by this situation, Snowden took to heart the 1945 Nuremberg principle that says, 'Individuals have international duties which transcend the national obligations of obedience. Therefore individual citizens have the duty to violate domestic laws to prevent crimes against peace and humanity from occurring.' – Having concluded that the NSA's real and potential secret access to the communications of almost every American, and a growing number of non-citizens, was criminal in nature (perhaps totalitarianism in the making), he leaked the classified information that would bring the NSA's activities into public view. 'That moral decision to tell the public about spying that affects all of us has been costly, but it was the right thing to do and I have no regrets'. (Davidson, 16 July 2013)

To conclude, this section introduced the term 'quasi-totalitarianism' to explain digital surveillance as leaked by Edward Snowden to the global mediascape. The resemblance (quasi), but not the reality, of historical totalitarianism is based on the following elements, which the argumentation supports: (1) the monopoly of digital planning on surveillance rests on back-channel secret communication between government and tech corporate elites; (2) enterprise association politics ensures that the dual goal of state (security) and capital (profit) continues unabated and unaccounted for; (3) at the very least there is a Western intelligence matrix of surveillance of unprecedented proportions in the form of total structural data acquisition; (4) journalists, whistleblowers, and transparency movements are prosecuted in the clumsiest manner possible, resembling historical totalitarian practices of the past; (5) there is significant anger and frustration not just from the usual organizations fighting for digital rights and freedom of information and privacy, but also by the public about the infringement on civil liberties and against what is currently resembling (i.e., quasi) totalitarianism. Our redeveloped study of the Snowden revelations with Martin Gak also includes the co-optation of advocacy and NGOs accepting donations from government and industry in this area of work (Karatzogianni and Gak, forthcoming).

The case studies we have looked at show that where there is digital materialization, the Real follows suit, so in the defence of civil association politics in the digital public sphere, the quasi-totalitarian practices of enterprise association style politics, conducted by global trusted networks (state, capital, co-opted civil society) and led by the United States, has to be seriously reconsidered.

4
The Future of Digital Activism and Its Study

4.1 Definition of digital activism and cyberconflict as an area of study

With the rise and spread of digital activism and cyberconflict, a proliferation of linked research subjects has emerged. This kind of breadth involves the following areas:

- *The individual*: privacy and security in cyberspace.
- *Class, gender, minority, and migration* issues, individuals and groups (e.g., the digital gap, the digital have-lesses, the digital working class, digital diaspora networks, and the digital development of migrants).
- *Private corporations* in the IT industry and elsewhere and their corporate, social, and moral responsibility (e.g., issues coming up in the Google-China cyberconflict, issues of human rights, censorship, the cybersecurity professionals hawks vs doves).
- *Civil society* – nonstate actors (e.g., the role of these actors in ensuring digital freedom, the methods used and the ethical debates and issues raised by the collaboration of governments and corporations with NGOs).
- *The state* – the role of the state and the difficulties of the boundary-less character of cyberspace, and the inability of the state to embrace ICTs fast, adequately, and if at all depending on its position in the global system. Also, questions of e-government as the last effort at state relevancy and survival.
- *International Relations* – international regulation–international law regarding cyberspace (e.g., the problems related to the nonexistence of these for situations such as Estonia, NATO, the UN, the EU, and major INGOs, and serious problems in addressing violations

and cyberattacks between states; see for example the Sony hack in December 2014). Also debates surrounding 'posthuman agency' in relation to drones, for example.

- *Global politics, political economy* – wider implications for global politics beyond states, with grassroots diplomacy, citizen journalism, social movement organizations and their demonstrated use of ICTs, and the transformations due to network forms of organization, mobilization, and recruitment. The empowerment of the user/citizen.
- *Media convergence, digital economy regulations* – illegal file sharing, fandom, and purity brand control; transmedia marketing and storytelling.
- *Global media* – the effect of social media on older forms of media ownership, media coverage, security implications stemming from cybersecurity problems, and radicalization media.
- *Global resistances, uprisings, and movements* and their organization, mobilization, recruitment, and ideological development/framing through digital networked everyday media and commercial platforms.

In terms of movements that make extensive use of digital social media networks, there is a wide spread of issues as well:

- Demanding global justice, countering capitalist crisis and austerity
- Challenging hegemony: secession, insurgency, and extremist movements
- Demanding regime change, opposition movements
- Countering the state, transparency, anti-surveillance movements
- Offering alternative socioeconomic, lifeworld, and political reforms: peer production, ecological, LGBT/queer/feminist movements.

The kind of theories and epistemologies that scholars of digital activism have used include political communication, social movement, network, framing, performativity, critical, continental, cultural, and comparative approaches. The research techniques used in the past two decades include critical discourse analysis, social network analysis, big data quantitative approaches, interviews, focus groups, theoretical sampling, netnography, as well as techniques related to media and communication, political science, sociology, anthropology, psychology, management, and social computing. Scholars have focused on specific events, countries, or themes, and in the future they will focus in areas such as

- country, for example, a European focus comparative
- comparative across continents, for example, Europe, Asia, Americas

- issue, for example, what issue people are protesting about as per issues above
- theme, for example, citizenship, participation, governance, agency, visibility, publics
- class, race, gender, difference as reproduced themes in several case studies (standard media representation studies).

There are specific debates for the study of digital activism that have not been resolved over the past two decades. These are the most critical in my opinion:

- The relationship between digital activism and cybersecurity, and under what circumstances it should be prosecuted by governments as a crime.
- The difficulty in understanding where attacks originate, whether they are state sponsored or by ad hoc assemblages.
- The problem of ideology and consensus in the global public sphere in defining whether digital activist events are legitimate.
- The securitization of digital networks and the crackdown on dissent by authoritarian regimes, as well as by liberal democratic states.
- The effect of digital activists' dependence on commercial platforms and the broader importance of this dependence.
- How to effectively measure digital media's impact on ideology, identity, privacy, organization, mobilization, leadership emergence, and coordination of digital activist communities.
- The central problem of assigning agency in distributed systems overall, which impacts digital activism greatly as there is no single actor to whom to attribute specific activities.
- The ability to measure effectively the impact of digital activism in the Real.
- Understanding the mechanisms through which digital protests materialize in the Real.
- Understanding to what extent affect plays a more central role in digital communication in comparison to other communication.

4.2 The agency problematique

Let me take a shot at some of these questions. One of the main areas of concern in the study of digital activism is understanding notions of individual and collective agency in an intensely multimodal, hybrid-mediated contemporary world. These notions complicate and underlie our understandings of digitality and virtuality at both theoretical and ontological levels.

As an example, recent research regarding conflict in digital migrant networks (MIG@NET, 2012) shows that new forms of agency enabled by digital networks and social media unsettle closed and fixed 'tribal' identities that rely on religion or ethnicity. However, migrants are more inclined to 'stick' to such 'thick' identities of religion, nationality, ethnicity, and culture than agents engaged in sociopolitical networks of resistance, a finding consistent with previous research on resistance networks (Karatzogianni and Robinson, 2010). Resistance networks operate in affective durations, so to speak: active-affective structures dominate more in sociopolitical affinity networks, while reactive-affective structures dominate more in ethnoreligious groups and reactive insurgent collectives more generally.

In the first and second phases in this book, we saw that ethnoreligious groups adhere to hierarchical notions of ethnicity, nationality, and religion to form and transfer 'real' communities to digitally networked spaces. The reliance on nationality, ethnicity, and religion to repress (or utilize) emotions such as fear, suspicion, and hatred demonstrates the operation of the politics of emotion and affect in digital cultures. In migrant networks, meanwhile, the migrant mixes and matches her loyalties and tests the primacy of one identity, identification, and subjectivity (home country, ethnicity) against others (host country, new social affiliations), depending on the immediate social context and the fear and uncertainty that needs to be exorcised at any given time in the diverse, hybrid media environments in which she lives. Research into religious practices in digital networks (MIG@NET, 2012) reinforces the idea that agency, especially communicative agency, is extremely contingent and volatile and is used by migrants to defend older loyalties or new religious revivals, old and new friends and enemies, in a constant negotiation of many different – often dissonant – worlds (home country, host country, online and offline) at the same time, and to be loved, appreciated, and safe in each of them.

The evolving forms of agency available to individual actors negotiating such identities are directly afforded by networked communications technologies and social media, but they are not (and cannot be) solely technological. These novel agentic forces are highly political/intentional and affective/motivated (Karatzogianni and Schandorf, 2015). Emotions, affect, and technologies get negotiated in rapid rhythms against the old constants of religion, nationality, ethnicity, generation, and public life, all of which digital networks make somewhat ephemeral and far more contingent than in the past.

In the case studies we conducted for the European Commission MIG@ NET project (Karatzogianni et al., 2013), we observed the centrality of ethnic and religious affiliation, chauvinism, and national identity (e.g., the 'foreigners' in the Greek case; the 'non-European immigrants' in Russian discourse, or ethnic divisions among post-Soviet migrants; the chauvinism displayed by ultra-right-wing racist groups in the Cypriot case). Secondly, discourses of inclusion and exclusion are present in all case studies (e.g., us the Greek nationals vs them the criminal foreigner enemies in the Greek case; us the good Russians vs them the niggers who riot in the UK study; us the pure Cypriots vs them who want to take over our squares and country). There is strong evidence in all case studies that offline hierarchies, identities, and discourses are also reproduced online, thus creating a continuum of hybridity. In all cases, digital media were used as a mobilization tool (in organizing the activism against Putin, for instance, in the UK case). If one looks at the effect of ICTs on mobilization, organization, and the opportunity structure, digital media were used to organize and raise awareness against racism in the Cypriot case and to refute each side's argumentation in terms of propaganda. In Greece, through social media and blogs, digital activism played a role in framing the racist–antiracist discourse.

Individuals are recruited online to participate in events, and their tactics and goals are influenced by digitality. The protest against Putin in the United Kingdom is a major case in point, but we also see an influence of social media in activism/protest in the other two case studies. The effect on framing processes points to a considerable influence of digitality on the strategies of the groups involved, as the elliptical Internet discourse, interactivity, and speed with which individuals and groups connect means there is a low-cost participation of an amalgam of organizations, which might not always have a common ideological platform, just a common single issue (this proved a major problem for WikiLeaks as discussed previously). The network style of some of these groups means that there is also a greater difficulty in leadership emergence and sustainability of their struggles and conflicts.

The mainstream media and the level of their influence was different in the three case studies. In Cyprus and Greece, for instance, we see more mainstream media influence than in the United Kingdom, and in the UK case what is also relevant is the censorship and closure of the Russian mainstream media, where alternative media flourished early and significantly continued to impact the communication of

Russian-speaking migrants. Wolfsfeld's (1997) political contest model was especially relevant to the Cypriot study, as there was a true hybridity in online and offline contestation of the physical space in the racist-antiracist discourse. The fact that mainstream media tended to support more the racist discourse and alternative, newer media supported the antiracist one meant that while on the one hand antiracist groups were able to mobilize faster, they were not able to dominate political discourse and get the support of the government in their efforts in a substantial way. In terms of media effects on policy, we see far more effect in the UK study than in the Greek case. In the Cypriot case, although it is too early to tell, it seems that the events organized and communicated by the antiracist groups seem to have a certain effect, in that they are being contested in the mainstream media, far more than they are currently in Greece, where Xrysi Avgi (Golden Dawn) managed to get into the Greek parliament in the June 2012 elections.

Nevertheless, so far the most significant impact of ICTs has been on the political opportunity structure (it was first theorized with the example of 1989 and the revolutions caused by the collapse of the USSR). The speed with which an opening in the structure can be grasped, with key examples being the recent Occupy movement, the Arab Spring in 2011, and WikiLeaks before that, means that we will be encountering more collaboration between digital migrant networks and sociopolitical organizations that seek radical change or reform of the capitalist system.

In turn, this might project into the future as a more open and less reliant identity, subjectivity, and agency on closed and fixed notions of being/becoming for migrant populations, consistent with technologically created transformations in agency. Resistances seem to be moving toward more networked, rhizomatic, and open forms of identification, despite the short-term reliance on nationality, ethnicity, and religion to defend local and regional cultures against globalization.

4.3   The structure problematique

This takes us to the global political environment as the broad sphere that digital activism and cyberconflict aim to influence. There is no doubt that digital media have put more power into the hands of nonstate actors. Arquilla and Ronfeldt (2001) were the first to theorize this arguing that 'sprawling multi-organizational networks' are more flexible and responsive than hierarchies in reacting to outside developments and appear to be better than hierarchies at using information to improve decision making. The rise of networks has indeed, very much as they predicted, reshaped activism, resistance, protest, revolution, insurgency, and war, as much as everything else. Hammond (2009) explains that beyond high-tech weaponry, war is becoming postmodern both in the sense of intrastate conflicts where we witness wars about identity politics, in the cosmopolitanism versus exclusivism fashion, but also wars of humanitarian intervention, of 'spreading democracy'. He argues that the West's crisis of meaning after the end of the Cold War and the collapse of the grand narratives has caused a shift first to the therapeutic war (salvaging the reality of war in our own eyes – humanitarianism) to the war on terror (postmodern terror, as the West at war with itself, with the Other regarding imperialism and nihilistic terrorism as products of the crisis of meaning). In Hammond's explanation of postmodern politics, he revokes Žižek's argument that the elite takes over the language of the left – from identity politics to official multiculturalism as the ideal form of ideology of global capitalism, which does not disturb the circulation of capital. The idea of war as distraction is replaced by war used to engage a disengaged citizenry. The postmodern war becomes an exercise in risk management.

In this kind of logic, Stahl (2010) talks of the fusion of the military and entertainment as *militainment*: the transformation of war aesthetics from the 1991 Gulf War, where we consume a clean surgical sanitized war, a computer game technofetishism with the citizen spectator, to Iraq 2003 were we have depictions of war as sports coverage, reality television, and video games, with similarities to all these entertainment genres. Identity is absorbed into the military-entertainment matrix: a migration of identity to the interactive war. The spectator of 1991 becomes a virtual citizen-soldier, annihilating the viewer's capacity to distinguish between fact and fiction. This is similar to embodying the body in the military machine, as in the movie *Iron Man*: 'An integrated machine of hardware and software interfacing the subject with the military apparatus'. As Stahl explains, conflict becomes a celebratory event, an exercise in recreational violence within a larger sea of fictitious violent entertainment.

In turn, Der Derian (2009) in his *Virtuous War* argues that the global media is e-motive: a transient electronic affect conveyed at speed, where it is difficult to maintain the distinction between war and peace: 'In this high tech rehearsal for war, one learns how to kill but not to take responsibility for it, one experiences "death" but not the tragic consequences of it'. In this type of infowar, Der Derian tells us, they did not invent a new game: they made the virtuous war the only game worth playing.

Cyberconflict, the role of networks, and communication technology infrastructures will be of paramount importance, not only in the way wars are fought, but also in the way wars are communicated and justified to the global public. Not only that, but the acceleration of protest, due to the digital virtual enabling the grasping of political opportunity, when there is a crack in the global political structure by ad hoc assemblages, allows protest networks and other resistant movements to have spectacular spillover effects and points to the critical importance of political communication in the global transformations taking place all over the world. The move to overthrow repression, violence, and fear through peaceful means and virtual protest and its real-life materialization of revolution seems to be perhaps rendering war an extraordinary response to be used only to protect and not maim life. The politics of justifying war beyond the protection of life will likely be debated for a long time to come, but the importance of ICTs as a factor in the political communication of future wars, protests, and resistance is unquestionable.

4.4   The affect problematique

The reason for this assertion is that new media complicate subjecthood, they denaturalize the project of subject formation, and they question the interiority of the subject and its coherence. The shift from real to hyperreal occurs in transit from mere representation to simulation, a movement that already exists in the virtual world. Now that there is total connectivity, this metaphorical cyberspace has become the hyperreal; as Baudrillard formulated, it is more real than the place it once simulated.

This is where Grusin's concepts of remediation and premediation prove useful. Grusin splits remediation into immediacy (unconstrained connectivity) and hypermediacy (multiplicity – affective participation with the distribution of one's networked identity across multiple networks). Hypermediacy operates within a paradigm of securitization but with the proliferation of interconnected media formats of social networking and is no longer limited within the binary logics of reality versus mediation but is all about connectivity, mobility, and flow. Grusin's premediation focuses on the desire to make sure that the future has already been premediated in order to proliferate multiple remediations to maintain a low level of fear and to prevent media shock. Premediation depends on affect and mediality. Grusin explains that premediation is not prediction. Premediation does not want to get the future right, but to map out a multiplicity of possible futures in order to prevent anxiety, as a kind of affective prophylactic. The example he used to illustrate this concept was premediation from 9/11 leading to the Iraq War and the war on terror. Grusin's work points to the inseparability of affect and emotion from cognition and rational judgement. What should concern media and communication scholars is the media *not just as representation systems, but how they function to govern human affectivity.*

During 2011, in an effort to map the affective processes involved in the reactions to WikiLeaks, which were discussed in the third chapter, I faced the problem of conceptualizing the spectrum and mechanisms of the in-between space of the actual and digital virtual. My solution was to conceptualize affective structures as the structures residing between the actual and the digital virtual. I use the term 'digital virtual' as technologically simulated, while the term 'virtual' is used in the Deleuzian sense, as a potentiality for change (Deleuze and Guattari, 1987). When affective structures, residing on the interface between the actual and the digital virtual, enable revolutionary moments, I view this as an actualization of the Deleuzian virtual – the virtual full of potentialities that may or may not happen. I use the term 'Revolutionary Virtual' to denote the result of this process: the materialized mass of potentiality for change. In that sense, the Revolutionary Virtual is different from the Deleuzian virtual, in that the 'blocs of affect' that Deleuze and Guattari refer to are materialized in the Real.

Every time there is an incident, which is attributed to information communication technologies, particularly the Internet, it ends up disturbing the hierarchies in the global system. In that sense, I understand cyberspace as another topos, a time-space compression spectrum, which exists in the interface between the spiritual and the material, the imaginary and the actual, digitally enabling virtuality as a potentiality for change. I view cyberspace as a playground for affective movements, of the active or the reactive type in the Nietzschean sense, the way Deleuze qualifies our relation to power (Deleuze, 2006, 40). From that theoretical platform, I explore the public feelings expressed through hacktivism, or other ethically and politically blurred digital methods of dissent. The focus is more on the tensions and the psycho-political formations that digital movements and antagonistic organizations tap into in order to produce and inspire virtualities of hope, truth, freedom, and revolution, and equally paranoia, suspicion, hatred, and fear.

I used affect theory to illuminate the hidden interface between the actual and the digital virtual, as a necessary ontological resolution, before mapping the affective structures involved in the WikiLeaks example. Drawing from Deleuze and Guattari (1987), Massumi (2002), and Clough

(2000; 2007), I argued that the strong active and reactive affective flows directed for or against the two actual personalities – Julian Assange and his organization WikiLeaks, and Bradley Manning as his source – their biographies, and their actions, snowballed eventually beyond the digital virtual to a Revolutionary Virtual, helping to actualize the potential of what are still modernist revolutions in the Middle East and to inspire postmodern desires across wider revolutionary plateaus already in the making.

The digital virtual poses challenges to the actual world, through the Deleuzian virtual, as the place of potentiality, which encompasses the revolutionary window for change, in the sense of movement, affect, and sensation, as described by Massumi in his *Parables for the Virtual*. Massumi understands emotion as subjective, the sociolinguistic fixing of the quality of an experience, qualified intensity into semiotically formed progressions, into narrativizable action-reaction circuits. Emotion is intensity, and by that Massumi means affect, which is owned and recognized (2002, 28). As Shaviro helpfully notes, 'Subjects are overwhelmed and traversed by affect, but they *have* or *possess* their own emotions' (2010, 3). What occurs with our interaction with contemporary media is operating beyond the representational, beyond the semantic and semiotic level, so it is not emotion but affect that is our sociotechnical subjectivity's response to the digital environment. As Clough argued in relation to television, '[r]ather than calling for the subject's unconscious identification through a narrative representation, television hopes for a continuous body-machine attachment' (Clough, 2000, 70).

Further, Massumi views this virtual as lived paradox, 'where what are normally opposites coexist, coalesce, and connect; where what cannot be experienced cannot but be felt – albeit reduced and contained ... The organization of multiple levels that have different logics and temporal organizations, but are locked in resonance to each other and recapitulate the same event in divergent ways, recalls the fractal ontology and nonlinear causality underlying theories of complexity' (Massumi, 2002, 30).

What then are these affective structures of the virtual? For Massumi, the levels at play could be multiplied to infinity: already mentioned are mind and body, but also volition and cognition, at least two orders of language, expectation and suspense, body depth and epidermis, past and future, action and reaction, happiness and sadness, quiescence and arousal, passivity and activity, and so on (ibid., 30). Massumi understands affect itself as a two-sidedness:

> the simultaneous participation of the virtual in the actual and the actual in the virtual, as one arises from and returns to the other ... Affect

is the virtual point of view, provided the visual metaphor is used guardedly... The autonomy of affect is its participation in the virtual. Its autonomy is its openness. Affect is autonomous to the degree to which it escapes confinement in the particular body whose vitality, or potential for interaction, it is... Actually existing, structured things live in and through that which escapes them. Their autonomy is the autonomy of affect. (ibid., 35)

It is this Massumian affect that can be found on the interface between the actual and the digital virtual. This notion could be taken further if one implicates Deleuze and his understanding of history, whereby Lampert argues for zones of intensity on the body without organs, by which the body becomes a pure past and makes decisions on a libidinal future, and so the virtual body becomes the place that takes up the place of the concept of history. Lampert (2006) takes the Deleuzian philosophy to its logical conclusion when he writes: 'After all, when an event enters into the store-house of virtual possibilities, it enters into a realm of meaning, even if the event as such was not fully actualized. Events that were on the verge of occurring in history, effectively become a part of history or to put it simply, an event takes place in phases: as virtual potential, as activity, and as fact'. And elsewhere: 'Adding strategy to sense – i.e. adding power to knowledge – begins to explain how "time is auto-affection" (Deleuze, 1986, 114–115, quoted in Lampert, 2006, 110). But to turn autoaffective time into history, we need to add the third category of outsideness, namely the fold, the "inside of the outside"' (Deleuze, 1986, 104, quoted in Lampert, 2006, 110). Robinson in his 'Deleuze and Theory of Time' (forthcoming) argues that Deleuze seeks a type of history that gets between points in time 'by way of an anti-memory that deterritorializes what happened in between' (Lampert, 2006, 10). It constructs a type of memory that is nonrepresentational. Memory becomes not recollection but rather a way of relating sheets of the past to layers of reality. Contemplating something long enough can make it part of one's affective past (ibid., 62).

This is the affect, its structures, and the understanding of history that informs my analysis. I argue that the digital virtual offers a zone of intensity or affect, a system of affective structures, which enable the Revolutionary Virtual and actualize revolution. Governments, movements, or social media in the centre of emotional turmoil and on the surface of ephemeral politics are engaged through affective structures in enabling and disabling this Revolutionary Virtual. Thus, it is becoming less and less necessary to experience actuality first before the potential for revolution is felt and materialized.

The digital virtual is becoming more and more necessary for the Revolutionary Virtual to materialize than the necessity of the actual. The digital virtual then becomes, in a characteristically Baudrillardian (1994) turn, more real than the reality it simulates, and thus enables the transformation of the Deleuzian virtual into the Revolutionary Virtual. Routledge and Simons describe 'revolutionary moments of politics that can be most appropriately described as spiritual moments'. Spiritual because they are the manifestation of an inner experience that is felt during these irreducible moments 'when people are willing to risk their lives while resisting oppressive power', so Routledge and Simons 'focus on moments of resistance' and not on the political movements within which they frequently occur, because they believe that 'they cannot be tamed by co-option or coercion' (1995, 472). Meanwhile, 'spirits of resistance are tamed intellectually by turning the poetry of transgression into the prose of rationality... On one level, an effort is made to explain the action of those engaged in resistance in terms of instrumental rationality' (ibid., 475). This Routledge and Simons call a 'teleological taming' that 'operates by determining in advance the path that revolutionary change must take in order to realize the principle (Reason or Freedom)... all insurrection and resistance can thus be assessed according to it a progress along this unwinding sameness, this consensus-approved trajectory, this pre-calculated curve of history' (ibid., 477). In this sense, it is not surprising that the revolutions in the Middle East have already had this teleological taming in the public sphere, especially in Western liberal democracies.

It is compelling to theorize in future studies the contribution of new media publishers and social networking platforms in enabling revolutions all over the world, by taking into account the affective structures and politics of emotion produced, and not by merely applying the resource mobilization theories, identity paradigms in social movement theory, or network analysis. The possibility exists of theorizing the interface between the actual and the digital virtual by situating that interface within affective structures while defining the result of the overflow of affective structures as the Revolutionary Virtual: *the plane of consistency, or the field of virtual and affective forces, in which new zones of affect can be created, or old ones reactivated and brought into the present.* It also opens up the potential to analyse affective aspects of resistance by moving beyond the representational and the semiotic.

Orders of discursive and affective structures in digital activism

In collaborative work with Michael Schandorf (2015), we began to think about the agent/structure problem in digital activism and the revolutionary wave of 2010–2012. I reproduce a small part of my contribution to this discussion here. Our theoretical position is that we cannot continue with a conception of agency that is not embodied, or which views affect as immaterial or even spiritual. Such a view of agency does not take into account the technosocial transformations that must be addressed when we produce theory and analysis of resistances, movements, and especially digital activism. In developing another view of agency, we argue that different types of agency reflect different orders of dissent in ideological terms and different possibilities for resistance to the established order, however contingent this order may be.

The highly contingent contemporary global order and its hierarchical social logic expressed in state and capital has been unable to negotiate and productively harness the energies unleashed by technologically enabled networks for the equitable betterment of global society. Systemic problems have manifested in the global financial crisis, permanent conflicts (e.g., 'the war on terror'), and constant pressure for reform and revolution by radical media movements and ad hoc mobilized networks. This pressure has achieved some partial success, in regime change in the Arab world for example, but has failed to intervene meaningfully at most levels of governance to reform or radically replace aggressive capitalisms of profit accumulation and uneven development or to respond effectively to demands for equal rights, struggles against censorship and electoral authoritarianism, social marginalization, or forced migration, displacement, and poverty (Morozov, 2010; Fuchs, 2011; Shirky, 2011; Castells, 2012; Harvey, 2012; Lovink, 2012). 'The question remains why does this network logic fail to transform the global system for the better?' (Karatzogianni and Robinson, 2010, 26), whether through the fluid channels of power available to networked capital, or through the possibilities for networked resistances afforded by social media and other digital communications technologies. The answer would seem to lie at the intersection of individual agency (as the power and capacity to take effective and significant action) and social structure. This was the idea behind the critical problem of agent versus structure that Giddens sought to resolve with his structuration theory – the focus on social practices across space and time (*The Constitution of Society*, 1984), that Latour (1987) proposed to solve with his actor-network theory to accommodate agency for nonhumans, and which Deleuze and Guattari's *A Thousand Plateaus* (1987) theorized as rhizomatic versus arborescent mappings of the world in material-semiotic terms.

During 2011, various resistances arose against the current workings of society by social movements and protest organizations across physical, digital, and affective spaces of everyday life. The Arab Spring movements across the Middle East and the Occupy movement in the United States, for example, were organized, and their demands reached the global public through ICTs, particularly social media. Such movements render a theorization of the various modes and forms of capitalism a critical undertaking because protesters and social movement activists communicate and organize their dissent in countries with vastly different modes of production, levels of development, and political systems. At the same time, the agencies and ideologies driving protests that challenge the capitalist system in its global, regional, and national manifestations operate and communicate at diverse and distinct orders of dissent.

The logical order at which political dissent is communicated is a critical issue for theorizing resistance. The schematic proposed here is that at the first order of dissent, primary concerns revolve around basic human liberties and rights of a universal kind, such as the rights to education, health, and justice. At the second order of dissent, demands are more overtly political, encompassing demands for democracy and equality of political participation, equal distribution of power and resources, and freedom of speech and movement. At the third order of dissent, concern for the global predominates, a critique which points to the failing of the capitalist order as a whole and to a recognition of postnational or transnational issues and demands for a reform or radical change of capitalism to address issues of global inequality and poverty, as well as national financial and economic realities, such as unemployment, exploitation, corruption, unequal distributions of wealth, and so on.

These orders of dissent derive from Baudrillard's view of capitalism as an 'indeterminate random machine', something comparable to a genetic social code (Poster, 2001, 141). The thesis here is that contemporary dissent against this capitalist code, in any of its manifestations, such as protest, uprising, or revolution, fails when the dissent is not of a higher logical order than that to which it is opposed. The Arab Spring regime changes, for example, were (and are) motivated by and activated by concerns of a specific order of dissent, an order that can change throughout the life of a protest movement. The initial Egyptian protests, for example, aimed at the removal of President Hosni Mubarak and were dominated by concerns of the first order over those of the second order. The failure and consequent struggle to reform and disentangle the military control of government in Egypt is linked to the fact that the original protests promoted first-order concerns over second-order concerns, while third-order concerns were not even in the picture. The regional impact of the Arab Spring as a whole was more about the second order – democracy, power, participation – and did not address the capitalist order as such. During the protests in Greece, dissent was of the second order against political corruption and the national elites, but also of the third order against global capital in the face of the IMF and regional capitalism in the face of the EU. The Occupy movement, as an abstract assemblage, communicates an ideological amalgam of the third order; however, local concrete assemblages make demands of the second order as well. Regardless, dissent at these orders has generally failed to affect material change, because they are of a lower logical order than the overarching capitalist code to which they are opposed.

In the logic of the current capitalist order, according to Baudrillard (Poster, 2001), capital and the state collide to reproduce a systemic neutralization of dissent, eliminate the opportunity for a determinate reversal, and as a result render 'revolutions' meaningless at the present level of random processes of control:

> You cannot beat randomness with finality; you cannot beat programmed dispersion with *prises de conscience* or dialectical transcendence; you cannot defend against the code with political economy or 'revolution.' All these political weapons (including those of the first order, the ethics and metaphysics of man and nature, use value, and other liberatory referentials) have been progressively neutralized by the general system, which is of a higher order. Everything that gets inserted into the definalized space-time of the code, or tries to interfere with it, is disconnected from its own finalities, disintegrated and absorbed – this is the well-known effect of recuperation, or manipulation: cycling and recycling at each level. (ibid., 122)

The hegemonic capitalist code simply absorbs social action and dissent of lower logical types. In this way the system itself has come to operate as or serve the function formerly attributed to the unconscious: an unreality that forms the basis of reality. Recall Margaret Thatcher's infamous, 'There is no alternative'. The capitalist code operates, according to Baudrillard, by putting an end to its own myth of origin and the reference values from which it developed.

> The industrial machine corresponds [to] the rational, referential, functional, historical consciousness. But it is the unconscious – nonreferential, transreferential, indeterminate, floating – that corresponds to the aleatory machinations of the code. Yet even the unconscious has been reinserted into the game: it long ago relinquished its own reality principle in order to become an operational simulacrum. At the exact point where its psychic principle of reality is confused with

its psychoanalytic reality principle, the unconscious becomes like political economy, another simulation model. (ibid., 121)

Baudrillard argues that current revolutions arm themselves with 'a nostalgic resurrection of the real in all its forms; in other words, with simulacra of the second order: dialectics, use value, the transparency and the finality of production, the "liberation" of the unconscious, or of repressed meaning (of the signifier, or of the signified called desire), and so on'. For Baudrillard, all of these liberations offer, as ideal content, 'the phantoms which the system has devoured in successive revolutions and which it subtly resuscitates as revolutionary fantasies. All these liberations are just transitions toward a generalized manipulation. The revolution itself is meaningless at the present level of random processes of control' (ibid., 121).

The technologies that enable the current protest movements, for example, are themselves produced under the social logic of capitalism and its random processes of control. It is for this reason that Žižek and others are critical of the 'netocracy' concept introduced by Alexander Bard and Jan Soderqvist: it makes the same mistake as the 'post-industrial society' and the 'information society'; 'all too many of the features of the netocratic class are sustainable only within a capitalist regime' (Žižek, 2004, 192, cites Bard and Soderqvist, 2002). This is because, according to Terranova (2003), the Internet is rather 'a mutation that is totally immanent to late capitalism, not so much a break as an intensification, and therefore a mutation, of a widespread cultural and economic logic'. She explains that cultural flows are originating within a field that is always already capitalism, which is channelling collective labour into monetary flows and its structuration within capitalist business practices. For Terranova, Lazzarato's description of the knowledge worker as 'immaterial labor' is, therefore, a useful way to conceptualize this contemporary form of labour power, which 'is not limited to highly skilled workers but is a form of activity of every productive subject within post-industrial societies. ... [I]mmaterial labor is a virtuality (an undetermined capacity) that belongs to the postindustrial productive subjectivity as a whole' (ibid.). Nevertheless, even if one calls this labour 'immaterial' in order to point to its underdetermined capacity and virtuality, such labour is inevitably operating in a very material capitalist order.

Hardt and Negri (2000) enumerate three types of immaterial labour that drive the postmodernization of the global economy:

> The first is involved in an industrial production that has been informationalized and has incorporated communication technologies in a

way that transforms the production process itself. ... Second is immaterial labor of analytical and symbolic tasks, which itself breaks down into creative and intelligent manipulations on the one hand and routine symbolic tasks on the other. Finally, a third type of immaterial labor involves the production and manipulation of affect and requires (virtual or actual) human contact, labor in the bodily mode. (2000, 293)

Hardt and Negri, therefore, view affective labour as 'immaterial' and argue that the manipulation of affect is essential to its function: '[E]ven if it is corporeal ... its products are intangible, a feeling of ease, well-being, satisfaction, excitement, passions ... Such affective production, exchange, and communication are generally associated with human contact, but that contact can be either actual or virtual, as it is in the entertainment industry' (ibid., 292). Affective labour instantiates (potentially and actually) one of the core points of potential resistance against the capitalist code. Affective labour is where individual action and agency meet collective and corporate action and behaviour in the reproduction of ideologies and disciplines that both reproduce the capitalist code itself and present a vital point of potential resistance: affective labour is the nexus of the ideologically reproductive act.

Such a conceptualization explains how the capitalist code subjectivizes, at a certain order (local, national, global), a certain type of agent (motivated, intentional, distributed) enabled by a particular form of agency (human, technological, assemblage) that mobilizes a dominant labour process (symbolic, informational, affective) with a specific logic (affective, hierarchical, rhizomatic). This theorization can help specify what occurs when we witness resistance movements, dissident individuals, organizations, and agencies communicating their opposition and alternative conceptions and practices of modes of production to those of capitalism. The modes of being in the world and the solidarities projected when these circles overlap – in spite of and despite how these are currently repressed and fought under the state or neoliberal democratic society signifiers and their sociopolitical logics. The overlapping fields where new zones and new forms of agency can be activated or reactivated are the critical interfaces whereby the remoulding of the material order through revolutionary virtual spaces might indeed be possible. In our collaborative work with Michael Schandorf (2015), this results in the following schema of orders of dissent:

Table 4.1 Orders of dissent

Order of dissent	Loci of concern	Examples
Third: Transnational/global	The failing of the capitalist order as a whole and a recognition of postnational or transnational issues and demands for a reform or radical change of capitalism to address issues of global inequality and poverty, as well as national financial and economic realities such as unemployment, exploitation, corruption, unequal distribution of wealth, etc.	Occupy Movement, 2011 Global Justice, antiglobalization movement (Seattle 1999 and onward), peace movement, anti-Iraq War mobilizations, 2003 environmental movements, freedom of information and anticensorship, Anonymous.
Second: National	Democracy and equality of political participation, equal distribution of power and resources, freedom of speech and movement, and demands against censorship.	EU crisis: Greece, Spain, Italy, Ireland; Arab Spring: Egypt, Tunisia, Libya, Syria, Bahrain, Yemen, Algeria, Iraq, Kuwait, Jordan, Lebanon, Morocco, Sudan, Oman, Saudi Arabia, Djibouti, Mauritania, Brazil.
First: Local	Basic human liberties and rights of a universal kind, such as the rights to education, health, justice, human rights, civil rights, minority struggles, group recognition, statehood, succession.	From demands for recognition, sovereignty, autonomy, or statehood (South Ossetia, Abkhazia, Transnistria, Palestine, and others) to indigenous struggles, to demands for equal rights by women (MENA region and elsewhere), gay rights (equal marriage for instance in the United Kingdom), ethnic minority group rights.

Source: Karatzogianni and Schandorf (2015).

Table 4.2 Agency, action, and order of dissent

Order of dissent	Dominant 'immaterial' labour process	Dominant agency	Dominant agent	Logic of action
Third: Global – Post/trans-National	Affective	Distributed	Subject: assemblage, collective, technosocial ensemble.	Technosocial, rhizomatic: programmatic manipulation and extension of affect through networks of motivated and intentional agents.
Second: National – political representation	Informational	Intentional	Agent: technological, programmed, determined.	Serial, linear, hierarchical.
First: Tribal – social rights and obligations	Symbolic	Motivated	Person: embodied, self-conscious, emotional (human) being.	Embodied, affective, parallel, distributed.

Source: Karatzogianni and Schandorf (2015).

In subsequent work on 'Agency in Posthuman IR: Solving the Problem of Technosocially Mediated Agency' (Schandorf and Karatzogianni, forthcoming), we propose that technosocially distributed agency can be explained as the possibilities of action of an agent generatively constrained by a subject-constituting assemblage, which has intentionality but no motivations of its own because it is not located in or centred upon a symbolically and socially identified person. The problem of the relation between 'agent' and 'structure' has continued to pose significant problems for explaining political agency and, more broadly, technologically mediated human conduct in individual or collective terms. There is an explanation of what we think is a way out: differentiating between active versus reactive desire; motivation versus intentionality; motivational forces stemming from the structural interaction of person-subject versus intentional forces stemming from the structural interaction of subject-agent.

Concluding thoughts

My journey researching and teaching digital activism and cyberconflict is reflected directly on the structure of this book. The first two phases (1994–2001 and 2001–2007) are periods I researched for my doctoral thesis. This embryonic romantic first period was characterized by tit-for-tat attacks in ethnoreligious cyberconflicts with nationalist and ethnic digital activism on the one hand, and sociopolitical cyberconflicts with the use of the Internet in real-world mobilizations. This phase revealed initial impact of the Internet on organizational forms (more networked organizations and more organized networks) and the first sight of networks fighting hierarchies. The second period was affected greatly by 9/11, 'the war on terror', and the mobilizations against the Iraq War of 2003. Small and unrecognized states as well as minorities used the Internet in unprecedented ways in post-Soviet states for instance. Social media effects were felt more in the third period (2008–2010), which meant that the financial crisis was debated heavily in the digital public sphere. The peak of those effects were obvious in the fourth phase (2010–2014) with WikiLeaks, the Arab Spring uprisings, the Occupy movement, and anti-austerity movements in Europe, Turkey, Brazil. In Nigeria, India, and other hotspots, online feminist movements exploded. Issues around privacy and new technologies were already brewing around Google, Facebook, Instagram, and other platforms before Snowden revealed the extent of the quasi-totalitarian matrix involving governments, corporations, and potentially other 'civil society' actors, all supposedly trusted networks for consumers, citizens, and activists. There is a limitation to my work, of course, especially because I have not researched Occupy, Anonymous, environmental movements, specific country case studies, and the use of social media by extremists and so on. I also did not address digital activism in relation to Internet studies, digital inequality, net neutrality, or other areas of Internet governance or e-government (see Tsatsou, 2014).

As examples of future trends in digital activism, I am lucky to be able to offer the PhD students I supervise. Dennis Nguyen proposes an integrative theoretical framework for the identification and classification of transnational web spheres by conducting a complementary frame and network analysis of a representative sample of political online media content that focuses on issues related to EU politics during the Eurozone crisis. Ioanna Ferra does research on the Greek crisis and the impact of digital media on anti-austerity mobilization. Adrija Dey examines gender-related sociopolitical digital activism in India; Shola Olabode works on a cross-comparison of digital activism and cyberconflict for Occupy Nigeria, MEND, and Boko Haram. Identity, memory, privacy, agency, and the network self in mobile phoneography are other related areas researched by Elisa Serafinelli and Patricia Routh. For me, these projects reflect the possibility for digital activism and cyberconflict to be central areas in Internet studies.

Reality leads scholarship. My own prediction, if one is rational in offering one – I am not a believer in rationality – is that in the short term we will witness

- extreme events of violence against civilians by reactive, insurgent, and terrorist movements that will use digital media to coordinate and publicize their exploits in a highly accelerated manner (e.g., the Islamic State, Boko Haram, the Paris attack on Charlie Hebdo, a critical predictor event);
- apolitical, criminal, as well as political proliferation of high-information infrastructure attacks against governments, corporations, and civil society actors and individuals;
- social media enabled mobilizations of every creed, which will force regime change; and
- information age movements demanding open governance, transparency, and reform or radical change to alternative modes of production against capitalism.

Long term, 'digital' activism will become less important, because it will be part and parcel of any sociopolitical activity. However, high-information warfare attacking infrastructure and network penetrations will become more important, because they provide another battle space for humanity to negotiate difference, power, inequality, competition, and affect.

Bibliography

Abbott, J.P. (2001) 'Democracy@internet.Asia? The Challenges to the Emancipatory Potential of the Net: Lessons from China and Malaysia', *Third World Quarterly*, 22 (1), 99–114.

Africa, D. (18 February 2011) 'Stealing Egypt's Revolution', Al Jazeera English, online available at: http://english.aljazeera.net/indepth/opinion/2011/02/201 121710152468629.html.

Ajami, F. (1 March 2012) 'The Arab Spring at One – A Year of Living Dangerously', *Foreign Affairs*, 91 (2), online available at: http://www.foreignaffairs.com/articles/137053/fouad-ajami/the-arab-spring-at-one.

Alakhdar, M.G. (2012) 'Cyber Text: Orality Online and the Promotion of Cultural Diversity', PhD dissertation, Cairo University, Faculty of Arts English Department, November 2012.

Al-Karoui, H. (2011) 'WikiLeaks: International and Regional Ramifications, Arab Center for Research and Policy Studies', online available at: www.dohainstitute.org.

Alleyne, B. (2011) '"We Are All Hackers Now": Critical Sociological Reflections on the Hacking Phenomenon', Goldsmiths Research Online, online available at: http://eprints.gold.ac.uk/6305/1/alleyne_-_we_are_all_hackers_now_-_critical_sociological_reflections_on_the_hacking_phenomenon.pdf.

Althusser, L. (1970) 'Ideology and Ideological State Apparatuses', in *Lenin and Philosophy and Other Essays* (1971), trans. Ben Brewster.

Altinay, H. (ed.) (2011) *Global Civics: Responsibilities and Rights in an Interdependent World*, Washington: Brookings.

Al-Zubaidi, L., Khoury, D., Abu-Ayyash, A., and Paul, J. (2 May 2011) People's Power: The Arab World in Revolt, Special Issue, *Perspectives: Political Analysis and Commentary from the Middle East*, Heinrich Böll Stiftung, online available at: http://boell-meo.org/downloads/02_Perspectives_ME_2011_The_Arab_World_in_Revolt.pdf.

Al Otaibi, M., and Thomas, O.W. (October 2011) 'Women Candidates and Arab Media: Challenging Conservatism in Bahraini Politics', *Westminster Papers in Communication and Culture*, 8 (2), 137–158.

Amnesty International (2 November 2012) 'China: Amnesty Warns of Intense Crackdown Ahead of Leadership Change', online available at: http://www.amnesty.org.uk/news_details.asp?NewsID=20421.

Anderson, J.W. (2003) 'New Media, New Publics: Reconfiguring the Public Sphere of Islam', *Social Research*, 70 (3), 887–906.

Anderson, J.W. (1999) 'The Internet and Islam's New Interpreters', in D.F. Eickelman and J.W. Anderson (eds) *New Media in the Muslim World: The Emerging Public Sphere*, Bloomington: Indiana University Press.

Anderson, L. 'Demystifying the Arab Spring: Parsing the Differences between Tunisia, Egypt and Libya', *Foreign Affairs*, 90 (3), 2–7.

Appadurai, A. (2006) *The Fear of Small Numbers: An Essay on the Geography of Anger*, Durham and London: Duke University Press.

Appadurai, A. (1990) 'Disjuncture and Difference in the Global Cultural Economy', *Theory, Culture, Society*, 7, 295–310.

Arendt, H. (1951) *The Origins of Totalitarianism*, New York: Harcourt, Brace.

Armbrust, W. (23 February 2011) 'The Revolution against Neoliberalism', *Jadaliyya*, online available at: http://www.jadaliyya.com/pages/index/717/the-revolution-againstneoliberalism.

Arquilla, J., and Ronfeldt, D. (2001) 'The Advent of Netwar (Revisited)', in J. Arquilla and D. Ronfeldt (eds) *Networks and Netwars: The Future of Terror, Crime, and Militancy*, Santa Monica, CA: RAND Corporation, online available at: http://www.rand.org/pubs/monograph_reports/MR1382.

Arrighi, G. (2007) *Adam Smith in Beijing*, London: Verso.

Associated Press-NORC Center for Public Affairs Research (2013) 'Balancing Act: The Public's Take on Civil Liberties and Security: A Trend Study', online available at: http://www.apnorc.org/PDFs/Balancing%20Act/AP-NORC%202013_Civil%20Liberties%20Poll_Topline_Trend.pdf.

Atlantic (17 February 2012) 'Rising Protests in China', online available at: http://www.theatlantic.com/infocus/2012/02/rising-protests-in-china/100247.

Augstein, J. (16 July 2013) 'The Chancellor and the NSA: Merkel Has Abandoned the Germans', *Spiegel*, online available at: http://www.spiegel.de/international/germany/editorial-merkel-has-left-germans-high-and-dry-a-911425.html#spLeserKommentare.

Bandurski, D. (2008) 'China's Guerilla War for the Web', *Far Eastern Economic Review*, online available at: http://www.feer.com/essays/2008/august/chinas-guerrillawar-for-the-web.

Barabási, A.-L. (2002) *Linked: How Everything Is Connected to Everything Else*, London: Penguin.

Barabási, A.-L., and Albert, R. (1999) 'Emergence of Scaling in Random Networks', *Science*, 286, 509–512.

Barboza, D. (25 October 2012) 'Billions in Hidden Riches for Family of Chinese Leader', online available at: http://www.nytimes.com/2012/10/26/business/global/family-of-wen-jiabao-holds-a-hidden-fortune-in-china.html.

Barboza, D., and Bradsher, K. (16 June 2010) 'In China, Labor Movement Enabled by Technology', *New York Times*, online available at: http://www.nytimes.com/2010/06/17/business/global/17strike.html.

Barnard-Wills, D. (2011) '"This Is Not a Cyber War, It's a … ?" WikiLeaks, Anonymous and the Politics of Hegemony', *International Journal of Cyber Warfare and Terrorism*, 1 (1), 13–23.

Baudrillard, J. (1994) *Simulacra and Simulation*, trans. S. Glaser, Ann Arbor: University of Michigan, originally published in French by Editions Galilee, 1981.

Bauwens, M. (20 October 2007) 'The Political Implications of the Peer to Peer Revolution', online available at: http://www.masternewmedia.org/information_access/p2p-peer-to-peer-economy/peer – to-peer-governance-production-property-part-1-Michel-Bauwens-20071020.htm.

Bauwens, M. (2009) 'Some Notes on the Social Antagonism in Netarchical Capitalism', in A. Karatzogianni (ed.) *Cyber Conflict and Global Politics*, London and New York: Routledge.

BBC News (29 October 2003) 'Islamic Hackers Step Up Attacks', online available at: http://news.bbc.co.uk/1/hi/technology/2372209.stm.

Benhabib, S. (ed.) (1996) *Democracy and Difference: Contesting the Boundaries of the Political*, Princeton: Princeton University Press.

Benjamin, W. (1995) *Reflections*, London: Random House.

Benkler, Y. (2006) *The Wealth of Networks: How Social Production Transforms Markets and Freedom*, New Haven and London: Yale University Press.

Benkler, Y. (2011a) 'Networks of Power, Degrees of Freedom', *International Journal of Communication*, 5, 721–755.

Benkler, Y. (2011b)'A Free Irresponsible Press: WikiLeaks and the Battle over the Soul of the Networked Fourth Estate', *Harvard Civil Liberties Law Review*, 46, 311–397.

Bennett, I. (2010) 'Media Censorship in China', Washington, DC: Council for Foreign Relations, online available at: http://www.cfr.org/china/media-censorship-china/p11515.

Berry, D., and Moss, G. (2005) 'On the Creative Commons', online available at: http://www.fabricemous.nl/wordpress/wp-content/uploads/2007/01/berry.pdf.

Berry, D.M. (2012) 'The Relevance of Understanding Code to International Political Economy', *International Politics*, 49 (2), 277–296.

Betz, D., and Stevens, T. (2011) 'Chapter Two: Cyberspace and Sovereignty', *Adelphi Series*, 51 (424), 55–74.

Betz, J.D., and Stevens, T. (2011) 'Cyberspace and the State', *Adelphi Series*, 51 (424), 55–74.

Birchall, C. (2011) Transparency, Interrupted: Secrets of the Left. *Theory, Culture and Society*, 28 (7–8), 60–84.

Blecher, M.J. (2002) 'Hegemony and Workers' Politics in China', *China Quarterly*, 170, June, 283–303.

Bodó, B. (2011) *You Have No Sovereignty Where We Gather – WikiLeaks and Freedom, Autonomy and Sovereignty in the Cloud*, Budapest University of Technology and Economics; Stanford Law School Centre for Internet and Society, online available at: http://papers.ssrn.com/sol3/papers.cfm?abstract_id=1780519.

Bourdieu, P. (2005) *The Social Structures of the Economy*, Cambridge: Polity Press.

Bradsher, K. (8 February 2010) 'China Announces Arrests in Hacking Crackdown', *New York Times*, online available at: http://www.nytimes.com/2010/02/08/world/asia/09hacker.html.

Branigan, T. (6 April 2010) 'Cyber-spies Based in China Target Indian Government and Dalai Lama', *The Guardian*, online available at: http://www.guardian.co.uk/technology/2010/apr/06/cyber-spies-china-target-india.

Brenner, N. (1998) 'Global Cities, Glocal States: Global City Formation and State Territorial Restructuring in Contemporary Europe', *Review of International Political Economy*, 5 (1) 1–37.

Brevini, B., Hintz, A., and McCurdy, P. (eds) (2013) *Beyond WikiLeaks: Implications for the Future of Communications, Journalism and Society*, New York: Palgrave Macmillan.

Bronk, C. (2011) *Between War and Peace: Considering the Statecraft of Cyberspace from the Perspective of the U.S. State Department*, 52nd Convention of the International Studies Association, Montreal, Quebec.

Brooke, H. (2011) *The Revolution Will Be Digitised: Dispatches from the Information War*, London: William Heinemann.

Brown, A.J. (2011) *Flying Foxes, WikiLeaks and Freedom of Speech: Statutory Recognition of Public Whistleblowing in Australia*, International Whistleblowing Research Network Conference, Middlesex University, London.

Bruns, A. (2011) 'Towards Distributed Citizen Participation: Lessons from WikiLeaks and the Queensland Floods', in P. Parycek, M. Kripp, and N. Edelmann (eds) *CeDEM11: Proceedings of the International Conference for E-Democracy and Open Government*, Edition Donau-Universität Krems, Danube-University Krems, Austria, 35–52.

Bunt, G. (2005) 'Defining Muslim Interconnectivity', in M. Cooke and B.B. Lawrence (eds) *Muslim Networks from Hajj to Hip Hop*, Chapel Hill: University of North Carolina Press.

Bunt, G. (2003) *Islam in the Digital Age: E-jihad, Online Fatwas, and Cyber Islamic Environments*, London: Pluto Press.

Burt, R.S. (1992) *Structural Holes: The Social Structure of Competition*, Cambridge, MA: Harvard University Press.

Byman, D. (2011) 'Israel's Pessimistic View of the Arab Spring', *Washington Quarterly*, 34 (3), 123–136.

Cai, Y. (2008) 'Local Governments and the Suppression of Popular Resistance in China', *China Quarterly*, 193, 24–42.

Calabrese, A., and Sparks, C. (2004) *Towards a Political Economy of Culture: Capitalism and Communication in the Twenty-First Century*, Lanham, MD: Rowman and Littlefield.

Calhoun, C. (1994) *Neither God Nor Emperors: Students and the Struggle for Democracy in China*, Berkeley: University of California Press.

Castells, M. (2000) *The Rise of the Network Society*, vol. 1 of *The Information Age: Economy, Society and Culture*, 2nd ed., Oxford: Blackwell.

Castells, M. (11 December 2010) 'WikiLeaks Cyberwar', *La Vanguardia*, retrieved from: http://www.lavanguardia.com/opinion/articulos/20101211/54086305259/la-ciberguerra-de-WikiLeaks.html.

Castells, M. (2012) *Networks of Outrage and Hope: Social Movements in the Internet Age*, Cambridge: Polity Press.

Castells, M. (2012) 'WikiLeaks to Wiki-Revolutions: Internet and the Culture of Freedom', online available at: http://www.youtube.com/watch?v=0Y_4_jc-YPA.

Central European University, participants' reflections on workshop themes, 'Cyber Security: Europe and the Global Society Revisited: Developing a Network of Scholars and Agenda for Social Science Research on Cyber Security', *Budapest Hungary*, 7–8 June 2010, http://ww.cmcs.ceu.hu/cybersecurity/main.

Chadwick, A. (2006) *Internet Politics: States, Citizens, and New Communication Technologies*, Oxford: Oxford University Press.

Chadwick, A. (2011) 'The Hybrid Media System', paper presented at the European Consortium for Political Research General Conference, Reykjavik, Iceland.

Chan, A. (1996) Review of 'Mandate of Heaven: A New Generation of Entrepreneurs, Dissidents, Bohemians and Technocrats Lays Claim to China's Future', by Orville Schell, *Pacific Affairs*, 69 (1), 102–104.

Chase, M., and Mulvenon, J. (2002) *You've Got Dissent! Chinese Dissident Use of the Internet and Beijing's Counterstrategies*, Santa Monica, CA: Rand.

Chen, S. (1998) 'Leadership Change in Shanghai: Toward the Dominance of Party Technocrats', *Asian Survey*, 38, 671–688.

Chesterman, S. (2011) 'WikiLeaks and the Future of Diplomacy', Global-is-Asian, LKY School of Public Policy, Singapore.

China Post (15 October 2012) 'China Writers Laud Mo for Release Call', online available at: http://www.chinapost.com.tw/art/books/2012/10/15/357664/Chinawriters.htm.

Chomsky, N. (2010) 'WikiLeaks Cables Reveal "Profound Hatred for Democracy on the Part of Our Political Leadership"', *Democracy Now*, online available at: http://www.chomsky.info/interviews/20101130.htm.

Clary, G. (25 October 2012) 'Chinese Dissident Ai Weiwei's Art Becomes His Messenger', *CNN*, online available at: http://edition.cnn.com/2012/10/13/us/weiwei-exhibit-washington/index.html.

Clough, P. (2000) *Autoaffection: Unconscious Thought in the Age of Teletechnology*, Minneapolis: University of Minnesota Press.

Clough, P., and Halley, J. (eds) (2007) *The Affective Turn: Theorizing the Social*, Durham and London: Duke University Press.

Cohen-Almagor, R. (19 November 2012) interview with the author at the University of Hull.

Coleman, G. (2012) *Coding Freedom: Hacker Pleasure and the Ethics of Free and Open Source Software*, Princeton, NJ: Princeton University Press.

Coleman, G. (2014) 'Hacker', in *The John Hopkins Encyclopedia of Digital Textuality*, online available at: http://gabriellacoleman.org/wp-content/uploads/2013/04/Coleman-Hacker-John-Hopkins-2013-Final.pdf.

Coleman, I. (20 December 2011) 'Is the Arab Spring Bad for Women?', *Foreign Policy*, online available at: http://www.foreignpolicy.com/articles/2011/12/20/arab_spring_women.

Coll, S., and Glasser, S. (7 August 2005) 'Terrorists Turn to Web as Base of Operations', *Washington Post*.

Cull, N.J. (2011) 'WikiLeaks, Public Diplomacy 2.0 and the State of Digital Public Diplomacy', *Place Branding and Public Diplomacy*, 7, 1–8.

Cunningham, M.E., and Wasserstrom J.N. (2011) 'Interpreting Protest in Modern China', *Dissent*, 58 (1), 13–18.

Dafermos, G. (29 March 2009) 'Division of Labour in Free & Open Source Software Development: The FreeBSD Project', Powerpoint slides, http://www.oekonux.org/list-en/archive/msg05772.html.

Dahlberg, L., and Siapera, E. (eds) (2007) *Radical Democracy and the Internet: Interrogating Theory and Practice*, London and New York: Palgrave Macmillan.

Dann, E.G., and Haddow, N. (2008) 'Just Doing Business or Doing Just Business: Google, Microsoft, Yahoo! and the Business of Censoring China's Internet', *Journal of Business Ethics*, 79, 219–234.

Davidson, L. (16 July 2016) 'A National Debate about Government Spying?', NYTexaminer.com, online available at: http://www.nytexaminer.com/2013/07/a-national-debate-about-government-spying.

De Armond, P. (2001) 'Netwar in the Emerald City: WTO Protest Strategy and Tactics', in J. Arquilla and D. Ronfeldt (eds) *Networks and Netwars: The Future of Terror, Crime and Militancy*, Santa Monica, CA: Rand.

De Sola Pool, I. (1983) *Technologies of Freedom*, Cambridge, MA: Harvard University Press.

Deleuze G. (1994) *Difference and Repetition*, trans. Paul Patton, New York: Columbia University Press.

Deleuze, G. (1986) *Foucault*, Paris: Editions de Minuit.

Deleuze, G. (2006) *Nietzsche and Philosophy*, trans. Janis Tomlison, New York: Columbia University Press.

Deleuze, G., and Guattari, F. (1987) *A Thousand Plateaus*, trans. Brian Massumi, London: Continuum.

Denning, D. (2006) 'A View of Cyberterrorism Five Years Later', in K. Himma (ed.) *Readings in Internet Security: Hacking, Counterhacking, and Society*, Boston, MA: Jones and Bartlett.

Dennison, S., Dworkin, A., Popescu, N. & Witney, N. (2011) 'After the Revolution: Europe and the Transition in Tunisia', Policy Brief, European Council on Foreign Relations, retrieved from ecfr.eu.

Der Derian, J. (2009) *Virtuous War*, London and New York: Routledge.

Devin, G., and Toernquist-Chesnier, M. (2010) 'Burst Diplomacy. The Diplomacies of Foreign Policy: Actors and Methods', *Brazilian Political Science Review*, 4 (2), 60–77.

Diani, M., and McAdam, D. (2003) *Social Movements and Networks: Relational Approaches to Collective Action*, Oxford: Oxford University Press.

Dickie, M. (12 November 2007) 'China Traps Online Dissent', *Financial Times*, online available at: http://www.viet-studies.info/kinhte/China_traps_online_dissent.pdf.

Ding, X.L. (2002) 'The Challenges of Managing a Huge Society under Rapid Transformation', in J. Wongand and Y. Zheng (eds) *China's Post-Jiang Leadership Succession: Problems and Perspectives*, Singapore: Singapore University Press.

Dixon, M. (2001) 'An Arab Spring', *Review of African Political Economy*, 38 (128), 309–316.

Dowell, W.T. (2006) 'The Internet, Censorship, and China', *Georgetown Journal of International Affairs*, 7 (2), 111–119.

Dunlap, C.J. (2011) 'Perspectives for Cyber Strategists on Law for Cyberwar', *Strategic Studies Quarterly*, 5 (1), 81–99.

Dupont, C., and Passy, F. (2011) 'The Arab Spring or How to Explain these Revolutionary Episodes?', *Swiss Political Sciences Review*, 17 (4), 447–451.

Dyer-Witheford, N. (1999) *Cyber-Marx: Cycles and Circuits of Struggle in High-Technology Capitalism*, Urbana: University of Illinois Press.

Ebadi, S.A. (12 March 2012) 'A Warning for Women of the Arab Spring', *Wall Street Journal*, online available at: http://online.wsj.com/article/SB10001424052970203370604577265840773370720.html.

Economic Times (ET Bureau) (3 November 2012) 'Why China's Stability-Obsessed Rulers Are Taking No Chances, Avian or Otherwise', online available at: http://articles.economictimes.indiatimes.com/2012-11-03/news/34892120_1_pigeons-taxi-drivers-hu-jia (accessed 4 November 2012).

Economy, E. (2004) 'China's Flood of Protests', *Project Syndicate*, online available at: http://www.project-syndicate.org/commentary/china-s-flood-of-protests.

Elmhirst, S. (11 October 2012) 'Ai Wei Wei: "If Someone Is Not Free, I Am Not Free"', online available at: http://www.newstatesman.com/media/media/2012/10/ai-weiwei-if-someone-not-free-i-am-not-free.

El-Said, M. (2012) 'The Morning After: Trips-Plus, FTAs and WikiLeaks – Fresh Insights on the Implementation and Enforcement of IP Protection in Developing Countries', PIJIP Research Paper No. 2012–03, American University Washington College of Law, Washington, DC.

El Saadawi, N. (2007) *The Hidden Face of Eve: Women in the Arab World*, London: Zed Books.

Endeshaw, A. (2004) 'Internet Regulation in China: The Never-Ending Cat and Mouse Game', *Information and Communications Technology Law*, 13 (1), 41–57.

Erbacher, R.F. (2011) 'Preparing for the Next WikiLeaks: Making Forensics Techniques Work', Proceedings of the 6th IEEE International Workshop on Systematic Approaches to Digital Forensic Engineering, Oakland, CA, May 2011, 1–8.

Erkin, A. (2009) 'Locally Modern, Globally Uyghur: Geography, Identity and Consumer Culture in Contemporary Xinjiang', *Central Asian Survey*, 28 (4), 417–428.

Eschenfelder, K.R., Desai, A.C., Alderman, I., Sin, J., and Shen Yi (2005) 'The Limits of DeCSS Posting: A Comparison of Internet Posting of DVD Circumvention Devices in the European Union, the People's Republic of China, Hong Kong and Macau', *Journal of Information Science*, 31 (4): 317–331.

Falk, B. (2008/2009) 'Learning from History: Why We Need Dissent and Dissidents', *International Journal*, 64 (1), Electoral Politics and Policy: Annual John W. Holmes Issue on Canadian Foreign Policy, 243–253.

Fattah, M. (2006) *Democratic Values in the Muslim World*, Boulder, CO: Lynne Rienner.

Fenster, M. (2011) Disclosure's Effects: WikiLeaks and Transparency', from the Selected Works of Mark Fenster, online available at: http://works.bepress.com/mark_fenster/10.

Feuerberg, G. (6 October 2012) 'US House Members Seek Answers on Transplant Abuse in China', *Epoch Times*, online available at: ttp://www.theepochtimes. com/n2/world/us-house-members-want-answers-on-transplantation-abuse-in-china-300526.html (accessed 4 November 2012).

Findlay, R. (14 March 2010) 'Royal Bank of Scotland Raiders' Huge £6m Haul in Just 12 Hours', online available at: http://www.dailyrecord.co.uk/news/business-news/2010/03/14/royal-bank-of-scotland-raiders-huge-6m-haul-in-12-hours-86908-22110087.

Flew, T., and Liu, B.R. (2011) 'Globally Networked Public Spheres? The Australian Media Reaction to WikiLeaks', *Global Media Journal* (Australian Edition), 5 (1), 1–13.

Fong, V. (2007) 'SARS, a Shipwreck, a NATO Attack, and September 11, 2001: Global Information Flows and Chinese Responses to Tragic News Events', *American Ethnologist*, 34 (3), 521–539.

Foucault, M. (1977) *Discipline and Punish*, Harmondsworth: Penguin.

Friedersdorf, C. (12 August 2013) 'The Surveillance Speech: A Low Point in Barack Obama's Presidency', online available at: http://www.theatlantic.com/politics/archive/2013/08/the-surveillance-speech-a-low-point-in-barack-obamas-presidency/278565.

Friedrich, C., and Brzezinski, A.K. (1956) *Totalitarian Dictatorship and Autocracy*, Cambridge: Harvard University Press.

Frontline (13 December 2005) interview with Xiao Qiang (edited transcript), posted 11 April 2006, online available at: http://www.pbs.org/wgbh/pages/frontline/tankman/interviews/xiao.html (accessed 19 October 2012).

Fu, Z.J. (2002) 'The State, Capital, and Urban Restructuring in Post-reform Shanghai', in J.R. Logan (ed.) *The New Chinese City: Globalization and Market Reform*, Oxford: Blackwell, 106–120.

Fuchs, C. (2011) *Foundation of Critical Media and Information Studies*, London and New York: Routledge.

Gardham, D. (4 December 2009) 'Cold War Enemies Russia and China Launch a Cyber Attack Every Day', *Telegraph*, online available at: http://www.telegraph.co.uk/technology/news/6727100/Cold-war-enemies-Russia-and-China-launch-a-cyber-attack-every-day.html.

Gaubatz, P. (1999) 'China's Urban Transformation: Patterns and Processes of Morphological Change in Beijing, Shanghai and Guangzhou', *Urban Studies*, 36 (9), 1495–1521.

Gerecht, R.M. (6 February 2011) 'How Democracy Became Halal', *New York Times*, online available at: http://www.nytimes.com/2011/02/07/opinion/07gerecht.html.

Ghini, A. (2011) 'Barbarians from Without: The Role of External Forces in Xinjiang Uyghur Separatism', PhD thesis, University of Hull.

Giglio, M. (21 February 2011) 'The Facebook Freedom Fighters', *Newsweek*, online available at: http://www.thedailybeast.com/newsweek/2011/02/13/the-facebook-freedom-fighter.html.

Gillis, Justin (7 July 2010) 'British Panel Clears Scientists', *New York Times*, online available at: http://www.nytimes.com/2010/07/08/science/earth/08climate.html?_r=1.

Ginkel, J., and Smith, A. (1999) 'So You Say You Want a Revolution: A Game Theoretic Explanation of Revolution in Repressive Regimes', *Journal of Conflict Resolution*, 43 (3), 291–316.

Gladney, D.C. (2004) *Dislocating China: Reflections on Muslims, Minorities and Other Subaltern Subjects*, London: C. Hurst.

Glasner, J. (19 March 2003) 'Protests to Start When War Does', online available at: http://archive.wired.com/politics/law/news/2003/03/58101.

Global Voices Advocacy (2010) http://advocacy.globalvoicesonline.org.

Goble, P. (31 May 2007) 'Window on Eurasia: FSB Encourages, Guides Russia's "Hacker-Patriots"', online available at: http://windowoneurasia.blogspot.com/2007/05/window-on-eurasia-fsb-encourages-guides.html.

Goldkorn, J. (6 January 2013) '*Legal Daily* Report on Mass Incidents in China in 2012', online available at: http://www.danwei.com/a-report-on-mass-incidents-in-china-in-2012.

Gray, C. (2011) 'President Obama's 2010 United States National Security Strategy and International Law on the Use of Force', *Chinese Journal of International Law*, 10 (1), 35–53.

Greenberg, A. (29 November 2010) 'An Interview with WikiLeaks' Julian Assange', *Forbes*, online available at: http://blogs.forbes.com/andygreenberg/2010/11/29/an-interview-with-wikileaks-julian-assange/5.

Greenwald, G. (15 July 2013) 'The Crux of the NSA Story in One Phrase: "Collect It All"', *The Guardian*, online available at: http://www.theguardian.com/commentisfree/2013/jul/15/crux-nsa-collect-it-all.

Gregg, M., and Seigworth, G.J. (eds) (2010) *The Affect Theory Reader*, Durham, NC: Duke University Press.

Grusin, R. (2010) *Premediation: Affect and Mediality After 9/11*, Basingstoke: Palgrave Macmillan.

(*The*) *Guardian* (30 November 2010) 'Cablegate Roulette: Diplomatic Dispatches Like You've Never Seen Them', online available at: http://www.guardian.co.uk/media/pda/2010/dec/03/cablegate-roulette-wikileaks.

(*The*) *Guardian* (1 December 2010) 'Bradley Manning, in His Own Words: This Belongs in the Public Domain', online available at: http://www.guardian.co.uk/world/2010/dec/01/us-leaks-bradley-manning-logs#history-link-box.

(*The*) *Guardian* (1 November 2013) 'NSA Files Decoded: What the Revelations Mean for You', online available at: http://www.theguardian.com/world/interactive/2013/nov/01/snowden-nsa-files-surveillance-revelations-decoded.

Guiheux, G. (2009) 'Justifying the New Economic and Social Order: The Voice of a Private Entrepreneur', in Gilles Guiheux and Khun Eng Kuah-Pearce (eds) *Social Movements in China and Hong Kong: The Expansion of Protest Space*, Amsterdam: Amsterdam University Press, 135–154.

Haidary, A. (November/December 2012) 'Afghanistan: Young Women for Change', *Amnesty Magazine*, online available at: www.amnesty.org.uk.

Halpin, T. (7 December 2009) 'Is Russia behind the Climategate Hackers?', *Times Online*, online available at: http://www.timesonline.co.uk/tol/news/environment/article6946385.ece.

Hamilton, A. (29 November 2012) 'Egyptian President's Mohamed Morsi's Actions Are Driven by Inexperience Not Lust for Power', *Independent*, online available at: http://www.independent.co.uk/voices/comment/egyptian-president-mohamed-morsis-actions-are-driven-by-inexperience-not-lust-for-power-8368884.html.

Hammond, P. (2009) *Media, War and Postmodernity*, London and New York: Routledge.

Haraway, D. (1995) 'Preface', in C. Grey (ed.) *The Cyborg Handbook*, London: Routledge.

Harding, L. (27 January 2010) 'Alexander Lebedev Sells Aeroflot and Air-Leasing Stakes for $575m', *The Guardian*, online available at: http://www.guardian.co.uk/media/2010/jan/27/lebedev-sells-aeroflot-stake.

Hardt, M., and Negri, A. (2000) *Empire*, London and Cambridge, MA: Harvard University Press.

Harrigan, J. (2011) 'Did Food Prices Plant the Seeds of the Arab Spring?', online abstract available at: http://fsaw2012.ifpri.info/files/2012/01/Abstract_JaneHarrigan_DidFoodPricesPlanttheSeedsoftheArabSpring.pdf, and podcast of Birbeck university talk: http://backdoorbroadcasting.net/2012/05/jane-harrigan-the-politics-of-food-and-the-arab-spring.

Harvey, D. (2012) *Rebel Cities: From the Right to the City to the Urban Revolution*, New York: Verso.

Hawkins, A. (7 April 2010) '3 Year Sentence for Hacker who Ripped off Charles Schwab Accounts', *Forbes* blogs, online available at: http://blogs.forbes.com/moneybuilder/2010/04/07/3-year-sentence-for-hacker-who-ripped-off-charles-schwab-accounts.

Hayeck, F.A. (2007) *The Collected Works of F.A. Hayek*, vol. 2, *The Road to Serfdom – Text and Documents*, definitive edition, ed. Bruce Caldwell, Chicago: University of Chicago Press.

Healy, K., and Schussman, A. (29 January 2004) 'The Ecology of Open-Source Software', online available at: opensource.mit.edu.

Heickero, R. (March 2010) 'Emerging Cyber Threats and Russian Views on Information Warfare and Information Operations', Swedish Defence Research Agency, Defence Analysis, www.foi.se.

Herrera, L. (12 February 2011) 'Egypt's Revolution 2.0: The Facebook Factor', *Jadaliyaa*, online available at: http://www.jadaliyya.com/pages/index/612/egypts-revolution-2.0_thefacebook-factor.

Hoff, R. (2005) 'Dissident Watch: Arash Sigarchi', *Middle East Quarterly*, 12 (4), 96.

Ho-fung Hung and Iam-ching Ip (2012) 'Hong Kong's Democratic Movement and the Making of China's Offshore Civil Society', *Asian Survey*, 52 (3), 504–527.

Hollis, R. (2012) 'No Friend of Democratization: Europe's Role in the Genesis of the "Arab Spring"', *International Affairs*, 88 (1), 81–94.

Hopkins, N., and Taylor, M. (6 October 2013) 'Cabinet Was Told Nothing about GCHQ Spying Programmes, Says Chris Huhne', *The Guardian*, online available at: http://www.theguardian.com/uk-news/2013/oct/06/cabinet-gchq-surveillance-spying-huhne.

Houston, W.W. (9 July 2013) 'America against Democracy', *The Economist*, online available at: http://www.economist.com/blogs/democracyinamerica/2013/07/secret-government.

Howard, P.N. (23 February 2011) 'The Arab Spring's Cascading Effects', *Miller-McCune*, online available at: http://www.miller-mccune.com/politics/the-cascading-effects-of-the-arabspring-28575.

Howard, P.N., and Hussain, M.M. (July 2011) 'The Role of Digital Media: The Upheaval in Egypt and Tunisia', *Journal of Democracy*, 22 (3), 35–48.

Hu, J.J.H., and Zhou, H. (2002) 'Information Accessibility, User Sophistication, and Source Credibility: The Impact of the Internet on Value Orientations in Mainland China', *Journal of Communications and Media Studies*, 7 (2), online available at: http://jcmc.indiana.edu/vol7/issue2/china.html.

Huang, C. (6 June 2006) 'Facebook and Twitter Key to Arab Spring Uprisings: Report', *The National*, online available at: http://www.thenational.ae/news/uae-news/facebook-and-twitter-key-to-arab-spring-uprisings-report.

Huang, R.G., and Yip, N.M. (2012) 'Internet and Activism in Urban China: A Case Study of Protests in Xiamen and Panyu', *Journal of Comparative Asian Development*, 11 (2), 201–223.

Huet, N. (11 July 2013) 'French Lawsuit Targets NSA, FBI, Tech Firms over Prism', *Reuters*, online available at: http://www.reuters.com/article/2013/07/11/us-usa-security-france-idUSBRE96A0OF20130711.

Hughes, C.R. (2002) 'China and the Globalization of ICTs: Implications for International Relations', *New Media and Society*, 4 (2), 205–224.

Hung, C.F. (2010) 'The Politics of China's *Wei-Quan* Movement in the Internet Age', *International Journal of China Studies*, 1 (2), 331–349.

Jacobs, A. (1 November 2012a) 'From Toys to TV News, Jittery Beijing Clamps Down', *New York Times*, online available at: http://www.nytimes.com/2012/11/02/world/asia/chinas-heavy-hand-smooths-way-to-party-congress.html (accessed 4 November 2012).

Jacobs, A. (1 November 2012b) 'Chinese Café Owner Given 8-Year Sentence for Posting Online Messages', *New York Times*, online available at: http://www.

nytimes.com/2012/11/02/world/asia/chinese-cafe-owner-given-8-year-sentence-over-online-messages.html?ref=asia (accessed 4 November 2012).

Jarach, L. (2012) 'On the Winter of WikiLeaks', *Anarchy: Journal of Desire Armed*, 70–71, online available at: http://www.anarchymag.org/index.php/archive/38-70-71/47-issue-70-editorial.

Jenkins, H. (2006) *Convergence Culture: Where Old and New Media Collide*, New York: New York University Press.

Jenkins, H., and Thorburn, D. (2003) *Democracy and New Media*, Cambridge, MA: MIT Press.

Jessop, B., and Sum, N.L. (2000) 'An Entrepreneurial City in Action: Hong Kong's Emerging Strategies in and for (Inter)urban Competition', *Urban Studies*, 37 (12), 2287–2313.

Johnson, B. (16 April 2009) 'No One Is Ready for This', *The Guardian*, http://www.guardian.co.uk/technology/2009/apr/16/internet-hacking-cyber-war-nato.

Johnson, I. (2 November 2012) 'China's Emigrant Attrition', *International Herald Tribune*.

Johnstone, S., and Mazo, J. (2011) 'Global Warming and the Arab Spring', *Survival: Global Politics and Strategy*, 53 (2), 11–17.

Jordan, T. (1999) *Cyberpower: The Culture and Politics of Cyberspace and the Internet*, London and New York: Routledge.

Judge, P. (7 December 2009) 'Russia Accused of Climategate Hack', *E-Week Europe*, online available at: http://www.eweekeurope.co.uk/news/news-security/russia-accused-of-climategate-hack-2674.

Ibahrine, M. (2007) *New Media and Neo-Islamism: New Media's Impact on the Political Culture in the Islamic World*, Saarbrucken: VDM Verl. Muller.

ITN News (28 April 2012) 'Escaped Chinese Activist Chen Guangcheng Releases Online Video', *YouTube*, online available at: http://www.youtube.com/watch?v=Qe8sRywbjbs.

Kahney, L. (21 January 2003) 'Internet Strokes Anti-war Movement', online available at: www.wired.com/news/culture/0,1284,57310,00.html.

Kalathil, S., and Boas, T.C. (2003) *Open Networks, Closed Regimes: The Impact of the Internet on Authoritarian Rule*, Washington, DC: Carnegie Endowment for International Peace.

Karatzogianni, A. (February 2004) 'The Politics of Cyberconflict', *Journal of Politics*, 24 (1), 46–55.

Karatzogianni, A. (2006) *The Politics of Cyberconflict*, London and New York: Routledge.

Karatzogianni, A. (ed.) (2009) *Cyber Conflict and Global Politics*, London and New York: Routledge.

Karatzogianni, A. (10 March 2010) 'The Thorny Triangle: Cyber Conflict, Business and the Sino-American Relationship in the World-System', *e-International Relations*, online available at: http://www.e-ir.info/?p=3420.

Karatzogianni, A. (November 2010) 'Blame It on the Russians: Tracking the Portrayal of Russians during Cyber Conflict Incidents', *Digital Icons: Studies in Russian, Eurasian and Central European New Media*, no. 4: War, Conflict and Commemoration in the Age of Digital Reproduction, online available at: http://www.digitalicons.org/issue04/athina-karatzogianni.

Karatzogianni, A. (2012a) 'WikiLeaks Affect: Ideology, Conflict and the Revolutionary Virtual', in A. Karatzogianni and A. Kunstman (eds) *Digital*

Cultures and the Politics of Emotion: Feelings, Affect and Technological Change, Basingstoke: Palgrave Macmillan.

Karatzogianni, A. (2012b) 'Blame It on the Russians: Tracking the Portrayal of Russian Hackers during Cyber Conflict Incidents', in A. Karatzogianni (ed.) *Violence and War in the Media: Five Disciplinary Lenses,* London and New York: Routledge.

Karatzogianni, A. (2012c) 'From Innovative Democracy to Warfare State: Ancient Athens as a Model of Hegemonic Decline', in H. Gardner and O. Kobtzeff (eds) *Ashgate Research Companion to War: Origins and Prevention,* Farnham and Burlington: Ashgate.

Karatzogianni, A. (2013) 'A Cyberconflict Analysis of the 2011 Arab Spring', in G. Youngs (ed.) *Digital World: Connectivity, Creativity and Rights,* London and New York: Routledge.

Karatzogianni, A., and Kuntsman A. (eds) (2012) *Digital Cultures and the Politics of Emotion,* Basingstoke: Palgrave Macmillan.

Karatzogianni, A., and Michaelides, G. (January 2009) 'Cyberconflict at the Edge of Chaos: Cryptohierarchies and Self-Organization in the Open Source Movement', in P. Moore and A. Karatzogianni (eds) *Parallel Visions of P2P Production: Governance, Organization and the New Economies,* Special Issue, *Capital and Class,* no. 97, 143–159.

Karatzogianni, A., Morgunova, O., Kambouri, N., Lafazani, O., Trimikliniotis, N., and Ioannou, G. (2013) 'Transnational Digital Networks, Migration and Gender: Intercultural Conflict and Dialogue', online available at MIG@NET.EU portal: http://www.mignetproject.eu/?cat=10.

Karatzogianni, A., and Robinson, A. (2010) *Power, Resistance and Conflict in the Contemporary World: Social Movements, Networks and Hierarchies,* Routledge Advances in International Relations and Global Politics, London and New York: Routledge.

Karatzogianni, A., and Robinson, A. (2014) 'Digital Prometheus: WikiLeaks, the State-Network Dichotomy and the Antinomies of Academic Reason', *International Journal of Communication,* 8, Feature 1–20.

Karatzogianni, A., and Robinson, A. (2016) 'A Cyberconflict Analysis of Chinese Dissidents', in G.D. Rawnsley and M.Y.T. Rawnsley (eds) *The Routledge Handbook of Chinese Media,* London and New York: Routledge.

Karatzogianni, A., and Schandorf, M. (20 October 2012) 'Agency, Resistance, and Orders of Dissent against the Capitalist Code', presented at the Association of Internet Researchers Conference 13.0, Salford University.

Karatzogianni, A., and Schandorf, M. (2015) 'Surfing the Revolutionary Wave 2010–12: A Technosocial Theory of Agency, Resistance, and Orders of Dissent in Contemporary Social Movements', in Alexander D. Ornella (ed.) *Anthropotechnologies – Making Humans. Religious, Technological, and Aesthetic Perspectives,* Oxford: Inter-Disciplinary Press.

Keidel, A. (26 May 2005) 'The Economic Basis for Social Unrest in China', online available at: http://www.carnegieendowment.org/files/Keidel_Social_Unrest.pdf.

Keizer, G. (7 April 2010) 'Botnets "the Swiss Army Knife of Attack Tools"', online available at: http://www.computerworld.com/s/article/9174560/Botnets_the_Swiss_Army_knife_of_attack_tools.

Kelliher, D. (1993) 'Keeping Democracy Safe from the Masses: Intellectuals and Elitism in the Chinese Protest Movement', *Comparative Politics,* 25 (4), 379–396.

Khondker, H.H. (2011) 'Role of the New Media in the Arab Spring', *Globalizations*, 8 (5), 675–679.

Kiguradze, T. (13 November 2009) 'Public Debates on the War Report in Tbilisi', *The Messenger Online*, online available at: http://www.messenger.com.ge/ issues/1982_november_13_2009/1982_temo.html.

Kinsman, J. (February 2011) 'Truth and Consequence: The WikiLeaks Saga', *Policy Options*, 45–49.

Kirkpatrick, D.D., and Sanger, D.E. (13 February 2011) 'A Tunisian-Egyptian Link That Shook Arab History', *New York Times*, online available at: http:// www.nytimes.com/2011/02/14/world/middleeast/14egypt-tunisia-protests. html?pagewanted=all&_r=0.

Kluver, R. (2005) 'The Architecture of Control: A Chinese Strategy for E-Governance', *Journal of Public Policy*, 25 (1), 75–97.

Knightley, P. (14 June 2003) 'Turning the Tanks on Reporters', *The Guardian*, online available at: http://www.theguardian.com/media/2003/jun/15/broad- casting.Iraqandthemedia.

Kolasinski, T. (4 December 2009) 'An Inconvenient Hoax', *Daily Evergreen Online*, online available at: http://www.dailyevergreen.com/story/31800.

Korns, S.W., and Kastenberg, J.E. (2009) 'Georgia's Cyber Left Hook', *Parameters*, 38 (4), 60–76, USA Army War College, online available at: http://www.carlisle. army.mil/usawc/Parameters/08winter/korns.pdf.

Krieg, A. (2011) 'Egyptian Civil-Military Relations and Egypt's Potential Transition to Democracy', *Publications in Contemporary Affairs (PiCA)*.

Kuah-Pearce, K.E. (2009) 'Defining Hong Kong as an Emerging Protest Space: The Anti-Globalization Movement', in G. Guiheux (ed.) *Social Movements in China and Hong Kong: The Expansion of Protest Space*, Amsterdam: Amsterdam University Press, 91–116.

Kuntsman, A. (2009) *Figurations of Violence and Belonging: Queerness, Migranthood and Nationalism in Cyberspace and Beyond*, Oxford: Peter Lang.

Kurlantzick, J. (2003) 'The Dragon Still Has Teeth: How the West Winks at Chinese Repression', *World Policy Journal*, 20 (1), 49–58.

Lamborn, K. 'Chinese Dissident's Eemake of Gangnam Style Is Banned', Video, *ITN News*, online available at: http://www.itn.co.uk/World/59790/ chinese-dissidents-remake-of-gangnam-style-is-banned (accessed 4 November 2012).

Lampert, J. (2006) *Deleuze and Guattari's Philosophy of History*, New York: Continuum.

Larson, K. (29 October 2012) 'Protests in China Get a Boost from Social Media', *Bloomberg Business Week*, online available at: http://www.businessweek.com/ articles/2012-10-29/protests-in-china-get-a-boost-from-social-media.

Le Grignou, B., and Patou, C. (2004) 'ATTAC(k)ing Expertise', in W. Van de Donk, B. Loader, P. Nixon, and D. Rucht (eds), *Cyberprotest: New Media, Citizens and Social Movements*, London and New York: Routledge.

Lee, C.K. (2007) *Against the Law: Labor Protests in China's Rustbelt and Sunbelt*, Berkeley: University of California Press.

Lee, P. (31 October 2012) 'Insider Training, Chinese Style', *Asia Times*, online available at: http://www.atimes.com/atimes/China/NJ31Ad02.html.

Leigh, D., Arthur, C., and Evans, R. (4 February 2010) 'Climate E-mails: Were They Really Hacked or Just Sitting in Cyber Space?', *The Guardian*, online available at:

http://www.guardian.co.uk/environment/2010/feb/04/climate-change-email-hacker-police-investigation.

Leigh, D., and Harding, L. (1 February 2011) 'WikiLeaks: From Wales to a US Jail, via Iraq, the Story of Bradley Manning', *The Guardian*, online available at: http://www.guardian.co.uk/world/2011/feb/01/bradley-manning-WikiLeaks.

Leigh, D., Harding, L., Hirsch, A., and MacAskill (30 November 2010) 'WikiLeaks: Interpol Wanted Notice for Julian Assange', *The Guardian*, online available at: http://www.guardian.co.uk/media/2010/nov/30/interpol-wanted-notice-julian-assange.

Levsen, L. (7 December 2009) 'Comprehensive Network Analysis Shows Climategate Likely to Be a Leak', online available at: http://wattsupwiththat.com/2009/12/07/comprhensive-network-analysis-shows-climategate-likely-to-be-a-leak.

Lévy, P. (Spring–Summer, 2005) 'Collective Intelligence, a Civilisation: Towards a Method of Positive Interpretation', *International Journal of Politics, Culture, and Society*, 18 (3/4), *The New Sociological Imagination*, 189–198.

Lewis, H. (18 October 2012) 'Taking on the "Great Firewall of China"', *New Statesman*, online available at: http://www.newstatesman.com/staggers/2012/10/taking-great-firewall-china.

Leyden, J. (12 April 2010) 'Russian Trade Body Aims to Fight Cyber Crime', *Register*, online available at: http://www.theregister.co.uk/2010/04/12/russia_cybercrime_feature.

Li, D.T. (30 July 2008) 'The Weng'an Model: China's Fix-it Governance', *Open Democracy*, online available at: http://www.opendemocracy.net/article/the-wengan-model-china-s-fix-it-governance.

Li, L.J. (September 2006) 'Driven to Protest: China's Rural Unrest', *Current History*, 105, 250–254.

Lim, E. (2010) 'WikiLeaks, Anarchism, and the State', online available at: http://www.elvinlim.com/2010/12/WikiLeaks-anarchism-and-state.html.

Lin, G.C.S. (2002) 'The Growth and Structural Change of Chinese Cities: A Contextual and Geographic Analysis', *Cities*, 19 (5), 299–316.

Liu, J.F. (2011) 'Picturing a Green Virtual Public Space for Social Change: A Study of Internet Activism and Web-based Environmental Collective Actions in China', *Chinese Journal of Communication*, 4 (2), 137–166.

Liu, S.D. (2006) 'China's Popular Nationalism on the Internet: Report on the 2005 Anti-Japan Network Struggles', *Inter-Asia Cultural Studies*, 7 (1), 144–155.

Longman, L. (March 2005) 'From Virtual Public Spheres to Global Justice: A Critical Theory of Internetworked Social Movements', *Sociological Theory*, 23 (1), 42–74.

Lovink, G. (2007) *Zero Comments: Blogging and Critical Internet Culture*, New York: Routledge.

Lovink, G. (2012) *Networks without a Cause: A Critique of Social Media*, Cambridge: Polity Press.

Lovink, G. (24 October 2014) 'Speech at Franco Berardi's PhD Defence in Helsinki', online available at: http://networkcultures.org/geert/2014/10/24/speech-at-franco-berardis-phd-defence-in-helsinki.

Loyd, A. (8 March 2010) 'Britain Applies Military Thinking to the Growing Spectre of Cyber War', online available at: http://technology.timesonline.co.uk/tol/news/tech_and_web/article7053270.ece.

Ludlow, P. (4 October 2010) 'WikiLeaks and Hacktivist Culture', *Nation*.

Lum, T. (2006) 'Social Unrest in China', *Congressional Research Service Reports and Issue Briefs*, online available at: http://digitalcommons.ilr.cornell.edu/cgi/viewcontent.cgi?article=1018&context=crs&sei-redir=1&referer=http%3A%2F%2Fscholar.google.co.uk%2Fscholar%3Fstart%3D30%26q%3Dchina%2Bprotest%26hl%3Den%26as_sdt%3D0%2C5#search=%22china%20protest%22.

Ma, N. (2009) 'Social Movements and State-Society Relationship in Hong Kong', in G. Guiheux (ed.) *Social Movements in China and Hong Kong: The Expansion of Protest Space*, Amsterdam: Amsterdam University Press, 45–64.

Macdonald, C. (13 April 2010) 'FBI Agent Visits Monterey Trail High', *Elk Grove Citizen*, online available at: http://www.egcitizen.com/articles/2010/04/13/news/doc4bc4fe6887a33275902281.txt.

Mackell, A. (25 May 2011) 'The IMF versus the Arab Spring', *The Guardian*, online available at: http://www.guardian.co.uk/commentisfree/2011/may/25/imf-arab-spring-loans-egypt-tunisia.

MacKinnon, R. (2010) 'Networked Authoritarianism in China and Beyond: Implications for Global Internet Freedom', presented at Stanford University, Conference on Liberation Technology in Authoritarian Regimes, 11–12 October, online available at: http://iis-db.stanford.edu/evnts/6349/MacKinnon_Libtech.pdf.

MacNicol, G. (7 December 2009) 'Are Russian Hackers Responsible for Creating Climategate?', online available at: http://www.mediaite.com/online/are-russian-hackers-responsible-for-creating-climategate.

Madey, G.V., Freech, V., and Tynan, R. (2005) 'Modelling and F/OSS Communities: A Quantitative Investigation', *Eight Americas Conference on Information Systems*.

Magnuson, S. (May 2010) 'Russian Cyber Thief Case Illustrates Security Risks for U.S. Corporations', online available at: http://www.nationaldefensemagazine.org/archive/2010/May/Pages/RussianCyberthiefCaseIllustratesSecurityRisks.aspx.

Marlin, R. (2011) 'Propaganda and the Ethics of WikiLeaks', *Global Media Journal* (Australian Edition), 5 (1).

Massumi, B. (2002) *Parables for the Virtual: Movement, Affect, Sensation*, Durham and London: Duke University Press.

McCahill, M., and Finn, R.L. (2014) *Surveillance, Capital and Resistance: Theorizing the Surveillance Subject*, London: Routledge.

McCarthy, M., and Owen, J. (6 December 2009) 'Climate Change Conspiracies: Stolen E-mails Used to Ridicule Global Warming', *Independent*, online available at: http://www.independent.co.uk/environment/climate-change/climate-change-conspiracies-stolen-emails-used-to-ridicule-global-warming-1835031.html.

McCaughey, M., and Ayers, M. (2003) *Cyberactivism: Online Activism in Theory and Practice*, New York and London: Routledge.

McCoy, A. (15 July 2013) 'Surveillance Blowback: The Making of the US Surveillance State, 1898–2020', *Popular Resistance*, online available at: http://www.popularresistance.org/surveillance-blowback-the-making-of-the-us-surveillance-state-1898-2020.

McLuhan, M. (1989) *The Global Village: Transformations in World Life and Media in the 21st Century*, Oxford: Oxford University Press.

McNay, L. (1994) *Foucault: A Critical Introduction*, Cambridge: Polity Press.

Megerisi, H. (22 March 2010) 'Russia Arrests $9 million Cash Machine Hackers', online available at: http://www.pcpro.co.uk/news/security/356617/russia-arrests-9-million-cash-machine-hackers.

Meinrath, S. (14 October 2013) 'We Can't Let the Internet Become Balkanized', *Slate*, online available at: http://www.slate.com/articles/technology/future_tense/2013/10/internet_balkanization_may_be_a_side_effect_of_the_snowden_surveillance.html.

Mengyu Dong (3 November 2012) 'Looking for Song Ze', *China Digital Times*, online available at: http://chinadigitaltimes.net/2012/11/looking-for-song-ze (accessed 4 November 2012).

Merchant, B. (7 December 2009) 'Ex-KGB Officers May Be the Hackers behind ClimateGate', *Treehugger*, online available at: http://www.treehugger.com/files/2009/12/ex-kgb-officers-hackers-climategate.php.

Michaelides, G. (2006) 'Far from Equilibrium: Emergence, Self-Organization and Diversity in the KDE Community', PhD thesis, Business School, University of Nottingham.

Migdal, J. (1988) *Strong Societies and Weak States: State-Society Relations and State Capabilities in the Third World*, Princeton, NJ: Princeton University Press.

Minzner, C.F. (2009) 'Riots and Cover-Ups: Counterproductive Control of Local Agents in China', *University of Pennsylvania Journal of International Law*, 31 (1), 53–123.

Miskimmon, A., O'Loughlin, B., and Roselle, L. (n.d.) 'Forging the World: Strategic Narratives and International Relations', online available at: http://newpolcom.rhul.ac.uk/storage/Forging%20the%20World%20Working%20Paper%202012.pdf.

Moore, C. (11 October 2013) 'This Is Not Blitz Britain. We Sure as Hell Can't Lick Terrorism on Our Own', *Daily Telegraph*, online available at: http://www.telegraph.co.uk/news/uknews/defence/11154322/GCHQ-This-is-not-Blitz-Britain.-We-sure-as-hell-cant-lick-terrorism-on-our-own.html.

Morozov, E. (14 August 2008) 'An Army of Ones and Zeroes: How I Became a Soldier in the Georgia-Russia Cyber war', *Slate.com*, online available at: http://www.slate.com/id/2197514.

Morozov, E. (2011) *The Net Delusion: The Dark Side of Internet Freedom*, New York: Public Affairs.

Moussa, B.M. (October 2011) 'The Use of the Internet by Islamic Social Movements in Collective Action: The Case of Justice and Charity', *Westminster Papers in Communication and Culture*, 8 (2), 65–91.

Mu, Y., and Thomson, M. (1989) *Crisis at Tiananmen: Reform and Reality in Modern China*, San Francisco: China Books and Periodicals.

Mulvenon, J., and Yang, R. (1999) *The People's Liberation Army in the Information Age*, Santa Monica, CA: Rand.

Nardin, T. (2011) *The Philosophy of Michael Oakeshott*, University Park: Pennsylvania State University Press.

Neilson, B., and Rossiter, N. (2008) 'Precarity as a Political Concept, or Fordism as Exception', *Theory, Culture and Society*, 25 (7–8), 51–72.

Nepstad, S.E. (December 2011) 'Nonviolent Resistance in the Arab Spring: The Critical Role of Military-Opposition Alliances', *Swiss Political Science Review*, 17 (4), 485–491.

Niman, M.I. (2010) 'WikiLeaks and the End of Democracy', *ArtVoice*, online available at: http://mediastudy.com/articles/av12-16-10.html?referer=http%3A%2F%2Fscholar.google.co.uk%2Fscholar%3Fstart%3D50%26q%3DWikiLeaks%26hl%3Den%26as_sdt%3D0%2C5#search=%22WikiLeaks%22.

Oakeshott, M. (1991) *On Human Conduct*, Oxford: Clarendon.

Ober, J. (2010) *Democracy and Knowledge: Innovation and Learning in Classical Athens*, Princeton and Oxford: Princeton University Press.

O'Brien, K.J. (ed.) (2008) *Popular Protest in China*, Cambridge, MA: Harvard University Press.

O'Brien, K.J., and Li, L. (2006) *Rightful Resistance in Rural China*, New York and Cambridge: Cambridge University Press.

O'Loughlin, J., Witmer, F.D.W., Linke, A.M., and Thorwardson, N. (2010) 'Peering into the Fog of War: The Geography of the WikiLeaks Afghanistan War Logs, 2004–2009', *Eurasian Geography and Economics*, 51 (4), 472–495.

Opper, M.H. (2011) 'WikiLeaks: Balancing First Amendment Rights with National Security', *Loyola of Los Angeles Entertainment Law Review*, 31, 237, online available at: http://digitalcommons.lmu.edu/elr/vol31/iss3/2.

O'Sullivan, N. (2012) 'Oakeshott on Civil Association', in P. Franco and L. Marsh (eds) *A Companion to Michael Oakeshott*, University Park: Pennsylvania State University Press.

Page, M., and Spence, J.E. (2011) 'Open Secrets Questionably Arrived at: The Impact of WikiLeaks on Diplomacy', *Defence Studies*, 11 (2), 234–243.

Papacharissi, Z. (2002) 'The Virtual Sphere: The Internet as the Public Sphere', *New Media & Society*, 4 (1), 5–23.

Papacharissi, Z. (2004) 'Democracy On-line: Civility, Politeness, and the Democratic Potential of On-line Political Discussion Groups', *New Media & Society*, 6 (2), 259–284.

Parmar, I. (2011) 'American Power and Identities in the Age of Obama', *International Politics*, 48 (2/3), 153–163.

Pearce, F. (9 February 2010a) 'Search for Hacker May Lead Police Back to East Anglia's Climate Research Unit', *The Guardian*, online available at: http://www.guardian.co.uk/environment/2010/feb/09/hacked-emails-police-investigation.

Pearce, F. (9 February 2010b) 'How the "Climategate" Scandal Is Bogus and Based on Climate Sceptics' Lies', *The Guardian*, online available at: http://www.guardian.co.uk/environment/2010/feb/09/climategate-bogus-sceptics-lies.

Periscope It. (3 February 2003) 'Hacker Attack Takes Russian Newspaper Offline for Days', online available at: http://www.periscopeit.co.uk/website-monitoring-news/article/hacker-attack-takes-russian-newspaper-offline-for-days/594.

Perna, S. (9–12 February 2012) 'Social Media and New Technologies in Egypt and Tunisia: Two Examples of Innovative forms of Democratization', International Sociological Association, *From Social to Political. New Forms of Mobilization and Democratization*, Bilbao.

Perthes, V. (2011) 'Europe and the Arab Spring', *Survival: Global Politics and Strategy*, 53 (6), 73–84.

Pickard, V. 'United Yet Autonomous: Indymedia and the Struggle to Sustain a Radical Democratic Network', *Media, Culture and Society*, 28, 315.

Poitras, L., Rosenbach, M., Schmid, F., Stark, H., and Stock, J. (1 July 2013) 'Cover Story: How the NSA Targets Germany and Europe', *Spiegel*, online available at:

http://www.spiegel.de/international/world/secret-documents-nsa-targeted-germany-and-eu-buildings-a-908609.html.

Poster, M. (ed.) (2001) *Jean Baudrillard: Selected Writings*, 2nd ed., Cambridge: Polity Press.

Poulsen, K. (22 August 2007) 'Cyber War and Estonia's Panic Attack', *Wired*, online available at: http://www.wired.com/threatlevel/2007/08/cyber-war-and-e.

Powers, J. (2004) *History as Propaganda: Tibetan Exiles versus the People's Republic of China*, Oxford: Oxford University Press.

Prensky, M. (2001) 'Digital Natives, Digital Immigrants', online available at: http://www.marcprensky.com/writing/Prensky%20-%20Digital%20Natives,%20Digital%20Immigrants%20-%20Part1.pdf (accessed January 2009).

Pun, N. (2005) *Made in China: Women Factory Workers in a Global Workplace*, Durham and London: Duke University Press.

Pye, L.W. (1990) 'Tiananmen and Chinese Political Culture: The Escalation of Confrontation from Moralizing to Revenge', *Asian Survey*, 30 (4), 331–347.

Pye, L.W. (2001) 'Review Essay "Appealing the Tiananmen Verdict: New Documents from China's Highest Leaders"', *Foreign Affairs*, 80 (2), 148–154.

Qiao, L.A., and Wang, X.S. (2002) *Unrestricted Warfare*, Panama City: Pan-American.

Qiu, J.L. (2004) 'The Internet in China: Technologies of Freedom in a Statist Society', in M. Castells (ed.) *Network Society: A Cross-Cultural Perspective*, London: Edward Elgar.

Qiu, J.L. (2009) *Working-Class Network Society: Communication Technology and the Information Have-Less in Urban China*, Cambridge, MA, and London: MIT Press.

Radio Free Asia (3 November 2012) 'Court Rejects Chen Lawsuit', online available at: http://www.rfa.org/english/news/china/lawsuit-11022012103759.html (accessed 4 November 2012).

Radó, N. (2011) 'On WikiLeaks Diplomacy: Secrecy and Transparency in the Digital Age', MA thesis, Department of International Relations and European Studies, Central European University, Budapest, Hungary.

Rainsford, S. (11 March 2010) 'Inside the Mind of a Russian Hacker', *BBC*, online available at: http://news.bbc.co.uk/1/hi/8561910.stm.

Ramzy, A. (7 October 2012) 'The Artist Who Can't Leave China: An Interview with Ai Weiwei', online available at: http://world.time.com/2012/10/07/the-artist-who-cant-leave-china-an-interview-with-ai-weiwei (accessed 4 November 2012).

Rawnsley, G.D. (November 2006) 'The Media, Internet and Governance in China', China Discussion Paper No. 12, China Policy Institute, University of Nottingham, online available at: http://www.nottingham.ac.uk/china-policy-institute/publications/discussionpapers.php.

Rawnsley, G.D. (2007) 'Virtual China: The Internet as Threat or Opportunity?', *St. Antony's International Review*, 3 (1), 42–57.

Rawnsley, G.D., and Rawnsley, M.Y.T. (2003) *Political Communications in Greater China*, London: RoutledgeCurzon.

Rawnsley, M.Y.T. (2012) 'The Media in Democratic Taiwan', in D. Blundell (ed.) *Taiwan since Martial Law: Society, Culture, Politics, Economy*, Berkeley: University of California, Berkeley & National Taiwan University Press.

Raymond, G. (1998) 'The Cathedral and the Bazaar', *First Monday*, 3 (3), 395–417.

Reese, S., and Dai, J. (2009) 'Citizen Journalism in the Global News Arena: China's New Media Critics', in S. Allan and E. Thorsen (eds) *Citizen Journalism: Global Perspectives*, New York: Peter Lang.

Reuters (28 March 2003) 'War Attacks Tit for Tat', online available at: http://archive.wired.com/politics/law/news/2003/03/58275.

Reuters (2 December 2009) 'Georgia Releases Ossetians in Likely Prisoner Swap', online available at: http://www.reuters.com/article/idUSATRE5B122Q20091202.

Reuters (30 June 2013) http://www.reuters.com/article/2013/06/30/us-usa-germany-spying-idUSBRE95T04B20130630.

Rheingold, H. (1991) *Virtual Reality*, London: Secker and Warburg.

Rheingold, H. (1994) *The Virtual Community: Surfing the Internet*, London: Minerva.

Rheingold, H. (2002) *Smart Mobs: The Next Social Revolution*, New York: Perseus.

Rimmer, P.J. (2002) 'Overview: Restructuring Chinese Space in the New Millennium', *Asia Pacific Viewpoint*, 43, 1–8.

Rosen, N. (2011) *WikiLeaks: Assange and the Death of Privacy*, New York: Andre Deutsch.

Rosenzweig, P. (2011) *Lessons of WikiLeaks: The U.S. Needs a Counterinsurgency Strategy for Cyberspace*, online available at: http://ssrn.com/abstract=1884336.

Ross, M.L. (September/October 2011) 'Will Oil Drown the Arab Spring?' *Foreign Affairs*, online available at: http://www.foreignaffairs.com/articles/68200/michael-l-ross/will-oil-drown-the-arab-spring.

Routledge, P., and Simons, J. (1995) 'Embodying Spirits of Resistance', *Environment and Planning D: Society and Space*, 13, 471–498.

Rozoff, R. (26 May 2010) 'USA Cyber Command: Waging War in World's Fifth Battlespace', online available at: http://rickrozoff.wordpress.com/2010/05/26/us-cyber-command-waging-war-in-worlds-fifth-battlespace.

RT (19 February 2008) 'Russia Named "Spam Superpower"', online available at: http://rt.com/Business/2008-02-19/Russia_named_spam_superpower_.html.

RT (11 July 2013) 'Microsoft Helped the NSA Bypass Encryption, New Snowden Leak Reveals', online available at: http://rt.com/usa/microsoft-nsa-snowden-leak-971.

Rupnik, J. (1988) 'Totalitarianism Revisited', in J. Keane (ed.) *Civil Society and the State*, London: Verso.

Rushe, D. (12 September 2013) 'Zuckerberg: US Government "Blew It" on NSA Surveillance', online available at: http://www.theguardian.com/technology/2013/sep/11/yahoo-ceo-mayer-jail-nsa-surveillance.

Saletan, W. 'Springtime for Twitter: Is the Internet Driving the Revolutions of the Arab Spring?', Future Tense, Slate.com, online available at: http://www.slate.com/articles/technology/future_tense/2011/07/springtime_for_twitter.html.

Sarikakis, K. (2011) 'Securitization and Legitimacy in Global Media Governance: Spaces, Jurisdictions and Tensions', online available at: http://homepage.univie.ac.at/katharine.sarikakis/wp-content/uploads/2011/11/Sarikakis_TM_v1-bib.pdf.

Saunders, R.A. (2011) 'WikiLeaks Are Not Terrorists: A Critical Assessment of the "Hacktivist" Challenge to the Diplomatic System', *Globality Studies Journal*, 25, 1–11.

Schandorf, M., and Karatzogianni, A. (forthcoming) 'Agency in Posthuman IR: Solving the Problem of Technosocially Mediated Agency', in E. Cudworth, S. Hobden, and E. Kavalski (eds) *Posthuman Dialogues in International Relations*, Farnham: Ashgate.

Schedler, A. (2006) 'The Logic of Electoral Authoritarianism', from his edited collection, *Electoral Authoritarianism: The Dynamics of Unfree Competition*, Boulder, CO: Lynne Rienner, online available at: www.ethiomedia.com/accent/ ea_schedler.pdf.

Schluessel, E.T. (2009) 'History, Identity and Mother-Tongue Education in Xinjiang', *Central Asian Survey*, 28 (4), 383–402.

Schow, A. (1 July 2013) 'US Government Declares Hacking an Act of War, Then Hacks Allies', *Washington Examiner*, online available at: http://washingtonex-aminer.com/article/2532594.

Schumacher, T. (2011) 'The EU and the Arab Spring: Between Spectatorship and Actorness', *Insight Turkey*, 13 (3), 107–119.

Scott, J.C. (2012) 'Infrapolitics and Mobilizations: A Response by James C. Scott', online available at: http://www.cairn.info/resume.php?ID_ARTICLE= RFEA_131_0112.

Secrest, B. (29 April 2010) 'Cyber Crime: Russian Hackers Threaten the World', online available at: http://www.conservativerefocus.com/blog5.php/2010/04/ 29/cyber-crime-russian-hackers-threaten-the-world.

Severo, M., Giraud, T., and Douay, N. (2011) 'Citizen Protest in Online Networks: The Case of China's Bloody Map', paper presented to the 7th Social Network Conference, London, UK, online available at: http://hal.archives-ouvertes.fr/ docs/00/67/55/17/PDF/BloodyMap_Severo_inviato.pdf.

Shadid, A. (21 November 2011) 'Bahrain Nervously Awaits Report on Revolt', *New York Times*, online available at: http://www.nytimes.com/2011/11/22/world/ middleeast/bahrain-nervouslyawaits-revolt-reports-findings.html.

Shah, N., and Abrahan, S. (2009) Digital Natives with a Cause? Engaging with the Physical-Virtual Dialectic', Hivos Knowledge Programme Report, online available: http://www.hivos.net/Hivos-Knowledge-Programme/Themes/ Digital-Natives-with-a-Cause/Publications/New-Publication-Digital-Natives-with-a-Cause.

Shan, R. (16 October 2012) 'Exiled Dissidents Should Leave Hatred Behind', *Global Times*, online available at: http://www.globaltimes.cn/content/738704.shtml.

Shan, W., and Chen, G. (n.d.) 'The Urumqui Riots and China's Ethnic Policy in Xinjiang', online available at: http://www.eai.nus.edu.sg/Vol1No3_Shanwei ChenGang.pdf.

Shane, P. (ed.) (2005) *Democracy Online: The Prospects for Political Renewal through the Internet*, London: Routledge.

Shao, J. (1 November 2012) 'Weighty Times, Aggressive Measures: China Must End Heightened Crackdown Ahead of Party Congress', *Amnesty International UK/Blogs*, online available at: http://www2.amnesty.org.uk/blogs/count-down-china/weighty-times-aggressive-measures-china-must-end-heightened-crackdown-ahead.

Shaviro, S. (2010) *Post Cinematic Affect*, Hants: Zero Books.

Shi, Y.L., and Hamnett, C. (2002) 'The Potential and Prospect for Global Cities in China: In the Context of the World System', *Geoforum*, 33, 121–135.

Shirky, C. (2011) 'The Political Power of Social Media', *Foreign Affairs*, 90 (1), 28–41.

Shu-Yun Ma (1993) 'The Exit, Voice, and Struggle to Return of Chinese Political Exiles', *Pacific Affairs*, 66 (3), 368–385.

Siegel, A. (ed.) (1998) *The Totalitarian Paradigm after the End of Communism*, Amsterdam: Radopi.

Sifry, M. (2011) *WikiLeaks and the Age of Transparency*, New Haven, CT: Yale University Press.

Sikkink, K. (1993) 'Human Rights, Principled Issue-Networks, and Sovereignty in Latin America', *International Organization*, 47 (3), 411–441.

Simmons, B.A. (2011) 'International Studies in the Global Information Age', *International Studies Quarterly*, 55, 589–599.

Sinclair, G. (2002) 'The Internet in China: Information Revolution or Authoritarian Solution?', dissertation, online available at: http://www.geocities.ws/gelaige79/intchin.pdf.

Skinner, J. (2011) 'Social Media and Revolution: The Arab Spring and the Occupy Movement as Seen through Three Information Studies Paradigms', *Sprouts: Working Papers on Information Systems*, 11 (169), online available at: http://sprouts.aisnet.org/11-169.

Smith, M., and Warren, P. (6 June 2010) 'NATO Warns of Strike against Cyber Attackers', *Sunday Times*, online available at: http://www.timesonline.co.uk/tol/news/world/article7144856.ece.

Snapple (7 January 2010) 'Tomsk Hackers Part III: FBI Investigating Death Threats against Global Warming Scientists', online available at: http://legendofpineridge.blogspot.com/2010/01/tomsk-hackers-part-iii-fbi.html.

Snapple (21 March 2010) 'The BBC Interviews of a Reformed Hacker', online available at: http://legendofpineridge.blogspot.com/2010/03/bbc-interviews-reformed-russian-hacker.html.

Snow, D., Zurcher, L., and Olson, S. (October 1980) 'Social Networks and Social Movements: A Micro-structural Approach to Differential Recruitment', *American Sociological Review*, 45 (5), 787–801.

Sommerville, M. (11 December 2010) 'Wikileaks, Wikileakers and Wiki-ethics', online available at: http://www.mercatornet.com/articles/view/wikileaks_wikileakers_and_wiki-ethi.

Soueif, A. (8 March 2012) 'This Year Let's Celebrate the Women of Egypt's Revolution', *The Guardian*, online available at: http://www.guardian.co.uk/commentisfree/2012/mar/08/egypt-revolution-international-womens-day.

Soueif, A. (16 November 2012) 'Gaza Is No Longer Alone', *The Guardian*, online available at: http://www.guardian.co.uk/commentisfree/2012/nov/16/gaza-no-longer-alone?INTCMP=ILCNETTXT3487.

Southern Perspectives (2011) 'When Silence Must Be Heard: Knowledge in the Pacific', online available at: http://www.southernperspectives.net/region/pacific/when-silence-must-be-heard-knowledge-in-the-pacific-a-dialogue-with-sana-balai-and-kirk-huffman.

Springborg, R. (2011) 'Whither the Arab Spring? 1948 or 1989?', *International Spectator: Italian Journal of International Affairs*, 46 (3), 5–12.

Springer, S., Chi, H., Crampton, J., Mcconnell, F., Cupples J., Glynn, K., Warf, B., and Attewell, W. (2012) 'Leaky Geopolitics: The Ruptures and Transgressions of WikiLeaks', *Geopolitics*, 17 (3), 681–711.

Stack, M. (17 March 2010) 'Russian Secrets for Sale, No Questions Asked', *LA Times*, online available at: http://articles.latimes.com/2010/mar/17/world/la-fg-secrets-for-sale17-2010mar17.

Stahl, R. (2010) *Militainment Inc.: War, Media and Popular Culture*, London and New York: Routledge.

Stallman, R.M. (2010) *Free Software, Free Society: Selected Essays of Richard M. Stallman*, 2nd ed., Boston: GNU Press.

Steinmetz, K. (2012) 'WikiLeaks and Realpolitik', *Journal of Theoretical and Philosophical Criminology*, 4 (1), 14–52.

Stepanova, E. (May 2011) 'The Role of Information Communication Technologies in the "Arab Spring": Implications beyond the Region', Ponars Eurasia Policy Memo No. 159.

Sterner, E. (2011) 'WikiLeaks and Cyberspace Cultures in Conflict', *Marshall Policy Outlook*.

Stewart, W., and Delgado, M. (6 December 2009) 'Were Russian Security Services behind the Leak of "Climategate" E-mails?', online available at: http://www. climateark.org/shared/reader/welcome.aspx?linkid=144998&keybold=climat e%20AND%20%20deal%20AND%20%20post%20AND%20%20Kyoto.

Sui-Lee Wee (6 November 2012) 'Chinese Women's Rights Activist Sent to Labour Camp Again', *Reuters*, online available at: http://uk.reuters.com/ article/2012/11/06/uk-china-labour-idUKBRE8A50DG20121106.

Sun, W. (2010) 'Scaling Chinese Media: A Geographic Turn to Future Research', *International Journal of Communication*, 4, 537–543.

Sunstein, C. (1999) 'The Law of Group Polarization', The Law School, University of Chicago.

Sunstein, C. (2003) *Why Societies Need Dissent*, Cambridge: Harvard University Press.

Tai, Z. (2006) *The Internet in China: Cyberspace and Civil Society*, New York: Routledge.

Talmon, J.L. (1961) *The Origins of Totalitarian Democracy*, London: Mercury Books.

Tapscott, J. (2008) *Grown-Up Digital: How the Net Generation Is Changing Your World*, New York: Vintage.

Tatlow, D.K. (17 October 2012a) 'Dissident Writer Calls for the Breakup of the Chinese Empire', *IHT Rendezvous*, online available at: http://rendezvous.blogs. nytimes.com/2012/10/17/dissident-writer-calls-for-the-breakup-of-the-chi- nese-empire (accessed 4 November 2012).

Tatlow, D.K. (17 October 2012b) 'In 3 Awards, 3 Ways of Seeing China', *New York Times*, online available at: http://www.nytimes.com/2012/10/18/world/ asia/18iht-letter18.html (accessed 4 November 2012).

Taubman, G. (1998) 'A Not-So World Wide Web: The Internet, China, and the Challenges to Nondemocratic Rule', *Political Communication*, 15 (2), 255–272.

Taylor, P.J. (2000) 'World Cities and Territorial States under Conditions of Contemporary Globalization II: Looking Forward, Looking Ahead', *Geoforum*, 52, 157–162.

Taylor, P.J., and Jordan, T. (2004) *Hacktivism and Cyberwars: Rebels with a Cause?*, London: Routledge.

Taylor, P.J., Ni, P., Derudder, B., Hoyler, M., Huang, J., Pain, F.L.K., Witlox, F., Yang, X., Bassens, D., and Shen, W. (2009) 'The Way We Were: Command- and-Control Centres in the Global Space-Economy on the Eve of the 2008 Geo-economic Transition', *Environment and Planning A*, 41, 7–12.

Taylor, P.J., Walker, R.F., Catalano, G., and Hoyler, M. (2002) 'Diversity and Power in the World City Network', *Cities*, 19 (4), 231–241.

Telegraph (6 December 2009) 'Climategate: Was Russian Secret Service behind Email Hacking plot?', online available at: http://www.telegraph.co.uk/earth/

copenhagen-climate-change-confe/6746370/Climategate-was-Russian-secret-service-behind-email-hacking-plot.html.

Terranova, T. (2003) 'Free Labor: Producing Culture for the Digital Economy', *Electronic Book Review*, http://www.electronicbookreview.com/thread/technocapitalism/voluntary.

Thornton, P.M. (2009) 'Manufacturing Dissent in Transnational China: Boomerang, Backfire or Spectacle?', in K. O'Brien (ed.) *Popular Protest in China*, Harvard: Harvard University Press.

Tong, Y.Q., and Lei, S.H. (2010) 'Creating Public Opinion Pressure in China: Large-Scale Internet Protest', EIA Background Brief No. 534, online available at: http://www.eai.nus.edu.sg/BB534.pdf.

Tsatsou, P. (2014) *Internet Studies: Past, Present and Future Directions*, Farnham: Ashgate.

Tuinstra, F. (2009) 'Internet Censorship: The Myth, Oft Told, and the Reality', *Nieman Reports*, online available at: http://www.nieman.harvard.edu/reports/article/101905/Internet-Censorship-The-Myth-Oft-Told-and-the-Reality.aspx.

UNCHR (16 February 2009) 'Attacks on the Press 2009 – Georgia', *Refworld*, online available at: http://www.unhcr.org/refworld/country,,,,GEO,,4b7bc2e82d,0.html.

Van Aelst, P., and Walgrave, S. (2004) 'New Media, New Movements?', in W. Van de Donk, B. Loader, P. Nixon, and D. Rucht, *Cyberprotest: New Media, Citizens and Social Movements*, London and New York: Routledge.

Van de Donk, W., Loader, B., Nixon, P., and Rucht, D. (eds) (2004) *Cyberprotest: New Media, Citizens and Social Movements*, London and New York: Routledge.

Van Laer, J., and van Aelst, P. (2009) 'Cyber-Protest and Civil Society: The Internet and Action Repertoires in Social Movements', in Y. Jewkes and M. Yar (eds) *Handbook on Internet Crime*, Cullompton: Willan, 230–254.

Vegh, S. (2003) 'Classifying Forms of Online Activism', in M. McCaughey and M. Ayers (eds) *Cyberactivism: Online Activism in Theory and Practice*, New York and London: Routledge.

Villeneuve, N. (10 April 2010) 'Blurring the Boundaries between Cyber Crime and Politically Motivated Attacks', online available at: http://www.nartv.org/2010/04/10/blurring-the-boundaries-between-cybercrime-and-politicaly-motivated-attacks.

Virilio, P. (1997) *Open Sky*, trans. Julie Rose, London: Verso.

Wacker, G. (2003) 'The Internet and Censorship in China', in C.R. Hughes and G. Wacker (eds) *China and the Internet: Politics of the Digital Leap Forward*, London and New York: Routledge.

Wacquant, L. (2008) *Urban Outcasts: A Comparative Sociology of Advanced Marginality*, Cambridge: Polity.

Walker, S. (7 December 2009) 'Was Russian Secret Service behind Leak of Climate-Change E-mails?', *Independent*, online available at: http://www.independent.co.uk/news/world/europe/was-russian-secret-service-behind-leak-of-climate-change-emails-1835502.html.

Walton, G. (2001) *China's Golden Shield: Corporations and the Development of Surveillance Technology in the People's Republic of China*, International Centre for Human Rights and Democratic Development.

Wang, X.R. (2009) *Behind the Great Firewall: The Internet and Democratization in China*, PhD dissertation, University of Michigan, online available at: http://141.213.232.243/bitstream/handle/2027.42/64681/wangx_1.pdf;jsessio nid=5E157B3861C0405E66420FBB7B68A65F?sequence=1.

Warf, B., and Grimes, J. (1997) 'Counterhegemonic Discourses and the Internet', *Geographical Review*, 87 (2), 259–274.

Wark, M. (2004) *A Hacker Manifesto*, Cambridge, MA: Harvard University Press.

Warwick, S. (2000) *I, Cyborg*, London: University of Reading Press.

Watts, A. (6 December 2009) 'Media Now Blaming Russians for Climategate Leak', online available at: http://wattsupwiththat.com/2009/12/06/media-now-blaming-russians-for-climategate-leak.

Watts, D.J., and Strogatz, S.H. (June 1998) 'Collective Dynamics of "Small-World" Networks', *Nature*, 393, 440–442.

Way, L. (October 2011) 'Comparing the Arab Revolts: The Lessons of 1989', *Journal of Democracy*, 22 (4), 17–27.

Weber, S. (2004) *The Success of Open Source*, Cambridge, MA, and London, England: Harvard University Press.

Wei, Y.D., and Leung, C.K. (2005) 'Development Zones, Foreign Investment, and Global City Formation in Shanghai', *Growth and Change*, 36 (1), 16–40.

Weinberger, D. (2008) *Everything Is Miscellaneous: The Power of the Digital Disorder*, New York: Times Books.

Weinberger, S. (14 May 2010) 'Hackers Are Internet Shock Troops', *Aviation Week*, online available at: http://www.aviationweek.com/aw/generic/story_channel. jsp?channel=defense&id=news/dti/2010/05/01/DT_05_01_2010_p19-218221. xml&headline=Hackers%20Are%20Internet%20Shock%20Troops.

Wenfang, T. (2001) 'Political and Social Trends in the Post-Deng Urban China: Crisis or Stability?', *China Quarterly*, 168, 890–909.

Williams, S. (2002) *Free as in Freedom: Richard Stallman's Crusade for Free Software*, Farnham: O'Reilly.

Wissinger, E. (2007) 'Always on Display: Affective Production in the Modeling Industry', in Patricia Clough and Jean Halley (eds) *The Affective Turn: Theorizing the Social*, Durham and London: Duke University Press.

Wolfsfeld, G. (1997) *Media and Political Conflict*, Cambridge: Cambridge University Press.

Wolpe, H. (1972) 'Capitalism and Cheap Labour-Power in South Africa: From Segregation to Apartheid', *Economy and Society*, 1 (4), 425–456.

Wu, F.L. (2000) 'The Global and Local Dimensions of Place-Making: Remaking Shanghai as a World City', *Urban Studies*, 37 (8), 1359–1377.

Wu, X. (2007) *Chinese Cybernationalism: Evolution, Characteristics, and Implications*, Lanham, MD: Lexington Books.

Yamaguchi, K. (2012) 'American Responses to 9/11: Orientalism(s) in a State of Exception', *Journal of Postcolonial Writing*, 48 (3), 241–251.

Yang, G.B. (August 2003) 'The Internet and Civil Society in China: A Preliminary Assessment', *Journal of Contemporary China*, 12 (36), 453–475.

Yang, G.B. (2005) 'Environmental NGOs and Institutional Dynamics in China', *China Quarterly*, 181, 46–66.

Yang, G.B. (2009a) 'Contention in Cyberspace', in K.J. O'Brien (ed.) *Popular Protest in China*, Cambridge, MA: Harvard University Press, 126–143.

Yang, G.B. (2009b) *The Power of the Internet in China: Citizen Activism Online*, New York: Columbia University Press.

Yu, V. (16 January 2010) 'Big Brother' a Constant, Chilling Presence for Bloggers and Activists', *South China Morning Post*.

Yusuf, S., and Wu, W. (2002) 'Pathways to a World City: Shanghai Rising in an Era of Globalisation', *Urban Studies*, 39 (7), 1213–1240.

Zeitzoff, T. (2011) 'Using Social Media to Measure Conflict Dynamics: An Application to the 2008–2009 Gaza Conflict', *Journal of Conflict Resolution*, 55 (6), 938–969.

Zhao, K. (2011) 'Boundary-Spanning Contention: The Panyu Anti-Pollution Protest in Guangdong, China', *Stanford Journal of East Asian Affairs*, 11 (1), online available at: http://www.stanford.edu/group/sjeaa/journal111/China2.pdf.

Zhao, S.S. (1998) 'A State-Led Nationalism: The Patriotic Education Campaign in Post-Tiananmen China', *Communist and Post-Communist Studies*, 31 (3), 287–302.

Zhao, Y. (1998) *Media, Market and Democracy in China*, Urbana: University of Illinois Press.

Zheng, Y. (1999) *Discovering Chinese Nationalism in China: Modernization, Identity, and International Relations*, Cambridge: Cambridge University Press.

Zheng, Y. (2008) *Technological Empowerment: The Internet, State, and Society in China*, Stanford, CA: Stanford University Press.

Zhou, Q. (n.d.) 'The Emerging Environmental Protest in China and Its Impacts on the Growth of Chinese Civil Society', online available at: http://www.inter-disciplinary.net/wp-content/uploads/2011/06/zhouqianepaper.pdf.

Zhou, Y. (2005) 'Living on the Cyber Border: *Minjian* Political Writers in Chinese Cyberspace', *Current Anthropology*, 46 (5), 779–803.

Zhou, Y. (2006) *Historicizing Online Politics: Telegraphy, the Internet, and Political Participation in China*, Stanford, CA: Stanford University Press.

Zhou, K. (28 August 2008) 'China's Grassroots Movement toward Greater Freedom', *Economic Reform Freedom Service*, Washington: Centre for international Private Enterprise.

Zhou, M., and Logan, J.R. (2002) 'Market Transition and the Commodification of Housing in Urban China', in J.R. Logan (ed.) *The New Chinese City: Globalization and Market Reform*, Oxford: Blackwell, 137–152.

Zittrain, J., and Edelman, B. (2003) *Empirical Analysis of Internet Filtering in China*, Cambridge, MA: Berkman Center for Internet and Society, Harvard Law School.

Zittrain, J., and Palfrey, J. (2010) 'Internet Filtering: The Politics and Mechanisms of Control', in R. Deibert, J. Palfrey, R. Rohozinski, and J. Zittrain (eds) *Access Controlled: The Shaping of Power, Rights and Rule in Cyberspace*, Cambridge, MA: MIT Press, 15–35.

Žižek, S. (1989) *The Sublime Object of Ideology*, London and New York: Verso.

Žižek, S. (2004) *Iraq: The Borrowed Kettle*, London and New York: Verso.

Žižek, S. (2005) *Interrogating the Real*, London and New York: Continuum.

Žižek, S. (2011) *Did Somebody Say Totalitarianism?*, London: Verso.

Žižek, S. (17 January 2011) 'Good Manners in the Age of WikiLeaks', *London Review of Books*, online available at: http://www.lrb.co.uk/v33/n02/slavoj-zizek/good-manners-in-the-age-of-WikiLeaks.

Zweig, D. (2002) *Internationalizing China: Domestic Interests and Global Linkages*, Ithaca, NY: Cornell University Press.

Index

GPSR Compliance
The European Union's (EU) General Product Safety Regulation (GPSR) is a set
of rules that requires consumer products to be safe and our obligations to
ensure this.

If you have any concerns about our products, you can contact us on

ProductSafety@springernature.com

In case Publisher is established outside the EU, the EU authorized
representative is:

Springer Nature Customer Service Center GmbH
Europaplatz 3
69115 Heidelberg, Germany